THE DEVELOPMENT OF
POLITICAL THOUGHT
IN CANADA

The Development of
POLITICAL THOUGHT
in Canada

An Anthology

edited by
KATHERINE FIERLBECK

broadview press

Library and Archives Canada Cataloguing in Publication

The development of political thought in Canada : an anthology / edited by Katherine Fierlbeck.

Includes bibliographical references.
ISBN 1-55111-710-X

1. Political science—Canada—History—20th Century—Sources. 2. Canada—Politics and government—20th Century—Sources. I. Fierlbeck, Katherine

JA84.C3D48 2005   320'.0971'0904   C2005-903770-9

Broadview Press Ltd. is an independent, international publishing house, incorporated in 1985. Broadview believes in shared ownership, both with its employees and with the general public; since the year 2000 Broadview shares have traded publicly on the Toronto Venture Exchange under the symbol BDP.

We welcome comments and suggestions regarding any aspect of our publications–please feel free to contact us at the addresses below or at broadview@broadviewpress.com / www.broadviewpress.com

North America
PO Box 1243, Peterborough, Ontario, Canada K9J 7H5
Tel: (705) 743-8990; Fax: (705) 743-8353
email: customerservice@broadviewpress.com
3576 California Road, PO Box 1015, Orchard Park, NY, USA 14127

UK, Ireland, and continental Europe
NBN Plymbridge
Estover Road
Plymouth PL6 7PY UK
Tel: 44 (0) 1752 202 301
Fax: 44 (0) 1752 202 331
Fax Order Line: 44 (0) 1752 202 333
Customer Service: cservs@nbnplymbridge.com
Orders: orders@nbnplymbridge.com

Australia and New Zealand
UNIREPS, University of New South Wales
Sydney, NSW, 2052
Australia
Tel: 61 2 9664 0999; Fax: 61 2 9664 5420
email: info.press@unsw.edu.au

Broadview Press Ltd. gratefully acknowledges the financial support of the Government of Canada through the Book Publishing Industry Development Program for our publishing activities.

PRINTED IN CANADA

This book is dedicated to Donald Smiley, James Aitchison,
and all the previous generations of political scientists
who committed their lives to the understanding of this country.

CONTENTS

PART 3: THE THIRD WAVE (1980s to the present)

PREFACE

"What do you *mean*, 'Who's George Grant?'" I asked, incredulously. The class regarded me with some annoyance. They wanted to know about the effects of globalization, the relevance of state sovereignty, and the moral imperative of culture. They did not want to hear about the writings of dead Canadians. But who else, I wondered, could articulate so clearly and eloquently those very issues with which current generations struggle so passionately? How could one comprehend the ongoing protests against the World Trade Organization or the International Monetary Organization unless one could understand Innis's study of the geography of economic development, Levitt's analysis of the nature of multinationals, or Grant's cry to remember exactly what there was to be lost with the envelopment of Canada in an Americanized world?

This book was written to remind Canadians that many of the issues and ideas they engage in so determinedly today have been the subject of reflection and debate for several generations. It is also intended to help readers understand *why* Canadian political thought takes the shape that it does. What, historically, were the events, and who were the individuals, that defined the way in which we now argue about politics and political values? If Queen Victoria, for example, had executed Lord Durham's recommendations to the word, would the contemporary concern over minority rights be as emphatic? Or more so?

I would like very much to acknowledge the invaluable intellectual contributions of my colleagues, who never fail to astound me with their collective ability to respond spontaneously and eruditely to any queries that I might throw out to them: what was the nationality of David Easton? how did Methodism evolve in Canada? what was the nature of Pearsonian multilateralism? what caused the Frog Lake rebellion? and so on. I would especially like to thank two of my very favourite political thinkers—Louise Carbert and Florian

Bail—for their endless patience with all my questions and for their ongoing enthusiasm for this project. Not least, I owe my husband my usual debt of gratitude for his support (technical and otherwise) through the course of writing and editing this book.

Halifax

INTRODUCTION

"We have achieved political autonomy and economic maturity," wrote Frank Underhill, directly after the end of the Second World War. "But to the discussion of those deep underlying intellectual, moral, and spiritual issues which have made such chaos of the contemporary world we Canadians are making very little contribution."[1] Underhill would be relieved and heartened to learn that Canadians are now very well represented within modern political thought, and that we are quite articulate in probing the reasons for, and solutions to, the chaos of the contemporary world. But he would also undoubtedly be curious as to the reasons for this recent flourishing in political thought. Why do Canadians now have so much to say? Why are the ideas of Charles Taylor, Will Kymlicka, and Michael Ignatieff currently the ideas that people everywhere find so relevant? One possibility is that Canada is a cultural canary in a global coalmine; its small size, historical composition, and proximity to a powerful neighbour make it vulnerable to the vicissitudes of globalization much sooner than stronger nations. Issues of national sovereignty and cultural rapport dominated political debate prior even to the formal establishment of this country as a sovereign entity, yet these are the issues that now vex and perplex most modern states.

So how are we to understand political thought in Canada? Even as ideas do not flame into being within an intellectual vacuum, the popular resonance of particular theories and approaches must be understood by more closely peering into the political and social context within which these ideas fermented and grew. A deeper appreciation of the works of modern Canadian theorists can only occur with an understanding of the historical evolution of the debates they now address.

This book traces the development of Canadian political thought historically and thematically. While the contents are generally arranged chronologically, one can also follow the intellectual growth of particular debates for well over the past century. Thus, if one wishes to examine the discussion between liberal democracy and multiculturalism with which Taylor and Kymlicka, amongst others, are grappling, one should understand how this debate was influenced, both philosophically and politically, by Trudeau and Lévesque in the sixties, seventies, and early eighties. And to understand the positions taken by Trudeau, Lévesque, and others in this period, one must look, in turn, at the writings of Lionel Groulx and Henri Bourassa, whose ideas were influenced very dramatically by the same issues that had faced Lord Durham in the early 1800s.

One can trace the development of Canadian nationalism in the same way. Durham, again, was well aware of the political consequences of proximity to the United States for Britain's North American colonies; these concerns were reiterated by Henri Bourassa, noted by Harold Innis, and influential in the development of Pearson's foreign policy. Fears for national sovereignty also formed the basis for two of the most powerful works of Canadian political thought: Kari Levitt's *Silent Surrender* and George Grant's *Lament for a Nation*. Philosophers have castigated these works as overly emotive and insufficiently rationalist, political scientists have argued that they are simply empirically wrong, and politicians have condemned them for breeding a dangerous form of nationalism. Both works have nonetheless left an indelible mark upon generations of Canadians. The same themes and concerns articulated by Levitt and Grant, for better or for worse, now underlie the widespread anxiety about domination by American business interests and American cultural values expressed by so many anti-globalization activists.

The third theme that runs throughout these readings is another ambivalent Canadian trait: the prevalent, if amorphous, belief in some degree of common social responsibility for the well-being of citizens. There are many sources for this mild resistance to American frontier individualism, including, as Gad Horowitz argues, the "cultural fragments" that made their way to Canada. Immigration policies encouraged a massive influx of Europeans (and later, Asians) who brought with them a strong sense of community and a much weaker sense of individual right. (Also, as Donald Smiley would remind his students, Canadians were well represented by those who had found themselves on the losing side of revolutions.) Another reason for Canadians' more muted sense of individualism is the impact of Methodism on Canadian political thought. J.S. Woodsworth, Nellie McClung, and Tommy Douglas were all very much a part of the "social gospel" movement of the early twentieth century. Pearson's foreign policy was not immune to the influence of Methodism,[2] and even George Grant's grandfather was a strong Methodist. The "progressivism" of the Canadian Methodists would likely shock young self-identified "progressive" activists today, as the former also believed strongly in temperance, the sanctity of motherhood, and the clear superiority of British-Canadian culture.

A thread that runs concurrently with, but is independent of, the influence of Methodism in Canada is regional influence. Quebec's influence is fairly self-evident, both through its political aspirations and the Thomist philosophy that emerged from the Roman Catholic political culture.[3] A less-examined variable, however, is the political culture of the western provinces, which served as a breeding ground for radical political movements of all kinds. Many early Canadian feminists, such as Emily Murphy and Nellie McClung, lived on the prairies; Woodsworth's attempts at progressive urban reform and Tommy Douglas's successful implementation of a publicly-insured health care system were based respectively in Manitoba and Saskatchewan. The Winnipeg General Strike of 1919 and the "social credit" experiment of Alberta (and later British Columbia) were also significant western political phenomena.

One fascinating aspect of political thought that this volume has not been able to address is the role that Canadian thinkers played in the debates over social science methodology. Throughout the 1950s and 1960s, political science as a discipline was becoming dominated by a school of thought known as "behaviouralism," which was, simply put, a methodological approach based only upon observable, measurable data. While the social activism of the 1960s undermined the orthodoxy of behaviouralism, the approach has resurfaced in a more sophisticated school commonly referred to as rational choice theory; and, to many, it exemplifies, for better or for worse, the "American" practice of political science. Yet many of the early practitioners of behaviouralism, as well as some of its most vehement critics, were in fact "Canadian" by birth or by association. David Easton, whose work on systems theory epitomized the behavioural approach in political science for many years, was both born a Canadian and taught for many years at a Canadian university, while Ludwig von Bertalanffy, another systems theorist, also lived in Canada for several years. At the same time, two of the most articulate critiques of behaviouralism at this time were Charles Taylor's essay "Neutrality in political science" and Leon Dion's "Democracy as perceived by the public opinion analysists."

Another stream of thought neglected here is that of social theory, and most notably the works of Marshal McLuhan and Northrop Frye. Both were progenitors of what is now referred to as "cultural studies." McLuhan, a student of Harold Innis, was deeply influenced by Innis's analysis of the way that technological developments influenced how individuals thought and acted. Neither social theory nor methodological debates are included in this volume due to their ambivalent identity as "political" thought. Yet even within a more closely circumscribed field of "political thought," much is omitted from this volume. This introduction attempts to present a richer account of what might be included in the category of Canadian political thought; however, even this account should not be considered an exclusive or even definitive listing.

THE FIRST WAVE (PRE-WORLD WAR II)

To begin, a more meticulous account of the development of political thought in Canada would have to include Louis Joseph Papineau's critical response to the Durham Report, *Histoire de l'insurrection du Canada* (1839). To understand how early Canadian political figures saw the pre-eminent problems of the day (and the best solutions to them), an energetic reader would be well-advised to unearth speeches by Robert Baldwin, William Lyon Mackenzie, Etienne Parent, and, or course, Sir John A. Macdonald and Sir Wilfrid Laurier. Notable historical documents articulating key political debates of the pre-Confederation period include the "Ninety-Two Resolutions" and the "Six Counties" address. For slightly less energetic readers, H.D. Forbes's 1985 anthology *Canadian Political Thought* contains a number of these original sources while more recent accounts of early Canadian political thought (such as Ajzenstat and Smith's *Canada's Origins: Liberal, Tory, or Republican?*) present palatable discussions of the dominant themes and ideas of the time. Those who are comfortable reading in French are well-advised to find a copy of *Le rouge et le bleu: Une anthologie de la pensée politique au Québec de la Conquête à la Révolution tranquille* (Yvan Lamonde and Claude Corbo, eds., 1999). Those in the Maritimes would also be well-advised to read Joseph Howe's writings, including *The Organization of the Empire* (1866), to understand that opposition to (and support for) Confederation was not based solely upon issues of language and culture. Cultural nationalism has nonetheless played a dominant role in Canadian political discourse, and the most articulate statement of the position for Quebec sovereignty is perhaps that of Lionel Groulx. A prolific writer, Groulx's consistent theme was the essential need to protect and nurture the distinct vitality of the French Canadian people. One might wish to begin with *Notre maître, le passé* (1936) or *Vers l'indépendance politique* (1943); readers preferring an English text could look at *Why We Are Divided* (1943).

Those interested in following the development of feminist political thought in Canada can usefully begin with the "famous five" (Nellie McClung, Louise McKinney, Henrietta Muir Edwards, Emily Murphy, and Irene Parlby). Their writings are quite disparate, partly because of the expectations of propriety, the negligible academic opportunities, and the publication limitations faced by women. Much of their material takes the form of essays, speeches, fiction, and journalistic writing: many of the most interesting comments on the nature of "political womanhood" in this period, for example, can be found in pieces published in early women's periodicals such as *Chatelaine*. One (more formal) exception is Henrietta Muir Edwards's *Legal Status of Canadian Women* (1908).

An additional omission is Stephen Leacock. A trained political scientist, Leacock's early works include a popular textbook for political science students, *Elements of Political Science* (1906), and a study of responsible government in Canada, *Baldwin, Lafontaine, Hinks: Responsible Government* (1903). Not to dissuade readers from his works *Too Much College* (1940) or *Hellements of Hickonomics* (1936), one might recommend Alan Bowker's edited book *The Social Criticism of Stephen Leacock* (1973) as a good introduction to the more serious themes underlying his work.

THE SECOND WAVE (1950s-1970s)

Like Britain, Canada in the 1950s experienced a period of political introspection that permitted the serious consideration of radical economic alternatives, and, like the United States, Canada in the 1960s faced a period of intensely vociferous activism challenging the dominant relations of power. Modelled on Britain's massive efforts at creating a modern welfare state, Canada developed the prototype for its own social welfare agenda in the post-war period. Intellectual discussions challenging the "hegemony of capital" blossomed both in the political realm and in academia, and the most lasting contributions were those attempting to reconcile the virtues of liberal democracy with the material concerns of social justice and economic redistribution. While the CCF (later the NDP) did release programmatic statements in this vein, more readable are David Lewis's discussions of what Canadian social democracy stood for: see, for example, *Socialism Today* (1956) and *Louder Voices: The Corporate Welfare Bums* (1972). At the same time, it is worth mentioning that John Kenneth Galbraith, the liberal economist who refuses to ignore the issues of poverty in America, was in fact born and raised in southern Ontario. His most well-known books include *The Affluent Society* (1958), *The Age of Uncertainty* (1977), and *The Culture of Contentment* (1992). An excellent intellectual history of socialism in Canada is Norman Penner's *The Canadian Left: A Critical Analysis.*

Canada in the period between 1955 and 1965 was particularly introspective about the composition of Canadian identity, and was especially concerned to distinguish the country from its boisterous southern neighbour. Historians, legal scholars, and sociologists, amongst others, joined with political theorists to scrutinize the nature of "Canadianness" on the eve of the nation's centenary. One might, for example, begin with Frank Underhill's *In Search of Canadian Liberalism* (1955), examine Donald Creighton's *Dominion of the North* (1957) and *The Story of Canada* (1959), proceed to F.R. Scott's *Civil Liberties and Canadian Federalism* (1959), add W.L. Morton's *The Canadian Identity* (1961), and conclude with S.D. Clark's *The Developing Canadian Community* (1962). The concern with Canadian identity seemed to ignite in the mid-1960s, with works by George Grant, Gad Horowitz, and Walter Gordon (*A Choice for Canada: Independence or Colonial Status* [1966]). These works, along with Kari Levitt's *Silent Surrender*, provoked a sustained period of Canadian nationalism both in national politics (most explicitly under Pierre Trudeau) and in academia, where American political scientists who had enlarged faculty ranks in the 1970s became subject to a great deal of animosity throughout the 1980s.

THE THIRD WAVE (1980s TO THE PRESENT)

While Canadian nationalism was fashionable on university campuses throughout the 1980s (culminating in the Free Trade debate in the 1988 electoral campaign), it is best considered as the ebb of the Second Wave of Canadian political thought rather than as an aspect of the Third Wave. To a notable extent, and perhaps to a fault, issues of economic nationalism and economic redistribution have been muted in the Third Wave of Canadian political thought as the explosion of debate surrounding "liberal multiculturalism" invigorated academic and political debate in Canada. Fuelled by the theoretical discussions of postmodernism, in which scepticism of liberal rationalism and liberal universalism become wildly fashionable, the debate over multiculturalism arose in Canada as a challenge to Trudeau's evocatively clear articulation of liberal political values. Still, Kymlicka's argument was the spark. His idea that liberals could accommodate empowered minorities and remain liberal—in fact, become better liberals—and his observation that, in Canada, this already happens ignited widespread interest in liberal multiculturalism, an interest that now exists throughout the world.

Many notable contemporary political theorists have not been included in this volume, as the thrust of the book is predominantly historical. Nonetheless, Canada has produced a significant number of theorists whose contributions to the liberal-multinationalist debate have been acclaimed internationally. To one's reading list, then, one might add Joseph Carens's *Culture, Citizenship, and Community: A Contextual Exploration of Justice as Evenhandedness* (2000) and Margaret Moore's *The Ethics of Nationalism* (2001). Embedded within this debate, but with a more substantive focus, are Alan Cairns's *Citizens Plus: Aboriginal Peoples and the Canadian State* (2000), Tom Flanagan's *First Nations? Second Thoughts* (2000), and Matthew Mendelsohn's essay "Public brokerage: constitutional reform and the accommodation of mass publics" (2000).4 This is, again, not an exhaustive list. It omits, for example, those political theorists whose works focus upon the history of political thought or even upon the debates in political theory that are currently less fashionable, such as works on distributive justice, including G.A. Cohen's *If You're an Egalitarian, How Come You're So Rich?* (2000).

But the issue of missing voices is more complex still. Some readers will already have noted that, notwithstanding the books about aboriginal policy cited above, there is no credible aboriginal voice. My one great regret is that the speeches of Big Bear to be found in Rudy Wiebe's *The Temptation of Big Bear* are (unsurprisingly, for a work of fiction) not actually those of Big Bear himself. The only real historical record of Big Bear's oral contributions are 150-year-old court records, in which Big Bear's replies are minimal, and the records of Alexander Morris, the government's "Indian Agent," who, some might argue, filtered the words of the First Nations' representatives through his own.5 Poignantly, Big Bear, at his trial, asked that his speech be reprinted verbatim in the newspapers of the day. It never was. Another source of aboriginal voice could arguably be Louis Riel; although it is not clear, upon inspection of Riel's copious writings, which document would stand out as a reflective piece of political theory. Much of Riel's work is personal or theological, and the explicitly political documents penned by Riel are quite programmatic (although one might wish to uncover one of Riel's petitions to the President of the United States or his essay "L'amnistie aux Métis du Manitoba: mémoire sur les causes de troubles du Nord-Ouest et sur les négociations qui ont amené leur règlement amiable" [1874]). There is a great deal more modern work written explicitly by aboriginal writers, but it is arguable whether much of it can be construed as political theory. One of the best contemporary books in print is Daniel Paul's *We Were Not the Savages* (2000), and some might well take issue with my decision that this book is too historical and insufficiently theoretical to be included here. Another rich source of historical, political, and sociological work on aboriginal issues worth consulting is the compilation of background documents for the Royal Commission on Aboriginal Peoples (1991).

Yet the question of a "Canadian voice" more broadly considered can also be quite contentious. Lord Durham, of course, was British to the core. Gerry Cohen, noted above, resides in Britain yet was born and raised in Canada. Charles Taylor and Michael Ignatieff, both Canadians, have appointments at American universities. And Christian Bay, the Norwegian political theorist who won the American Political Science Association prize for his 1958 work *The Structure of Freedom*, sought an appointment at a Canadian university because of his perceptions regarding Canadian political values.

So, what *is* Canadian political thought? How can it be considered distinctly *Canadian* if it is produced by Canadians living abroad or by non-Canadians living in the country? In the spirit of cosmopolitanism and tolerance, this volume contains works that contribute to the pre-eminent debates that shape the way that Canadians think about themselves and their country. Specifically, it addresses the issues of cultural integrity, national sovereignty, and social justice. This is also why, with somewhat more temerity, it includes politicians and political actors in the category of "political theorist," a decision that will not delight the purists. However, it would be impossible to discuss Canadian political values without any reference to the more substantive policies of, say, health care or multilateralism, and it is equally difficult to grasp fully the impact of contemporary arguments for minority rights without understanding the clear counterpoint offered by Trudeau's political vision.

The ideas presented by theorists in this volume are tentative, not definitive. They have not satisfactorily put political dilemmas to rest; nor have they conclusively settled theoretical differences. But they have made sense of these problems, both for Canadians and for others, and they have presented options for political actions. At the very least, Canadians can now add "contributions to those deeper underlying intellectual, moral, and spiritual issues" to Frank Underhill's list of "political autonomy and economic maturity" as real Canadian achievements.

NOTES

1 Frank Underhill, "Some reflections of the liberal tradition in Canada," *Canadian Political Thought*, ed. H.D. Forbes (Toronto: Oxford UP, 1985) 231.

2 See, for example, John English, *Shadow of Heaven: The Life of Lester Pearson* (Toronto: Lester and Orpen, 1989) and, more specifically, Denis Stairs, "Liberalism, Methodism, and statecraft: the secular life of a Canadian practitioner," *International Journal* 49.3 (Summer 1994): 673–80.

3 For a more modern analysis of the influence of Catholicism, see Gregory Baum, "Beginnings of a Canadian Catholic social theory," *Political Thought in Canada*, ed. Stephen Brooks (Toronto: Irwin, 1984) 80.

4 *Canadian Journal of Political Science* 33.2 (2000): 245–72.

5 See Alexander Morris, *The Treaties of Canada with the Indians of Manitoba and the North-West Territories, including the negotiations on which they were based, and other information relating thereto* (Toronto: P.R. Randall, 1862).

PART
1

THE FIRST WAVE
(PRE-WORLD WAR II)

1

LORD DURHAM

INTRODUCTION

After a tumultuous period of political upheaval in both Upper and Lower Canada, Lord Durham (1792–1840) arrived in British North America in 1838 to review "the form and future Government" of the two largest provinces. His Report is notable for two reasons. First, he argued emphatically for the need for a system of "responsible government" similar to that of Britain. The provinces did have "representative" government, insofar as they had elected Assemblies, but they also had Legislative Councils of individuals appointed by the Crown who were not accountable or "responsible" to the elected body. Thus, Durham's Report is the first great democratic statement underlying Canadian governance.

The second iconic feature of the Report is its depiction of relations between French and English groups. Durham's description of Canada as "two nations warring in the bosom of a single state" well delineates the subsequent history of the country, although his solution of amalgamating the two provinces in order to deter racial tensions was disregarded as early as the Union Act of 1840. It is this tension between "democracy" and "cultural assimilation or preservation" that continues to define so much of Canada's political thought.

LORD DURHAM'S REPORT ON THE AFFAIRS OF BRITISH NORTH AMERICA (1839)

The preceding pages have sufficiently pointed out the nature of those evils, to the extensive operation of which, I attribute the various practical grievances, and the present unsatisfactory condition of the North American Colonies. It is not by weakening, but strengthening the influence of the people on its Government; by confining within much narrower bounds than those hitherto allotted to it, and not by extending the interference of the imperial authorities in the details of colonial affairs, that I believe that harmony is to be restored, where dissension has so long prevailed; and a regularity and vigour hitherto unknown, introduced into the administration of these Provinces. It needs no change in the principles of government, no invention of a new constitutional theory, to supply the remedy which would, in my opinion, completely remove the existing political disorders. It needs but to follow out consistently the principles of the British constitution, and introduce into the Government of these great Colonies those wise provisions, by which alone the working of the representative system can in any country be rendered harmonious and efficient. We are not now to consider the policy of establishing representative government in the North American Colonies. That has been irrevocably done; and the experiment of depriving the people of their present constitutional power, is not to be thought of. To conduct their Government harmoniously, in accordance with its established principles, is now the business of its rulers; and I know not how it is possible to secure that harmony in any other way, than by administering the Government on those principles which have been found perfectly efficacious in Great Britain. I would not impair a single prerogative of the Crown; on the contrary, I believe that the interests of the people of these Colonies require the protection of prerogatives, which have not hitherto been exercised. But the Crown must, on the other hand, submit to the necessary consequences of representative institutions; and if it has to carry on the Government in unison with a representative body, it must consent to carry it on by means of those in whom that representative body has confidence....

The means which have occasionally been proposed in the Colonies themselves appear to me by no means calculated to attain the desired end in the best way. These proposals indicate such a want of reliance on the willingness of the Imperial Government to acquiesce in the adoption of a better system, as, if warranted, would render an harmonious adjustment of the different powers of the State utterly hopeless. An elective executive council would not only be utterly inconsistent with monarchical government, but would really, under the nominal authority of the Crown, deprive the community of one of the great advantages of an hereditary monarchy. Every purpose of popular control might be combined with every advantage of vesting the immediate choice of advisers in the Crown,

were the Colonial Governor to be instructed to secure the co-operation of the Assembly in his policy, by entrusting its administration
to such men as could command a majority; and if he were given to
understand that he need count on no aid from home in any difference with the Assembly, that should not directly involve the relations between the mother country and the Colony. This change
might be effected by a single dispatch containing such instructions;
or if any legal enactment were requisite, it would only be one that
would render it necessary that the official acts of the Governor should
be countersigned by some public functionary. This would induce
responsibility for every act of the Government, and, as a natural
consequence, it would necessitate the substitution of a system of
administration, by means of competent heads of departments, for
the present rude machinery of an executive council. The Governor,
if he wished to retain advisers not possessing the confidence of the
existing Assembly, might rely on the effect of an appeal to the people,
and, if unsuccessful, he might be coerced by a refusal of supplies,
or his advisers might be terrified by the prospect of impeachment.
But there can be no reason for apprehending that either party would
enter on a contest, when each would find its interest in the maintenance of harmony; and the abuse of the powers which each would
constitutionally possess, would cease when the struggle for larger
powers became unnecessary. Nor can I conceive that it would be
found impossible or difficult to conduct a Colonial Government
with precisely that limitation of the respective powers which has
been so long and so easily maintained in Great Britain.

I know that it has been urged, that the principles which are
productive of harmony and good government in the mother country, are by no means applicable to a colonial dependency. It is said
that it is necessary that the administration of a colony should be
carried on by persons nominated without any reference to the
wishes of its people; that they have to carry into effect the policy,
not of that people, but of the authorities at home; and that a colony
which should name all its own administrative functionaries, would,
in fact, cease to be dependent. I admit that the system which I
propose would, in fact, place the internal government of the colony
in the hands of the colonists themselves; and that we should thus
leave to them the execution of the laws, of which we have long
entrusted the making solely to them. Perfectly aware of the value

of our colonial possessions, and strongly impressed with the necessity of maintaining our connexion with them, I know not in what respect it can be desirable that we should interfere with their internal legislation in matters which do not affect their relations with the mother country. The matters, which so concern us, are very few. The constitution of the form of government—the regulation of foreign relations, and of trade with the mother country, the other British Colonies, and foreign nations—and the disposal of the public lands, are the only points on which the mother country requires a control. This control is now sufficiently secured by the authority of the Imperial Legislature; by the protection which the Colony derives from us against foreign enemies; by the beneficial terms which our laws secure to its trade; and by its share of the reciprocal benefits which would be conferred by a wise system of colonization. A perfect subordination, on the part of the Colony, on these points, is secured by the advantages which it finds in the continuance of its connexion with the Empire. It certainly is not strengthened, but greatly weakened, by a vexatious interference on the part of the Home Government, with the enactment of laws for regulating the internal concerns of the Colony, or in the selection of the persons entrusted with their execution. The colonists may not always know what laws are best for them, or which of their countrymen are the fittest for conducting their affairs; but, at least, they have a greater interest in coming to a right judgment on these points, and will take greater pains to do so than those whose welfare is very remotely and slightly affected by the good or bad legislation of these portions of the Empire. If the colonists make bad laws, and select improper persons to conduct their affairs, they will generally be the only, always the greatest, sufferers; and, like the people of other countries, they must bear the ills which they bring on themselves, until they choose to apply the remedy. But it surely cannot be the duty or the interest of Great Britain to keep a most expensive military possession of these Colonies, in order that a Governor or Secretary of State may be able to confer colonial appointments on one rather than another set of persons in the Colonies. For this is really the only question at issue. The slightest acquaintance with these Colonies proves the fallacy of the common notion, that any considerable amount of patronage in them is distributed among strangers from the mother country. Whatever inconvenience a consequent frequency of changes among the holders of office may produce, is a necessary disadvantage of free government, which will be amply compensated by the perpetual harmony which the system must produce between the people and its rulers. Nor do I fear that the character of the public servants will, in any respect, suffer from a more popular tenure of office. For I can conceive no system so calculated to fill important posts with inefficient persons as the present, in which public opinion is too little consulted in the original appointment, and in which it is almost impossible to remove those who disappoint the expectations of their usefulness, without inflicting a kind of brand on their capacity or integrity....

It is necessary that I should also recommend what appears to me an essential limitation on the present powers of the representative bodies in these Colonies. I consider good government not to be attainable while the present unrestricted powers of voting public money, and of managing the local expenditure of the community, are lodged in the hands of an Assembly. As long as a revenue is raised, which leaves a large surplus after the payment of the necessary expenses of the civil Government, and as long as any member of the Assembly may, without restriction, propose a vote of public money, so long will the Assembly retain in its hands the powers which it everywhere abuses, of misapplying that money. The prerogative of the Crown which is constantly exercised in Great Britain for the real protection of the people, ought never to have been waived in the Colonies; and if the rule of the Imperial Parliament, that no money vote should be proposed without the previous consent of the Crown, were introduced into these Colonies, it might be wisely employed in protecting the public interests, now frequently sacrificed in that scramble for local appropriations, which chiefly serves to give an undue influence to particular individuals or parties.

The establishment of a good system of municipal institutions throughout these Provinces is a matter of vital importance. A general legislature, which manages the private business of every parish, in addition to the common business of the country, wields a power which no single body, however popular in its constitution, ought to have; a power which must be destructive of any constitutional balance. The true principle of limiting popular power is that apportionment of it in many different depositaries which has been adopted in all the most free and stable States of the Union. Instead of confiding the whole collection and distribution of all the revenues raised in any country for all general and local purposes to a single representative body, the power of local assessment, and the application of the funds arising from it, should be entrusted to local management. It is in vain to expect that this sacrifice of power will be voluntarily made by any representative body. The establishment of municipal institutions for the whole country should be made a part of every colonial constitution; and the prerogative of the Crown should be constantly interposed to check any encroachment on the functions of the local bodies, until the people should become alive, as most assuredly they almost immediately would be, to the necessity of protecting their local privileges....

*　　*　　*　　*　　*

These general principles apply, however, only to those changes in the system of government which are required in order to rectify disorders common to all the North American Colonies; but they do not in any degree go to remove those evils in the present state of Lower Canada which require the most immediate remedy. The fatal feud of origin, which is the cause of the most extensive mischief, would be aggravated at the present moment by any change, which should give the majority more power than they have hitherto possessed. A plan by which it is proposed to ensure the tranquil government of Lower Canada, must include in itself the means of putting an end to the agitation of national disputes in the legislature, by settling, at once and for ever, the national character of the Province. I entertain no doubts as to the national character which must be given to Lower Canada; it must be that of the British Empire; that of the majority of the population of British America; that of the great race which must, in the lapse of no long period of time, be predominant over the whole North American Continent. Without effecting the change so rapidly or so roughly as to shock the feelings and trample on the welfare of the existing generation, it must henceforth be the first and steady purpose of the British Government to establish an English population, with English laws and language, in this Province, and to trust its government to none but a decidedly English Legislature.

It may be said that this is a hard measure to a conquered people; that the French were originally the whole, and still are the bulk of the population of Lower Canada; that the English are newcomers, who have no right to demand the extinction of the nationality of a people, among whom commercial enterprize has drawn them. It may be said, that, if the French are not so civilized, so energetic, or so money-making a race as that by which they are surrounded, they are an amiable, a virtuous, and a contented people, possessing all the essentials of material comfort, and not to be despised or ill-used, because they seek to enjoy what they have, without emulating the spirit of accumulation, which influences their neighbours. Their nationality is, after all, an inheritance; and they must be not too severely punished, because they have dreamed of maintaining on the distant banks of the St. Lawrence, and transmitting to their posterity, the language, the manners, and the institutions of that great nation, that for two centuries gave the tone of thought to the European Continent. If the disputes of the two races are irreconcileable, it may be urged that justice demands that the minority should be compelled to acquiesce in the supremacy of the ancient and most numerous occupants of the Province, and not pretend to force their own institutions and customs on the majority.

But before deciding which of the two races is now to be placed in the ascendant, it is but prudent to inquire which of them must ultimately prevail; for it is not wise to establish today that which must, after a hard struggle, be reversed tomorrow. The pretensions of the French Canadians to the exclusive possession of Lower Canada, would debar the yet larger English population of Upper Canada and the Townships from access to the great natural channel of that trade which they alone have created, and now carry on. The possession of the mouth of the St. Lawrence concerns not only those who happen to have made their settlements along the narrow line which borders it, but all who now dwell, or will hereafter dwell, in the great basin of that river. For we must not look to the present alone. The question is, by what race is it likely that the wilderness which now covers the rich and ample regions surrounding the comparatively small and contracted districts in which the French Canadians are located, is eventually to be converted into a settled and flourishing country? If this is to be done in the British dominions, as in the rest of North America, by some speedier process than the ordinary growth of population, it must be by immigration from the English Isles, or from the United States—the countries which

supply the only settlers that have entered, or will enter, the Canadas
in any large numbers. This immigration can neither be debarred
from a passage through Lower Canada, nor even be prevented from
settling in that Province. The whole interior of the British dominions must ere long, be filled with an English population, every year
rapidly increasing its numerical superiority over the French. Is it
just that the prosperity of this great majority, and of this vast tract
of country, should be for ever, or even for a while, impeded by the
artificial bar which the backward laws and civilization of a part, and
a part only, of Lower Canada, would place between them and the
ocean? Is it to be supposed that such an English population will
ever submit to such a sacrifice of its interests?

I must not, however, assume it to be possible that the English
Government shall adopt the course of placing or allowing any check
to the influx of English immigration into Lower Canada, or any
impediment to the profitable employment of that English capital
which is already vested therein. The English have already in their
hands the majority of the larger masses of property in the country;
they have the decided superiority of intelligence on their side; they
have the certainty that colonization must swell their numbers to a
majority; and they belong to the race which wields the Imperial
Government, and predominates on the American Continent. If we
now leave them in a minority, they will never abandon the assurance of being a majority hereafter, and never cease to continue the
present contest with all the fierceness with which it now rages. In
such a contest they will rely on the sympathy of their countrymen
at home; and if that is denied them, they feel very confident of
being able to awaken the sympathy of their neighbours of kindred
origin. They feel that if the British Government intends to maintain its hold of the Canadas, it can rely on the English population
alone; that if it abandons its colonial possessions, they must become
a portion of that great Union which will speedily send forth its
swarms of settlers, and, by force of numbers and activity, quickly
master every other race. The French Canadians, on the other hand,
are but the remains of an ancient colonization, and are and ever
must be isolated in the midst of an Anglo-Saxon world. Whatever
may happen, whatever government shall be established over them,
British or American, they can see no hope for their nationality.
They can only sever themselves from the British Empire by waiting

till some general cause of dissatisfaction alienates them, together with the surrounding colonies, and leaves them part of an English confederacy; or, if they are able, by effecting a separation singly, and so either merging in the American Union, or keeping up for a few years a wretched semblance of feeble independence, which would expose them more than ever to the intrusion of the surrounding population. I am far from wishing to encourage indiscriminately these pretensions to superiority on the part of any particular race; but while the greater part of every portion of the American Continent is still uncleared and unoccupied, and while the English exhibit such constant and marked activity in colonization, so long will it be idle to imagine that there is any portion of that Continent into which that race will not penetrate, or in which, when it has penetrated, it will not predominate. It is but a question of time and mode; it is but to determine whether the small number of French who now inhabit Lower Canada shall be made English, under a Government which can protect them, or whether the process shall be delayed until a much larger number shall have to undergo, at the rude hands of its uncontrolled rivals, the extinction of a nationality strengthened and embittered by continuance.

And is this French Canadian nationality one which, for the good merely of that people, we ought to strive to perpetuate, even if it were possible? I know of no national distinctions marking and continuing a more hopeless inferiority. The language, the laws, the character of the North American Continent are English; and every race but the English (I apply this to all who speak the English language) appears there in a condition of inferiority. It is to elevate them from that inferiority that I desire to give to the Canadians our English character. I desire it for the sake of the educated classes, whom the distinction of language and manners keeps apart from the great Empire to which they belong. At the best, the fate of the educated and aspiring colonist is, at present, one of little hope, and little activity; but the French Canadian is cast still further into the shade, by a language and habits foreign to those of the Imperial Government. A spirit of exclusion has closed the higher professions on the educated classes of the French Canadians, more, perhaps, than was absolutely necessary; but it is impossible for the utmost liberality on the part of the British Government to give an equal position in the general competition of its vast population to those who speak a foreign language. I desire the amalgamation still more for the sake of the humbler classes. Their present state of rude and equal plenty is fast deteriorating under the pressure of population in the narrow limits to which they are confined. If they attempt to better their condition, by extending themselves over the neighbouring country, they will necessarily get more and more mingled with an English population: if they prefer remaining stationary, the greater part of them must be labourers in the employ of English capitalists. In either case it would appear, that the great mass of the French Canadians are doomed, in some measure, to occupy an inferior position, and to be dependent on the English for employment. The evils of poverty and dependence would merely be aggravated in a ten-fold degree, by a spirit of jealous and resentful nationality, which should separate the working class of the community from the possessors of wealth and employers of labour....

In these circumstances, I should be indeed surprised if the more reflecting part of the French Canadians entertained at present any hope of continuing to preserve their nationality. Much as they struggle against it, it is obvious that the process of assimilation to English habits is already commencing. The English language is gaining ground, as the language of the rich and of the employers of labour naturally will. It appeared by some of the few returns, which had been received by the Commissioner of the Inquiry into the state of Education, that there are about ten times the number of French children in Quebec learning English, as compared with the English children who learn French. A considerable time must, of course, elapse before the change of a language can spread over a whole people; and justice and policy alike require, that while the people continue to use the French language, their Government should take no such means to force the English language upon them as would, in fact, deprive the great mass of the community of the protection of the laws. But, I repeat that the alteration of the character of the Province ought to be immediately entered on, and firmly, though cautiously, followed up; that in any plan, which may be adopted for the future management of Lower Canada, the first object ought to be that of making it an English Province; and that, with this end in view, the ascendancy should never again be placed in any hands but those of an English population. Indeed, at the present moment this is obviously necessary: in the state of mind in which I have described the French Canadian population, as not only now being, but as likely for a long while to remain, the trusting them with an entire control over this Province, would be, in fact, only facilitating a rebellion. Lower Canada must be governed now, as it must be hereafter, by an English population: and thus the policy, which the necessities of the moment force on us, is in accordance with that suggested by a comprehensive view of the future and permanent improvement of the Province.

The greater part of the plans which have been proposed for the future government of Lower Canada, suggest either as a lasting or as a temporary and intermediate scheme, that the Government of that Province should be constituted on an entirely despotic footing, or on one that would vest it entirely in the hands of the British minority. It is proposed either to place the legislative authority in a Governor, with a Council formed of the heads of the British party, or to contrive some scheme of representation by which a minority, with the forms of representation, is to deprive a majority of all voice in the management of its own affairs.

The maintenance of an absolute form of government on any part of the North American Continent, can never continue for any long time, without exciting a general feeling in the United States against a power of which the existence is secured by means so odious to the people; and as I rate the preservation of the present general sympathy of the United States with the policy of our Government in Lower Canada, as a matter of the greatest importance, I should be sorry that the feeling should be changed for one which, if prevalent among the people, must extend over the surrounding Provinces. The influence of such an opinion would not only act very strongly on the entire French population, and keep up among them a sense of injury, and a determination of resistance to the Government, but would lead to just as great discontent among the English. In their present angry state of feeling, they might tolerate, for a while, any arrangement that would give them a triumph over the French; but I have greatly misunderstood their character, if they would long bear a Government in which they had no direct voice. Nor would their jealousy be obviated by the selection of a Council from the persons supposed to have their confidence. It is not easy to know who really possesses that confidence; and I suspect that there would be no surer way of depriving a man of influence over them, than by treating him as their representative, without their consent....

With respect to every one of those plans which propose to make the English minority an electoral majority by means of new and strange modes of voting or unfair divisions of the country, I shall only say, that if the Canadians are to be deprived of representative government, it would be better to do it in a straightforward way than to attempt to establish a permanent system of government on the basis of what all mankind would regard as mere electoral frauds. It is not in North America that men can be cheated by an unreal semblance of representative government, or persuaded that they are out-voted, when, in fact, they are disfranchised.

The only power that can be effectual at once in coercing the present disaffection, and hereafter obliterating the nationality of the French Canadians, is that of a numerical majority of a loyal and English population; and the only stable government will be one more popular than any that has hitherto existed in the North American Colonies. The influence of perfectly equal and popular institutions in effacing distinctions of race without disorder or oppression, and with little more than the ordinary animosities of party in a free country, is memorably exemplified in the history of the state of Louisiana, the laws and population of which were French at the time of its cession to the American Union. And the eminent success of the policy adopted with regard to that State, points out to us the means by which a similar result can be effected in Lower Canada....

Every provision was made in Louisiana for securing to both races a perfectly equal participation in all the benefits of the Government. It is true that the intention of the federal Government to encourage the use of the English language was evinced by the provision of the constitution with respect to the language of the records; but those who will reflect how very few people ever read such documents, and how very recently it is that the English language has become the language of the law in this country, will see that such a provision could have little practical effect. In all cases in which convenience requires it, the different parties use their respective languages in the courts of justice, and in both branches of the legislature. In every judicial proceeding, all documents which pass between the parties are required to be in both languages, and the laws are published in both languages. Indeed the equality of the two languages is preserved in the legislature by a very singular contrivance; the French and English members speak their respective languages, and an interpreter, as I was informed, after every speech, explains its purport in the other language....

The distinction still lasts, and still causes a good deal of division; the society of each race is said to be in some measure distinct, but not by any means hostile; and some accounts represent the social mixture to be very great. All accounts represent the division of the races as becoming gradually less and less marked; their newspapers are printed in the two languages on opposite pages; their local politics are entirely merged in those of the Union; and instead of discovering in their papers any vestiges of a quarrel of races, they are found to contain a repetition of the same party recriminations and party arguments, which abound in all other parts of the federation.

The explanation of this amalgamation is obvious. The French of Louisiana, when they were formed into a state, in which they were a majority, were incorporated into a great nation, of which they constituted an extremely small part. The eye of every ambitious man turned naturally to the great centre of federal affairs, and the high prizes of federal ambition. The tone of politics was taken from those by whose hands its highest powers were wielded; the legislation and government of Louisiana were from the first insignificant, compared with the interests involved in the discussions at Washington. It became the object of every aspiring man to merge his French, and adopt completely an American nationality. What was the interest of individuals, was also the interest of the State. It was its policy to be represented by those who would acquire weight in the councils of the federation. To speak only a language foreign to that of the United States, was consequently a disqualification for a candidate for the posts of either senator or representative; the French qualified themselves by learning English, or submitted to the superior advantages of their English competitors. The representation of Louisiana in Congress is now entirely English, while each of the federal parties in the State conciliates the French feeling, by putting up a candidate of that race. But the result is, that the Union is never disturbed by the quarrels of these races; and the French language and manners bid fair, in no long time, to follow their laws, and pass away like the Dutch peculiarities of New York.

It is only by the same means—by a popular government, in which an English majority shall permanently predominate, that Lower Canada, if a remedy for its disorders be not too long delayed, can be tranquilly ruled.

On these grounds, I believe that no permanent or efficient remedy can be devised for the disorders of Lower Canada, except a fusion of the Government in that of one or more of the surrounding Provinces; and as I am of opinion that the full establishment of responsible government can only be permanently secured by giving these Colonies an increased importance in the politics of the Empire, I find in union the only means of remedying at once and completely the two prominent causes of their present unsatisfactory condition.

Two kinds of union have been proposed, federal and legislative. By the first, the separate legislature of each Province would be preserved in its present form, and retain almost all its present attributes of internal legislation; the federal legislature exercising no power, save in those matters of general concern, which may have been expressly ceded to it by the constituent Provinces. A legislative union would imply a complete incorporation of the Provinces included in it under one legislature, exercising universal and sole legislative authority over all of them, in exactly the same manner as the Parliament legislates alone for the whole of the British Isles.

On my first arrival in Canada, I was strongly inclined to the project of a federal union, and it was with such a plan in view, that I discussed a general measure for the government of the Colonies, with the deputations from the Lower Provinces, and with various leading individuals and public bodies in both the Canadas. I was fully aware that it might be objected that a federal union would, in many cases, produce a weak and rather cumbrous government; that a Colonial federation must have, in fact, little legitimate authority or business, the greater part of the ordinary functions of a federation falling within the scope of the imperial legislature and executive; and that the main inducement to federation, which is the necessity of conciliating the pretensions of independent states to the maintenance of their own sovereignty, federation must have, in fact, little legitimate authority or business, the greater part of the ordinary functions of a federation falling within the scope of the imperial legislature and executive; and that the main inducement to federation, which is the necessity of conciliating the pretensions of independent states to the maintenance of their own sovereignty, could not exist in the case of Colonial dependencies, liable to be moulded according to the pleasure of the supreme authority at home. In the course of the discussions which I have mentioned, I became aware also of great practical difficulties in any plan of federal government, particularly those that must arise in the management of the general revenues, which would in such a plan have to be again distributed among the Provinces. But I had still more strongly impressed on me the great advantages of an united Government; and I was gratified by finding the leading minds of the various Colonies strongly and generally inclined to a scheme that would elevate their countries into something like a national existence. I thought that it would be the tendency of a federation sanctioned and consolidated by a monarchical Government gradually to become a complete legislative union; and that thus, while conciliating the French of Lower Canada, by leaving them the government of their own Province and their own internal legislation, I might provide for the protection of British interests by the general government, and for the gradual transition of the Provinces into an united and homogeneous community.

But the period of gradual transition is past in Lower Canada. In the present state of feeling among the French population, I cannot doubt that any power which they might possess would be used against the policy and the very existence of any form of British government. I cannot doubt that any French Assembly that shall again meet in Lower Canada will use whatever power, be it more or less limited, it may have, to obstruct the Government, and undo whatever has been done by it. Time, and the honest co-operation of the various parties, would be required to aid the action of a federal constitution; and time is not allowed, in the present state of Lower Canada, nor co-operation to be expected from a legislature, of which the majority shall represent its French inhabitants. I believe that tranquillity can only be restored by subjecting the Province to the vigorous rule of an English majority; and that the only efficacious government would be that formed by a legislative union....

I am, in truth, so far from believing that the increased power and weight that would be given to these Colonies by union would endanger their connexion with the Empire, that I look to it as the only means of fostering such a national feeling throughout them as would effectually counterbalance whatever tendencies may now exist towards separation. No large community of free and intelligent men will long feel contented with a political system which places them, because it places their country, in a position of inferiority to their neighbours. The colonist of Great Britain is linked, it is true, to a mighty Empire; and the glories of its history, the visible signs of its present power, and the civilization of its people, are calculated to raise and gratify his national pride. But he feels, also, that his link to that Empire is one of remote dependence; he catches but passing and inadequate glimpses of its power and prosperity; he knows that in its government he and his own countrymen have no voice. While his neighbour on the other side of the frontier assumes importance, from the notion that his vote exercises some influence on the councils, and that he himself has some share in the onward progress of a mighty nation, the colonist feels the deadening influence of the narrow and subordinate community to which he belongs. In his own, and in the surrounding Colonies, he finds petty objects occupying petty, stationary and divided societies; and it is only when the chances of an uncertain and tardy communication bring intelligence of what has passed a month before on the other side of the Atlantic, that he is reminded of the Empire with which he is connected. But the influence of the United States surrounds him on every side, and is for ever present. It extends itself as population augments and intercourse increases; it penetrates every portion of the continent into which the restless spirit of American speculation impels the settler or the trader; it is felt in all the transactions of commerce, from the important operations of the monetary system down to the minor details of ordinary traffic; it stamps, on all the habits and opinions of the surrounding countries, the common characteristics of the thoughts, feelings and customs of the American people. Such is necessarily the influence which a great nation exercises on the small communities which surround it. Its thoughts and manners subjugate them, even when nominally independent of its authority. If we wish to prevent the extension of this influence, it can only be done by raising up for the North American colonist some nationality of his own; by elevating these small and unimportant communities into a society having some objects of a national importance; and by thus giving their inhabitants a country which they will be unwilling to see absorbed even into one more powerful....

I see no reason, therefore, for doubting that, by good government, and the adoption of a sound system of colonization, the British possessions in North America may thus be made the means of conferring on the suffering classes of the mother country many of the blessings which have hitherto been supposed to be peculiar to the social state of the New World.

In conclusion, I must earnestly impress on Your Majesty's advisers, and on the Imperial Parliament, the paramount necessity of a prompt and decisive settlement of this important question, not only on account of the extent and variety of interests involving the welfare and security of the British Empire, which are perilled by every hour's delay, but on account of the state of feeling which exists in the public mind throughout all Your Majesty's North American possessions, and more especially the two Canadas....

All which is humbly submitted to Your Majesty.

DURHAM. London, 31st January 1839.

FURTHER READING

One of the best commentaries on Lord Durham's Report remains Sir Charles Lucas's introductory volume published in 1912 (Oxford: Clarendon Press), which offers a wealth of historical detail and analysis in a very accessible style. A shorter commentary is Gerald Craig's introduction to an abridged volume entitled *Lord Durham's Report* (Toronto: McClelland and Stewart, 1963). Ged Martin's study, *The Durham Report and British Policy* (Cambridge: Cambridge University Press, 1972) is another excellent source, while Janet Ajzenstat in *The Political Thought of Lord Durham* (Kingston and Montreal: McGill-Queen's University Press, 1988) presents a stimulating and thoughtful critique of those who hold that Durham's call for political assimilation was simply characteristic of the "prejudice and ignorance" of the day rather than a reasonable and defensible political strategy.

2   HENRI BOURASSA

INTRODUCTION

An iconoclast and intellectual, Henri Bourassa (1868–1952) was notable for defending both Canadian nationalism and a distinct Quebecois culture. Bourassa was a strong adversary of British imperialism, and most vociferous in his opposition to sending Canadian troops to help Britain in the Boer War, to the establishment of a Canadian navy, to conscription of Canadians in World War I, and to immigration policies that heavily favoured native English speakers. Yet Bourassa often antagonized French Canadian nationalists with his declaration that Quebec could thrive within the Canadian state and by his belief in "British liberal principles."

In this article, originally published in *Le Devoir* (founded by Bourassa in 1909), Bourassa attempts to alert English Canadians to the alienation French Canadians experienced in Canada's unequivocal support of all things British; and he adds the prophetic warning that support for Britain could not save Canada from the real threat: the "moral conquest" of Canada by the United States.

THE SPECTRE OF ANNEXATION (1912)

Whatever the near or distant future of Canada may be, the French Canadian is still essentially Canadian. Profoundly British he also remains—by habit, instinct, or reason, if not by a warmer sentiment which his partner of British origin has not cared much to cultivate. From that double point of view, Canadian and British, the French Canadian is prepared to make new sacrifices in order to maintain the unity and independence of Canada and its connection with Great Britain, and consequently to avert any danger of the absorption of Canada by the United States. But before he makes those sacrifices, he puts two conditions, equally essential in his mind to the object desired. First, the welfare of Canada should predominate over that of Britain herself, if necessary. Second, English-speaking Canadians should also make their share of sacrifice, cease to consider the French as outcasts of Confederation, and make up their minds to treat them as co-workers, partners, and brothers.

Really, the French Canadian is amazed at the attitude of his English-speaking fellow citizens. Of the sincerity of their patriotism and the genuineness of their love for the motherland, he, at times, doubts seriously. Their thunderous asseverations of loyalty he cannot reconcile with their stupefying blindness in the face of the real dangers that threaten the unity of Confederation, and still less with their persistency in letting the peril grow, and even in accelerating its progress.

He finds it difficult to admit that the most efficient contribution to the grandeur and safety of the Empire should be to wage war on all the seas of the globe, before the most elementary precautions have been taken to organise the defense of Canadian territory: especially when he reads upon every page of history, and even in the avowals of the Imperialists, the glaring evidence that the British fleet is impotent to protect Canada against the United States, the only nation really capable of conquering its territory.

That Canada can and must "save" Britain and France, preserve the neutrality of Belgium, sink the German fleet in the Northern Sea, keep Austria and Italy at bay in the Mediterranean, seems absurd to him when he has still so much to do to put his own house in order; when years of intense effort and fabulous sums of money are still required to build up, on Canadian territory, these essential works with which Great Britain has been amply supplied for centuries.

His opinions on these matters he does not pretend to impose; but he thinks he has the right to express them and to urge them, on this as on every other question of interest to Canada, without being taxed with disloyalty, he, the oldest and most thoroughly tested of all Canadians. He still believes in a policy that has been considered for a century, by British statesmen, as the most efficient to maintain the political unity of the Empire and assure its material safety. To that policy he thinks he can remain faithful without being constantly accused of cowardice, rebellion and ingratitude by people who have done less than he himself has done to preserve Canada as a British possession.

But his perceptions of the striking contrast between the Imperialists' professions of faith, and their attitude of questions of vital interest to Canada, astonishes him above all and leads him seriously to doubt the sincerity of most of those Canadians who make such a display of frantic loyalty and exalted imperialism.

"*Let the flag and constitution be saved,*" shout the jingoes.

"All right," replies the French Canadian; "but, before defending the flag and the constitution against enemies without, that have not yet attacked them, is it not more pressing to preserve them from enemies within, who tear down the flag of national unity and break the constitution?"

To worship the flag and constitution is quite proper; but it is better still to respect their principles, the traditions and the right, of which flag is but the emblem and constitution the formula.

The flag the French Canadian has ever respected; by the Constitution he always stood. Can they say as much, those who are making of the flag—the symbol of harmony—an object of national dissension, the signal of the assault of might against right, the standard of brutal domination by the majority over the minority? Can they testify the same of themselves, those who never cease to distort and restrict the letter of the Law in order to more effectively violate its spirit?

"*Let Canada be saved from American conquest, the consequence of German supremacy.*"

Why do you not seek first to guard yourselves against the universal contagion of American ideals, morals and mentality, with which your family life, your intellectual and social atmosphere are already permeated? This moral absorption, the prelude of political domination, is more to be dreaded than the catastrophes predicted by the howling dervishes of Imperialism.

Just test yourselves!

American you already are by your language, your nasal accent, your common slang, your dress, your daily habits; by the Yankee literature with which your homes and clubs are flooded; by your yellow journals and their rantings; by your loud and intolerant patriotism; by your worships of gold, snobbery and titles.

Americans you are precisely by what constitutes the deepest line of cleavage between both our races: your system of so called "national schools," a servile copy of the American model, under which your children's mind[s], passing through the same intellectual roller, is formed or rather deformed to the perfect imitation of little Yankees—whilst we have remained faithful to the old British principle of respect to the liberty of conscience of both father and child.

In all those spheres, French Canadians have been better preserved from American contagion, thanks to better language, their French speech, to Canada the safest of national preservatives, which some of you so foolishly endeavour to eradicate from our country.

Unfortunately, in the sphere of public life, where we live side by side with you, but where you dominate by your numbers and language, you are americanising us as thoroughly as yourselves.

"*Let British institutions be saved,*" say you.

Granted; but so much is worth the spirit, so much the letter, so much the soul, so much the body. The spirit that gives life to national institutions and determines their character is to be found in public morals, in the mentality of statesmen, politicians and publicists. These are the sources from which the national spirit springs and in which it takes its nature and tendencies.

In their external fabric, Canadian institutions are but partially British. Our federal regime is largely imitated from the American constitution. Moreover, the inner soul of our national life has passed through a period of deep evolution, and so becomes more and more every day a simple replica of American civilisation—with this difference, that in the United States, public morals and administration have made marked progress in reform, whilst in Canada their degradation is still increasing.

Americans we are by the despotism of party machines, by the abominable abuse of patronage, by the sway of corporations and bosses, by the venality of our politicians, by the pest of log-rolling and lobbying in our parliaments, by the boodling with which our public bodies, federal, provincial or municipal, are infested by the quick disappearance of the laws of honour from finance, from trade transactions, and even from the practice of liberal professions....

We are fast approaching the day when, as fifteen or twenty years ago in the United States, it will be forbidden to any man careful of his honour and reputation to aspire to representative functions. No one, unless possessed of ample wealth, will be able to satisfy the mob's cupidity without accepting dishonourable help; and how can the honourable wish to associate with a pack of crooked politicians?

In the social and economic order, where do we stand in Canada? Canadian labour organisation is practically in the hands of American unions. American capital is invading our industries, and grasping our forests, water powers and public lands. Speculation in the American stock-exchange is fed by the savings of our banks, to the deep detriment, in times of crisis, of Canadian trade. A large portion of our means of transportation are but the "adjuncts" of American railways.

To radically stop that process of economical penetration may be impossible. That Canada finds in it considerable material advantage nobody denies. But in our eyes, national safety is more than material wealth; and some effort should be made to diminish at least the direct consequences of that economical conquest.

On several instances, nationalist "demagogues" have called the attention of public powers to that menace. Statesmen laughed and shrugged their shoulders. Some of the stoutest patriots of today even struck very nice bargains with the invaders. Countless are those staunch loyalists, who dream of nothing but war and slaughter on behalf of Britain, but who are always ready to sell any part of the national patrimony, provided they get their commission.

When they writhe with anguish at the sole thought of the danger to be incurred by Canada in case we sold a few bales of hay to the Americans, or when they entreat us to go help and sink German ships in order to "save our institutions," it is our turn to shrug our shoulders and laugh at the comedians.

"Let our national character be preserved."

Very well, but how can we believe in the sincerity or lucidity of those who see nothing but threats in the Black Sea, the Mediterranean or the North Sea, but who obstinately shut their eyes on a peril growing in the midst of Canada, from Lake Superior to the Rockies.

The same people who wish now to entangle us in all imperial wars and difficulties, have either favoured or tacitly accepted a criminal immigration policy, thanks to which Manitoba, Alberta, and Saskatchewan are fast becoming foreign to the older provinces in population, habits, traditions, aspirations, requirements, and social and political ideals. This means that the formidable influence of heterogeneous human forces deepens still further the line of cleavage between East and West, already so profoundly marked by differences in climate, soil, and production. In order to check the force of segregation and help in the work of unification, we French Canadians have offered our aid in endeavouring to plant through those immense territories outposts from the old population of Quebec, so as to reproduce there, as far as possible, the traditional and basic conditions of Confederation, and oppose to the invasion of American language, morals, and traditions, the bulwark of French language, morals, and traditions.

How were such efforts and attempts received?

All sorts of obstacles and vexations were raised against us. The importance of Galacians, Doukobors, Scandinavians, Mormons, or Americans of all races, was more encouraged than the settlement of French Canadians or the immigration of French-speaking Europeans, whom we could have easily assimilated. To preserve Canada from the danger of being "Frenchified," as he so boldly stated, a deputy minister of the Interior was allowed, without the slightest blame, to claim from England the "graduates" of jails and workhouses, and proffer a helping hand to the human derelicts gathered up by the Salvation Army and the Church Army. Steamship and railway companies, subsidised by the Federal exchequer, which receives contributions from French Canadian as well as from other rate-payers, bring immigrants from the slums of Liverpool to Winnipeg, at a lesser cost than the hardy sons of Quebec and other eastern farmers must pay for transportation to Manitoba.

Within a few years, the French Canadians in the West were severely deprived of their schools, of the official recognition of their language, and of all that could have contributed in attracting them to the settlement of that national domain, one third of it paid for by their money. When, standing on the constitution of Canada and the solemn pledges of the most eminent statesmen who made Confederation, they demanded justice, this was the brutal rebuff: "You are less numerous than we are in the West; you are there outnumbered by the Mormons. Besides, this is an English country. If you are not satisfied, then stay in your 'reserve' or get out of the Dominion."

In Ontario, their increase is denounced as a national peril. "Ontario does not want a France of Louis the Fourteenth," wrote not long ago a missionary in the columns of the Toronto *Globe*. Presumably, Sicilians with their knives, Polish Jews and Syrians are nearer to the heart of that apostle.

After all that, can anyone wonder if the French Canadians no more feel the thrill of joy or pride when he hears of "Canadian unity," "British institutions," or "flag worship"?

In the true interest of their cause, the champions of the imperialist crusade have but one thing to do: to organise a set campaign for the purpose of bringing Confederation back to its former basis, to restore to French-Canadians possession of those rights of which they have been deprived in half the provinces of Canada, to uproot that idiotic hatred which designs their reduction to the legal situation of Red Skins, and above all to fight strenuously that microbe of Americanism which is infecting Canada as a whole, and English-speaking Canada in particular.

That would be the real test of their sincerity and the only means of their obtaining tangible and enduring results. Should they fail to make the attempt, those stout champions of Imperialism will bring cool-headed people to the conclusion that some of them are purely led by the thirst of decorations or the snobbishness of titled parvenus, and that the rest, animated by still more sordid motives, are under the sway of secret donations, or interested, like some members of the Admiralty Board, in the making of warships and weapons.

In the above pages, it may be found that I have rather severely brought to task our English-speaking fellow-citizens, or rather a certain class of their public men and journalists. In justice, the share which we, French-Canadians, have contributed to national degradation must be shown.

FURTHER READING

In *National Disintegration: Responsibility of French Canadians* (1912), Bourassa moves his critique from the behaviour and attitudes of English Canada and argues that French Canadians themselves were culpable in the destruction of their own culture. Perhaps the best contrast to Bourassa is Lionel Groulx (1878–1967), arguably the intellectual founder of modern Quebec nationalism. In his essay "Tomorrow's Tasks" (1936), for example, Groulx argues for the need "to be masters in our own house."

Two excellent secondary sources on Bourassa are Casey Murrow's *Henri Bourassa and French Canadian Nationalism* (Montreal: Harvest House, 1968), which gives a detailed chronological account of

Bourassa's life and political activism, and Joseph Levitt's *Henri Bourassa and the Golden Calf* (Ottawa: Les Éditions de l'Université d'Ottawa, 1972), which focuses more closely upon the social and political programs of the Nationalist movement under Bourassa.

3

NELLIE McCLUNG

INTRODUCTION

Nellie McClung (1875-1957), one of the "famous five" who pressed for the right of women to be considered "persons," was a feminist, nationalist, and social reformer who was strongly influenced by the Social Gospel movement, which advocated progressive social change. Her feminism was primarily informed by her observation of the grim working conditions and legal double standards experienced by the women of her day; yet it was also dependent upon her belief in the moral superiority of women. In 1921, she was elected to the Alberta legislature. Her political crusade for women's rights (including access to birth control and fair divorces), for public health, and for rural development may seem to modern eyes to sit oddly with her support for temperance and the sterilization of the "mentally unfit"; but her position on all issues lay coherently within the broader Methodist outlook which underpinned much agrarian progressivism in western Canada.

HARDY PERENNIALS (1915)

If prejudices belonged to the vegetable world they would be described under the general heading of "Hardy Perennials; will grow in any soil, and bloom without ceasing; requiring no cultivation; will do better when left alone."

In regard to tenacity of life, no old yellow cat has anything on a prejudice. You may kill it with your own hands, bury it deep, and sit on the grave, and behold! the next day, it will walk in at the back door purring.

Take some of the prejudices regarding women that have been exploded and blown to pieces many, many times and yet walk among us today in the fulness of life and vigor. There is a belief that housekeeping is the only occupation for women; that all women must be housekeepers, whether they like it or not. Men may do as they like, and indulge their individuality, but every true and womanly woman must take to the nutmeg grater and the o-Cedar Mop. It is believed that in the good old days before woman suffrage was discussed, and when woman's clubs were unheard of, that all women adored housework, and simply pined for Monday morning to come to get at the weekly wash; that women cleaned house with rapture and cooked joyously. Yet there is a story told of one of the women of the old days, who arose at four o'clock in the morning, and aroused all her family at an indecently early hour for breakfast, her reason being that she wanted to get "one of these horrid old meals over." This woman had never been at a suffrage meeting—so where did she get the germ of discontent?

At the present time there is much discontent among women, and many people are seriously alarmed about it. They say women are no longer contented with woman's sphere and woman's work—that the washboard has lost its charm, and the days of the hair-wreath are ended. We may as well admit that there is discontent among women. We cannot drive them back to the spinning wheel and the mathook, for they will not go. But there is really no cause for alarm, for discontent is not necessarily wicked. There is such a thing as divine discontent just as there is criminal contentment. Discontent may mean the stirring of ambition, the desire to spread out, to improve and grow. Discontent is a sign of life, corresponding to growing pains in a healthy child. The poor woman who is making a brave struggle for existence is not saying much, though she is thinking all the time. In the old days when a woman's hours were from 5 A.M. to 5 A.M., we did not hear much of discontent among women, because they had not time to even talk, and certainly could not get together. The horse on the treadmill may be very discontented, but he is not disposed to tell his troubles, for he cannot stop to talk.

It is the women, who now have leisure, who are doing the talking. For generations women have been thinking and thought without expression is dynamic, and gathers volume by repression. Evolution when blocked and suppressed becomes revolution. The introduction of machinery and the factory-made articles has given women more leisure than they had formerly, and now the question arises, what are they going to do with it?

Custom and conventionality recommend many and varied occupations for women, social functions intermixed with kindly deeds of charity, embroidering altar cloths, making strong and durable garments for the poor, visiting the sick, comforting the sad, all of which women have faithfully done, but while they have been doing these things, they have been wondering about the underlying causes of poverty, sadness and sin. They notice that when the unemployed are fed on Christmas day, they are just as hungry as ever on December the twenty-sixth, or at least on December the twenty-seventh; they have been led to inquire into the causes for little children being left in the care of the state, and they find that in over half of the cases, the liquor traffic has contributed to the poverty and unworthiness of the parents. The state which licenses the traffic steps in and takes care, or tries to, of the victims; the rich brewer whose business it is to encourage drinking, is usually the largest giver to the work of the Children's Aid Society, and is often extolled for his lavish generosity: and sometimes when women think about these things they are struck by the absurdity of a system which allows one man or a body of men to rob a child of his father's love and care all year, and then gives him a stuffed dog and a little red sleigh at Christmas and calls it charity!

Women have always done their share of the charity work of the world. The lady of the manor, in the old feudal days, made warm mittens and woolen mufflers with her own white hands and carried them to the cottages at Christmas, along with blankets and coals. And it was a splendid arrangement all through, for it furnished the lady with mild and pleasant occupation, and it helped to soothe the conscience of the lord, and if the cottagers (who were often "low worthless fellows, much given up to riotous thinking and disputing") were disposed to wonder why they had to work all year and get nothing, while the lord of the manor did nothing all year and got everything, the gift of blanket and coals, the warm mufflers, and "a shawl for granny" showed them what ungrateful souls they were.

Women have dispensed charity for many, many years, but gradually it has dawned upon them that the most of our charity is very ineffectual, and merely smoothes things over, without ever reaching the root. A great deal of our charity is like the kindly deed of the benevolent old gentleman, who found a sick dog by the wayside, lying in the full glare of a scorching sun. The tender-hearted old man climbed down from his carriage, and, lifting the dog tenderly in his arms, carried him around into the small patch of shade cast by his carriage.

"Lie there, my poor fellow!" he said. "Lie there, in the cool shade, where the sun's rays may not smite you!"

Then he got into his carriage and drove away.

Women have been led, through their charitable institutions and philanthropic endeavors, to do some thinking about causes.

Mrs. B. set out to be a "family friend" to the family of her wash-woman. Mrs. B. was a thoroughly charitable, kindly disposed woman, who had never favored woman's suffrage and regarded the new movement among women with suspicion. Her wash-woman's family consisted of four children, and a husband who blew in gaily once in a while when in need of funds, or when recovering from a protracted spree, which made a few days' nursing very welcome. His wife, a Polish woman, had the old-world reverence for men, and obeyed him implicitly; she still felt it was very sweet of him to come home at all. Mrs. B. had often declared that Polly's devotion to her husband was a beautiful thing to see. The two eldest boys had newspaper routes and turned in their earnings regularly, and, although the husband did not contribute anything but his occasional company, Polly was able to make the payments on their little four-roomed cottage. In another year, it would be all paid for.

But one day Polly's husband began to look into the law—as all men should—and he saw that he had been living far below his privileges. The cottage was his—not that he had ever paid a cent on it, of course, but his wife had, and she was his; and the cottage was in his name.

So he sold it; naturally he did not consult Polly, for he was a quiet, peaceful man, and not fond of scenes. So he sold it quietly, and with equal quietness he withdrew from the Province, and took the money with him. He did not even say good-by to Polly or the children, which was rather ungrateful, for they had given him many a meal and night's lodging. When Polly came crying one Monday morning and told her story, Mrs. B. could not believe it, and assured Polly she must be mistaken, but Polly declared that a man had come and asked her did she wish to rent the house for he had bought it. Mrs. B. went at once to the lawyers who had completed the deal. They were a reputable firm and Mrs. B. knew one of the partners quite well. She was sure Polly's husband could not sell the cottage.

But the lawyers assured her it was quite true. They were very gentle and patient with Mrs. B. and listened courteously to her explanation, and did not dispute her word at all when she explained that Polly and her two boys had paid every cent on the house. It seemed that a trifling little thing like that did not matter. It did not really matter who paid for the house; the husband was the owner, for was he not the head of the house? and the property was in his name.

Polly was graciously allowed to rent her own cottage for $12.50 a month, with an option of buying, and the two little boys are still on a morning route delivering one of the city dailies.

Mrs. B. has joined a suffrage society and makes speeches on the injustice of the laws; and yet she began innocently enough, by making strong and durable garments for her washwoman's children—and see what has come of it! If women would only be content to snip away at the symptoms of poverty and distress, feeding the hungry and clothing the naked, all would be well and they would be much commended for their kindness of heart; but when they begin to inquire into causes, they find themselves in the sacred realm of politics where prejudice says no women must enter.

A woman may take an interest in factory girls, and hold meetings for them, and encourage them to walk in virtue's ways all she likes, but if she begins to advocate more sanitary surroundings for them, with some respect for the common decencies of life, she will find herself again in that sacred realm of politics—confronted by a factory act, on which no profane female hand must be laid.

Now politics simply means public affairs—yours and mine, everybody's—and to say that politics are too corrupt for women is a weak and foolish statement for any man to make. Any man who is actively engaged in politics, and declares that politics are too corrupt for women, admits one of two things, either that he is a party to this corruption, or that he is unable to prevent it—and in either case something should be done. Politics are not inherently vicious. The office of lawmaker should be the highest in the land, equaled in honor only by that of the minister of the gospel. In the old days, the two were combined with very good effect; but they seem to have drifted apart in more recent years.

If politics are too corrupt for women, they are too corrupt for men; for men and women are one—indissolubly joined together for good or ill. Many men have tried to put all their religion and virtue in their wife's name, but it does not work very well. When social conditions are corrupt women cannot escape by shutting their eyes, and taking no interest. It would be far better to give them a chance to clean them up.

What would you think of a man who would say to his wife: "This house to which I am bringing you to live is very dirty and unsanitary, but I will not allow you—the dear wife whom I have sworn to protect—to touch it. It is too dirty for your precious little white hands! You must stay upstairs, dear. Of course the odor from below may come up to you, but use your smelling salts and think no evil. I do not hope to ever be able to clean it up, but certainly you must never think of trying."

Do you think any woman would stand for that? She would say: "John, you are all right in your way, but there are some places where your brain skids. Perhaps you had better stay downtown today for lunch. But on your way down please call at the grocer's, and send me a scrubbing brush and a package of Dutch Cleanser, and some chloride of lime, and now hurry." Women have cleaned up things since time began; and if women ever get into politics there will be a cleaning-out of pigeon-holes and forgotten corners, on which the dust of years has fallen, and the sound of the political carpet-beater will be heard in the land.

There is another hardy perennial that constantly lifts its head above the earth, persistently refusing to be ploughed under, and that is that if women were ever given a chance to participate in outside affairs, that family quarrels would result; that men and their wives who have traveled the way of life together, side by side, for years, and come safely through religious discussions, and discussions relating to "his" people and "her" people, would angrily rend each other over politics, and great damage to the furniture would be the result. Father and son have been known to live under the same roof and vote differently, and yet live! Not only live, but live peaceably! If a husband and wife are going to quarrel they will find a cause for dispute easily enough, and will not be compelled to wait for election day. And supposing that they have never, never had a single dispute, and not a ripple has ever marred the placid surface of their matrimonial sea, I believe that a small family jar—or at least a real lively argument—will do them good. It is in order to keep the white-winged angel of peace hovering over the home that married women are not allowed to vote in many places. Spinsters and widows are counted worthy of voice in the selection of school trustee, and alderman, and mayor, but not the woman who has taken to herself a husband and still has him.

What a strange commentary on marriage that it should disqualify a woman from voting. Why should marriage disqualify a woman? Men have been known to vote for years after they were dead!

Quite different from the "family jar" theory, another reason is advanced against married women voting—it is said that they would all vote with their husbands, and that the married man's vote would thereby be doubled. We believe it is eminently right and proper that husband and wife should vote the same way, and in that case no one would be able to tell whether the wife was voting with the husband or the husband voting with the wife. Neither would it matter. If giving the franchise to women did nothing more than double the married man's vote it would do a splendid thing for the country, for the married man is the best voter we have; generally speaking, he is a man of family and property—surely if we can depend on anyone we can depend upon him, and if by giving his wife a vote we can double his—we have done something to offset the irresponsible transient vote of the man who has no interest in the community.

There is another sturdy prejudice that blooms everywhere in all climates, and that is that women would not vote if they had the privilege; and this is many times used as a crushing argument against woman suffrage. But why worry? If women do not use it, then surely there is no harm done; but those who use the argument seem to imply that a vote unused is a very dangerous thing to leave lying around, and will probably spoil and blow up. In support of this statement instances are cited of women letting their vote lie idle and unimproved in elections for school trustee and alderman. Of course, the percentage of men voting in these contests was quite small, too, but no person finds fault with that.

Women may have been careless about their franchise in elections where no great issue is at stake, but when moral matters are being decided women have not shown any lack of interest. As a result of the first vote cast by the women of Illinois over one thousand saloons went out of business. Ask the liquor dealers if they think women will use the ballot. They do not object to woman suffrage on the ground that women will not vote, but because they will.

"Why, Uncle Henry!" exclaimed one man to another on election day. "I never saw you out to vote before. What struck you?"

"Hadn't voted for fifteen years," declared Uncle Henry, "but you bet I came out today to vote against givin' these fool women a vote; what's the good of givin' them a vote? they wouldn't use it!"

Then, of course, on the other hand there are those who claim that women would vote too much—that they would vote not wisely but too well; that they would take up voting as a life work to the exclusion of husband, home and children. There seems to be considerable misapprehension on the subject of voting. It is really a simple and perfectly innocent performance, quickly over, and with no bad after-effects.

It is usually done in a vacant room in a school or the vestry of a church, or a town hall. No drunken men stare at you. You are not jostled or pushed—you wait your turn in an orderly line, much as you have waited to buy a ticket at a railway station. Two tame and quiet-looking men sit at a table, and when your turn comes, they ask you your name, which is perhaps slightly embarrassing, but it is not as bad as it might be, for they do not ask your age, or of what disease did your grandmother die. You go behind the screen with your ballot paper in your hand, and there you find a seal-brown pencil tied with a chaste white string. Even the temptation of annexing the pencil is removed from your frail humanity. You mark your ballot, and drop it in the box, and come out into the sunlight again. If you had never heard that you had done an unladylike thing you would not know it. It all felt solemn, and serious, and very respectable to you, something like a Sunday-school convention. Then, too, you are surprised at what a short time you have been away from home. You put the potatoes on when you left home, and now you are back in time to strain them.

In spite of the testimony of many reputable women that they have been able to vote and get the dinner on one and the same day, there still exists a strong belief that the whole household machinery goes out of order when a woman goes to vote. No person denies a woman the right to go to church, and yet the church service takes a great deal more time than voting. People even concede to women the right to go shopping, or visiting a friend, or an occasional concert. But the wife and mother, with her God-given, sacred trust of molding the young life of our land, must never dream of going round the corner to vote. "Who will mind the baby?" cried one of our public men, in great agony of spirit, "when the mother goes to vote?"

One woman replied that she thought she could get the person that minded it when she went to pay her taxes—which seemed to be a fairly reasonable proposition. Yet the hardy plant of prejudice flourishes, and the funny pictures still bring a laugh.

Father comes home, tired, weary, footsore, toe-nails ingrowing, caused by undarned stockings, and finds the fire out, house cold and empty, save for his half-dozen children, all crying.

"Where is your mother?" the poor man asks in broken tones. For a moment the sobs are hushed while little Ellie replies: "Out voting!"

Father bursts into tears.

Of course, people tell us, it is not the mere act of voting which demoralizes women—if they would only vote and be done with it; but women are creatures of habit, and habits once formed are hard to break; and although the polls are only open every three or four years, if women once get into the way of going to them, they will hang around there all the rest of the time. It is in woman's impressionable nature that the real danger lies.

Another shoot of this hardy shrub of prejudice is that women are too good to mingle in everyday life—they are too sweet and too frail—that women are angels. If women are angels we should try to get them into public life as soon as possible, for there is a great shortage of angels there just at present, if all we hear is true.

Then there is the pedestal theory—that women are away up on a pedestal, and down below, looking up at them with deep adoration, are men, their willing slaves. Sitting up on a pedestal does not appeal very strongly to a healthy woman—and, besides, if a woman has been on a pedestal for any length of time, it must be very hard to have to come down and cut the wood.

These tender-hearted and chivalrous gentlemen who tell you of their adoration for women, cannot bear to think of women occupying public positions. Their tender hearts shrink from the idea of women lawyers or women policemen, or even women preachers; these positions would "rub the bloom off the peach," to use their own eloquent words. They cannot bear, they say, to see women leaving the sacred precincts of home—and yet their offices are scrubbed by women who do their work while other people sleep—poor women who leave the sacred precincts of home to earn enough to keep the breath of life in them, who carry their scrub-pails home, through the deserted streets, long after the cars have stopped running. They are exposed to cold, to hunger, to insult—poor souls—is there any pity felt for them? Not that we have heard of. The tender-hearted ones can bear this with equanimity. It is the thought of women getting into comfortable and well-paid positions which wrings their manly hearts.

Another aspect of the case is that women can do more with their indirect influence than by the ballot; though just why they cannot do better still with both does not appear to be very plain. The ballot is a straight-forward dignified way of making your desire or choice felt. There are some things which are not pleasant to talk about, but would be delightful to vote against. Instead of having to beg, and coax, and entreat, and beseech, and denounce as women have had to do all down the centuries, in regard to the evil things which threaten to destroy their homes and those whom they love, what a glorious thing it would be if women could go out and vote against these things. It seems like a straightforward and easy way of expressing one's opinion.

But, of course, popular opinion says it is not "womanly." The "womanly way" is to nag and tease. Women have often been told that if they go about it right they can get anything. They are encouraged to plot and scheme, and deceive, and wheedle, and coax for things. This is womanly and sweet. Of course, if this fails, they still have tears—they can always cry and have hysterics, and raise hob generally, but they must do it in a womanly way. Will the time ever come when the word "feminine" will have in it no trace of trickery?

Women are too sentimental to vote, say the politicians sometimes. Sentiment is nothing to be ashamed of, and perhaps an infusion of sentiment in politics is what we need. Honor and honesty, love and loyalty, are only sentiments, and yet they make the fabric out of which our finest traditions are woven. The United States has sent carloads of flour to starving Belgium because of a sentiment. Belgium refused to let Germany march over her land because of a sentiment, and Canada has responded to the SOS call of the Empire because of a sentiment. It seems that it is sentiment which redeems our lives from sordidness and selfishness, and occasionally gives us a glimpse of the upper country. For too long people have regarded politics as a scheme whereby easy money might be obtained. Politics has meant favors, pulls, easy jobs for friends, new telephone lines, ditches. The question has not been: "What can I do for my country?" but: "What can I get? What is there in this for me?" The test of a member of Parliament as voiced by his constituents has been: "What has he got for us?" The good member who will be elected the next time is the one who did not forget his friends, who got us a Normal School, or a Court House, or an Institution for the Blind, something that we could see or touch, eat or drink. Surely a touch of sentiment in politics would do no harm.

Then there is the problem of the foreign woman's vote. Many people fear that the granting of woman suffrage would greatly increase the unintelligent vote, because the foreign women would then have the franchise, and in our blind egotism we class our foreign people as ignorant people, if they do not know our ways and our language. They may know many other languages, but if they have not yet mastered ours they are poor, ignorant foreigners. We Anglo-Saxon people have a decided sense of our own superiority, and we feel sure that our skin is exactly the right color, and we people from Huron and Bruce feel sure that we were born in the right place, too. So we naturally look down upon those who happen to be of a different race and tongue than our own.

It is a sad feature of humanity that we are disposed to hate what we do not understand; we naturally suspect and distrust where we do not know. Hens are like that, too! When a strange fowl comes into a farmyard all the hens take a pick at it—not that it has done anything wrong, but they just naturally do not like the look of its face because it is strange. Now that may be very good ethics for hens, but it is hardly good enough for human beings. Our attitude toward the foreign people was well exemplified in one of the missions, where a little Italian boy, who had been out two years, refused to sit beside a newly arrived Italian boy, who, of course, could not speak a word of English. The teacher asked him to sit with his lately arrived compatriot, so that he might interpret for him. The older boy flatly refused, and told the teacher he "had no use for them young dagos."

"You see," said the teacher sadly, when telling the story, "he had caught the Canadian spirit."

People say hard things about the corruptible foreign vote, but they place the emphasis in the wrong place. Instead of using our harsh adjectives for the poor fellow who sells his vote, let us save them all for the corrupt politician who buys it, for he cannot plead ignorance—he knows what he is doing. The foreign people who come to Canada, come with burning enthusiasm for the new land, this land of liberty—land of freedom. Some have been seen kissing the ground in an ecstacy of gladness when they arrive. It is the land of their dreams, where they hope to find home and happiness. They come to us with ideals of citizenship that shame our narrow, mercenary standards. These men are of a race which has gladly shed its blood for freedom and is doing it today. But what happens? They go out to work on construction gangs for the summer, they earn money for several months, and when the work closes down they drift back into the cities. They have done the work we wanted them to do, and no further thought is given to them. They may get off the earth so far as we are concerned. One door stands invitingly open to them. There is one place they are welcome—so long as their money lasts—and around the bar they get their ideals of citizenship.

When an election is held, all at once this new land of their adoption begins to take an interest in them, and political heelers, well paid for the job, well armed with whiskey, cigars and money, go among them, and, in their own language, tell them which way they must vote—and they do. Many an election has been swung by this means. One new arrival, just learning our language, expressed his contempt for us by exclaiming: "Bah! Canada is not a country—it's just a place to make money." That was all he had seen. He spoke correctly from his point of view.

Then when the elections are over, and the Government is sustained, the men who have climbed back to power by these means speak eloquently of our "foreign people who have come to our shores to find freedom under the sheltering folds of our grand old flag (cheers), on which the sun never sets, and under whose protection all men are free and equal—with an equal chance of molding the destiny of the great Empire of which we make a part." (Cheers and prolonged applause.)

If we really understood how, with our low political ideals and iniquitous election methods, we have corrupted the souls of these men who have come to live among us, we would no longer cheer, when we hear this old drivel of the "folds of the flag." We would think with shame of how we have driven the patriotism out of these men and replaced it by the greed of gain, and instead of cheers and applause we would cry: "Lord, have mercy upon us!"

The foreign women, whom politicians and others look upon as such a menace, are differently dealt with than the men. They do not go out to work, en masse, as the men do. They work one by one, and are brought in close contact with their employers. The women who go out washing and cleaning spend probably five days a week in the homes of other women. Surely one of her five employers will take an interest in her, and endeavor to instruct her in the duties of citizenship. Then, too, the mission work is nearly all done for women and girls. The foreign women generally speak English before the men, for the reason that they are brought in closer contact with English-speaking people. When I hear people speaking of the ignorant foreign women I think of "Mary," and "Annie," and others I have known. I see their broad foreheads and intelligent kindly faces, and think of the heroic struggle they are making to bring their families up in thrift and decency. Would Mary vote against liquor if she had the chance? She would. So would you if your eyes had been blackened as often by a drunken husband. There is no need to instruct these women on the evils of liquor drinking—they are able to give you a few aspects of the case which perhaps you had not thought of. We have no reason to be afraid of the foreign woman's vote. I wish we were as sure of the ladies who live on the Avenue.

There are people who tell us that the reason women must never be allowed to vote is because they do not want to vote, the inference being that women are never given anything that they do not want. It sounds so chivalrous and protective and high-minded. But women have always got things that they did not want. Women do not want the liquor business, but they have it; women do not want less pay for the same work as men, but they get it. Women did not want the present war, but they have it. The fact of women's preference has never been taken very seriously, but it serves here just as well as anything else. Even the opponents of woman suffrage will admit that some women want to vote, but they say they are a very small minority, and "not our best women." That is a classification which is rather difficult of proof and of no importance anyway. It does not matter whether it is the best, or second best, or the worst who are asking for a share in citizenship; voting is not based on morality, but on humanity. No man votes because he is one of our best men. He votes because he is of the male sex, and over twenty-one years of age. The fact that many women are indifferent on the subject does not alter the situation. People are indifferent about many things that they should be interested in. The indifference of people on the subject of ventilation and hygiene does not change the laws of health. The indifference of many parents on the subject of an education for their children does not alter the value of education. If one woman wants to vote, she should have that opportunity just as if one woman desires a college education, she should not be held back because of the indifferent careless ones who do not desire it. Why should the mentally inert, careless, uninterested woman, who cares nothing for humanity but is contented to patter along her own little narrow way, set the pace for the others of us? Voting will not be compulsory; the shrinking violets will not be torn from their shady fence-corner; the "home bodies" will be able to still sit in rapt contemplation of their own fireside. We will not force the vote upon them, but why should they force their votelessness upon us?

"My wife does not want to vote," declared one of our Canadian premiers in reply to a delegation of women who asked for the vote. "My wife would not vote if she had the chance," he further stated. No person had asked about his wife, either.

"I will not have my wife sit in Parliament," another man cried in alarm, when he was asked to sign a petition giving women full right of franchise. We tried to soothe his fears. We delicately and tactfully declared that his wife was safe. She would not be asked to go to Parliament by any of us—we gave him our word that she was immune from public duties of that nature, for we knew the lady and her limitations, and we knew she was safe—safe as a glass of milk at an old-fashioned logging-bee; safe as a dish of cold bread pudding at a strawberry festival. She would not have to leave home to serve her country at "the earnest solicitation of friends" or otherwise. But he would not sign. He saw his "Minnie" climbing the slippery ladder of political fame. It would be his Minnie who would be chosen—he felt it coming, the sacrifice would fall on his one little ewe-lamb.

After one has listened to all these arguments and has contracted clergyman's sore throat talking back, it is real relief to meet the people who say flatly and without reason: "You can't have it—no—

I won't argue—but inasmuch as I can prevent it—you will never vote! So there!" The men who meet the question like this are so easy to classify.

I remember when I was a little girl back on the farm in the Souris Valley, I used to water the cattle on Saturday mornings, drawing the water in an icy bucket with a windlass from a fairly deep well. We had one old white ox, called Mike, a patriarchal-looking old sinner, who never had enough, and who always had to be watered first. Usually I gave him what I thought he should have and then took him back to the stable and watered the others. But one day I was feeling real strong, and I resolved to give Mike all he could drink, even if it took every drop of water in the well. I must admit that I cherished a secret hope that he would kill himself drinking. I will not set down here in cold figures how many pails of water Mike drank—but I remember. At last he could not drink another drop, and stood shivering beside the trough, blowing the last mouthful out of his mouth like a bad child. I waited to see if he would die, or at least turn away and give the others a chance. The thirsty cattle came crowding around him, but old Mike, so full I am sure he felt he would never drink another drop of water again as long as he lived, deliberately and with difficulty put his two front feet over the trough and kept all the other cattle away.... Years afterwards I had the pleasure of being present when a delegation waited upon the Government of one of the provinces of Canada, and presented many reasons for extending the franchise to women. One member of the Government arose and spoke for all his colleagues. He said in substance: "You can't have it—so long as I have anything to do with the affairs of this province—you shall not have it!"

Did your brain ever give a queer little twist, and suddenly you were conscious that the present mental process had taken place before. If you have ever had it, you will know what I mean, and if you haven't I cannot make you understand. I had that feeling then.... I said to myself: "Where have I seen that face before?... Then, suddenly, I remembered, and in my heart I cried out: "Mike!—old friend, Mike! Dead these many years! Your bones lie buried under the fertile soil of the Souris Valley, but your soul goes marching on! Mike, old friend, I see you again—both feet in the trough!"

FURTHER READING

Nellie McClung wrote extensively in both fiction and non-fiction genres. She also campaigned vigorously for a number of causes, and some of her best speeches and essays are contained in the volume she compiled in 1915 as *In Times Like These* (from which the selection above is taken). Many accounts of Nellie McClung's life and activism are available, including *Nellie McClung and Women's Rights* by Helen Wright (Agincourt: Book Society of Canada, 1980); *Nellie McClung: No Small Legacy* by Carol Hancock (Kelowna: Northstone, 1996); and *Nellie McClung: A Voice for the Voiceless* by Margaret Macpherson (Montreal: XYZ Publishing, 2003). A brief but succinct version is Veronica Strong-Boag's introduction to *In Times Like These*, published by the University of Toronto Press in 1972.

4   J.S. WOODSWORTH

INTRODUCTION

J.S. Woodsworth (1872–1942) is the founder of social democracy in Canada. Rejecting both his Methodist background because of its conservatism and Marxist theory because of its confrontational politics, Woodsworth established a more liberal form of progressivism in Canada. He argued that poverty and exploitation could be solved more constructively by involving government and business in social reform rather than through the overthrow of capitalism. Beginning in 1918, Woodsworth wrote a series of articles for the *Western Labor News*, in which he attempted to set out a "third way" for Canadian politics. In December 1921, he was elected to the House of Commons, and in 1933, he was instrumental in the founding of the Cooperative Commonwealth Federation, the precursor to the modern New Democratic Party.

ORGANIZING DEMOCRACY IN CANADA (1918)

Why is Canada so far behind the other countries? Various reasons may be given. "We have not yet attained full autonomy." That is also true of our sister commonwealths, Australia and New Zealand, which, nevertheless, have secured much progressive legislation. "We are under the shadow of the great republic to the south." Possibly, yet we must confess that many of our forward movements have been stimulated by similar movements in the United States. "We are a divided people." Switzerland and Belgium are composed of diverse people and yet have secured unity and advancement. "We have been under the curse of protectionism and the dominance of the railroads." But this is an effect rather than a cause. Why have we been cursed and dominated more than others? "We have lacked leadership." Again, why? Probably not one, but a combination of these and other reasons have led to the deplorable position in which we Canadians find ourselves today.

Undoubtedly, we need leadership and higher ideals and greater unselfishness and courage. Whence these come, and how they may be developed, are questions outside the scope of this article. We confine ourselves to the practical problem of mobilizing the already existing forces. We believe that if the scattered forces of democracy could only be drawn together into an effective fighting unit, they would sweep the country.

Confessedly, Canada is a difficult country to organize. It is a land of "magnificent distances" with a sparse and scattered population. It is divided into more or less water-tight compartments. Nova Scotia has little in common with Ontario, or the prairie provinces, with British Columbia. Each province has its own interests, its own institutions, its own set of newspapers, its own organizations. It is very difficult to unify public opinion in one organization or through one newspaper or outstanding personality.

Further, we have not a common language—Canada is officially a bilingual country. Any one who has attended, say, a meeting of the Montreal Trades and Labor Council, in which business is conducted in both English and French, perceives the difficulties of the situation. Few, however, realize that all through Western Canada the majority of our non-English immigrants, who in reality hold the balance of power, are unable to read an English newspaper. Each group maintains its own identity. The lingual, religious, national ties are stronger than those of class interest. This the political demagogues recognize and so at every election the vital issues are beclouded by appeals to national and religious prejudices.

The industrial East is sharply divided, in economic interests, from the agricultural West. Even the labor forces of Toronto and the grain growers of the prairies would hardly unite against "the interests" if the tariff question were the immediate issue.

Within any one province there are thorough-going democrats among the "labor people," among the farmers and among the professional and commercial classes in the town and cities, yet it is very difficult to unite in one organization the farmer, the labor man and the townsman. Here again each speaks a different language. They run up against "the system" from different angles. Yet as a matter of fact, in most constituencies at least, two of these groups must be united, if an election is to be won.

The returned soldier has introduced yet another element into the Canadian political situation. For various reasons strong "pacifist" tendencies are at work among the French in Quebec, the farmers in Ontario and the middle west and the labor-men in all the larger industrial centres. The soldier is professionally a man of war, yet he, too, has gained some insight into "the system." He is above all else against "graft." Coming from the common people and returning to the ranks of the common people, he has, as he is beginning to realize, much more in common with the labor man or the farmer than with those representing the privileged interests.

Still another weakness in our public life must be reckoned with. We have had little training in the actual working of democratic or co-operative institutions. The country is so young and the population is so drifting that local self-government is almost undeveloped. The illiterate Russian peasant, or the Belgian farmer, or the English co-operator, has much clearer ideas and much more experience in practical organization than we have in Canada. We are bred in the bone, dyed-in-the-wool individualists, nourished on an individualist religion and code of ethics and plunged into a civilization at the moment where individualism seemed the key to success.

It is under such conditions that we must organize the forces of democracy. What method will likely prove the most effective? We could wish that we could have one strong organization with a broad platform—along the lines of the British Labor Party—one which all could unite in. Probably that is too much to expect. Yet that should be the ultimate aim and the leaders in any one division of the army of democracy should in the meantime do everything possible to show that all were fighting a common foe, that the interests of all real producers are identical and that so far as practicable all should be drawn into one camp.

Now that the old parties have joined forces in a Union Government it would seem that the democrats have a splendid opportunity to develop a genuine people's party in which farmers, individual workers, returned soldiers and progressives could all find a place.

But, as J.A. Hobson points out in a pamphlet recently issued by the I.L.P., the fight will be long and severe. We fight not against abstract "capitalism," but against capitalism in league with militarism, with Imperialism, with protection, with authoritarianism in religion and education, with subsidized press and with soporifics and palliatives in the form of amusements and "welfare" provisions—the fight must be maintained all along the line. We must have our own press—a free and far-reaching press. We must have institutions to supplement and correct the work of the public schools and universities and churches which on the whole seek to maintain the status quo. We must train ourselves in local co-operative enterprises. We must resist the insidious propaganda which, under camouflage of military necessity or national advantage, seeks to perpetuate conditions that breed jealousy and war. We must in season and out of season emphasize the priority of the claims of social welfare over those of selfish interests.

This war, with all its waste, with all the evils it brings in its train, will not be in vain. Men are thinking—thinking as never before. Old ideas and institutions have gone by the board. All is in the melting pot. We cannot escape the confusion and welter and terror of the process. The end of the war may be only the beginning of the "evil days" for Canada. But out of it all a new civilization is being born—a new religion is rising.

FURTHER READING

Woodsworth's early thought is set out in his two books: *Strangers Within Our Gates* (1908), a study on the problem of immigration, and *My Neighbor* (1911), which discusses the issue of urban development. His later thought is reflected in the *Regina Manifesto*, written cooperatively, which sets out the principles of the Cooperative Commonwealth Federation. The classic biography of Woodsworth is Kenneth McNaught's *A Prophet in Politics* (Toronto: University of Toronto Press, 1959). Allen Mills's *A Fool for Christ: The Political Thought of J.S. Woodsworth* (Toronto: University of Toronto Press, 1991) is a superb analysis of Woodsworth's life and ideas. For a discussion of the social democratic movement, see Norman Penner's "The development of social democracy in Canada," in Stephen Brooks, ed., *Political Thought in Canada* (Toronto: Irwin, 1984). A more detailed account of socialist thought in Canada can be found in Norman Penner's *The Canadian Left: A Critical Analysis* (Scarborough: Prentice-Hall, 1977).

HAROLD INNIS

INTRODUCTION

An exemplary polymath, Harold Innis (1894–1952) is one of the most influential figures not only in the study of economics and history in Canada, but also in sociology, politics, and cultural studies. His early works on the fur trade, mining, and the cod industry in Canada led to the development of the "staples theory" which investigated the dynamic relationship between geography and technology. His analysis of the economic relationship between metropole and hinterland strongly influenced the "dependency theory" school of Canadian political economy. Innis's later study of the political economy of transportation sparked his interest in the nature of communication; and this underpinned his more abstract work in "communications studies," which investigated how economic and political institutions dealt with the exigencies of time and space. These ideas, in turn, were strongly influential for thinkers such as Marshall McLuhan and for the nascent discipline of cultural studies.

TRANSPORTATION AS A FACTOR IN CANADIAN ECONOMIC HISTORY (1933)

Transportation has been of such basic importance to Canadian economic history that the title of this paper may appear redundant and inclusive. The paper is intended, however, as an attempt to consider the general position of transportation in Canada, with special relation to its peculiar characteristics and their relationships to Canadian development, rather than to present a brief survey of Canadian economic history.

The early development of North America was dependent on the evolution of ships adapted to crossing the Atlantic. Water transportation, which had been of first importance in the growth of

European civilization, had improved to the extent that, by the beginning of the sixteenth century, long voyages could be undertaken across the north Atlantic.[1] These voyages were continued in relation to the acquisition of commodities for which a strong demand existed in Europe, and which were available in large quantities within short distances from the seaboard of the new countries. In the north Atlantic, cod was a commodity in the handling of which the advantages of water transportation were capitalized to the full. On the banks, ships from Europe caught and cured the fish in preparation for direct sale in the home market. Early in the seventeenth century, following the opening of the Spanish market and the new demand for dried cod, ships from England and France developed dry fishing in Newfoundland, the remote parts of the Gulf such as Gaspé, and the New England shore.

Mr. Biggar has shown the relationship between dry fishing and the fur trade.[2] Penetration to the interior brought Europeans in touch with the resources of the mainland. The continued overwhelming importance of water transportation for the development of the interior warrants a brief survey of the more important waterways and their characteristics. The course and volume of the waterways in the northeastern half of North America is largely determined by the geological background of the area. The Precambrian formation is in the form of an angle, with one side pointing toward the northeast, including northern Quebec and Labrador, and bounded on the north by Hudson Straits, and the other to the northwest and bounded by the western Arctic. Hudson Bay constitutes a large portion of the territory in the angle. The resistant character of the formation and its relatively level surface have been responsible for a network of lakes and rivers. Its youthful topography following the retreat of the ice sheets is shown in the number of rapids and obstructions to the tributaries and rivers. The major water courses flow roughly along the junction of the formation with later weaker formations, as in the St. Lawrence waterway which begins with the Great Lakes and flows northeast toward the Gulf, and the Mackenzie which flows northwest toward the Arctic. The St. Lawrence is fed from the north by important tributaries, such as the Saguenay, the St. Maurice, and the Ottawa, which are separated by low heights of land from rivers flowing to Hudson Bay. The main waterway[3] is broken by serious obstructions at Niagara and the St. Lawrence rapids above

Montreal, and the tributaries have numerous rapids. The drainage basins to the south, the Mississippi, the Ohio, and the rivers of New York, are separated by comparatively low heights of land.

The commodity supplied by this vast stretch of northern Precambrian territory, and demanded by Europe, was fur. The sailing ships were restricted to the mouth of the St. Lawrence River, and the opening of trade on the river and its tributaries necessitated the use of pinnaces.4 Tadoussac became the first terminus, but was displaced by Quebec after the French became more familiar with the river channel to that point. The relatively level stretch of water from Quebec to Montreal was adapted to the use of large boats, and with the improvement of the route the depot shifted from Tadoussac to Quebec, to Three Rivers, and thence to Montreal. In 1642 Montreal was established and the position of the French on this stretch of waterway consolidated. Beyond Montreal a third type of transport equipment—the canoe—became essential. The French were able to borrow directly from the equipment of the hunting Indians of the northern Precambrian area, and to adapt the transport unit, worked out by them, to their needs. With this unit French and English succeeded in bringing practically the whole of northern North America under tribute to the demands of the trade.

The canoe was adapted to the shorter Ottawa route to the upper country rather than to the longer and more difficult upper St. Lawrence and Great Lakes route. The trade of Georgian Bay, Green Bay on Lake Michigan, and Lake Superior was developed from this route to Montreal. Eventually La Verendrye and his successors extended it northwest to Lake Winnipeg and the Saskatchewan. The limitations of the birch-bark canoe, even after its enlargement and adaptation by the French, necessitated the establishment of depots for provisions at convenient points. Its labour costs were heavy.

The upper St. Lawrence and Great Lakes route was never developed as a satisfactory substitute by the French, and the difficulties of La Salle with Great Lakes transportation in its initial development characterized its later history. The problems of organization of the route were enhanced by the competition of the Dutch and English through the Iroquois and the Mohawk route to Oswego prior to 1722, and through direct trade after the establishment of Oswego in that year. As a result of this competition, the St. Lawrence and

Great Lakes route involved a substantial drain on the trade. Posts were established at Frontenac, Niagara, and Detroit as a means of checking English competition, and the upkeep of these posts involved heavy expenses for the colony. Eventually Toronto was added in 1749 as a further check to Indian trade with the English. The shorter route to Oswego and the use of large boats on the lake were factors which seriously weakened the position of canoe transport on the Ottawa.

Only with the disappearance of the French after 1760 did it become possible to combine satisfactorily the upper St. Lawrence—Great Lakes route for boats and vessels with the canoe route on the Ottawa. The lake boat became an ally to the canoe rather than an enemy. Heavy goods were carried by the lakes, and light goods were taken up and furs brought down by canoes. Cheaper supplies of provisions were available at Detroit and Niagara, and were carried at lower costs up the lakes to Grand Portage and later to Fort William. Niagara portage was organized and a canal was built at Sault Ste Marie. With the organization of Great Lakes transport it became possible to extend the trade far beyond the limits reached by the French. The Northwest Company succeeded in penetrating from Fort William to Lake Winnipeg and the Saskatchewan, by Cumberland House and Frog Portage to the Churchill, by Methye Portage to Athabaska, the Peace and the Mackenzie, and by the passes across the Rockies to the upper Fraser and the Columbia. Supply depots were organized on the Red River, on the Saskatchewan, and on the Peace.

The efficiency of the canoe in serving as a transport unit from Montreal along the edge of the Canadian shield almost to the Arctic was dependent in part on the efficient organization of water transport along the Ottawa to Montreal, and on the Great Lakes. In 1821 this elaborate system collapsed and the canoe ceased to be a basic factor in transport. The boat again became an important factor in contributing to its failure, but from the north or Hudson Bay and not from the south. Ocean transport, in addition to supremacy of the Bay with boats in inland transport, was overwhelmingly important.

Hudson Bay was developed as a trading area over fifty years later than the St. Lawrence basin, and its growth depended largely on experience acquired in the St. Lawrence. Radisson and Groseilliers saw the possibility of tapping the trade from the centre of the Precambrian angle rather than from the outer edges. Accordingly ships were despatched to the mouths of the rivers flowing into James Bay and into Hudson Bay, and after the formation of the Hudson's Bay Company in 1670 the trade of the drainage basin began to flow toward the north. Ships were unable to visit the posts at the foot of James Bay because of the shallow character of the bay, and smaller boats were used to collect fur and distribute goods from a central depot on Charlton Island.5 On Hudson Bay ships were able to visit the mouths of the Nelson and the Churchill rivers. The tributaries of the Hudson Bay drainage basin flowing from the east and the south were similar to those on the opposite side of the height of land flowing toward the St. Lawrence. But the vast interior of the continent to the west poured its waters toward Hudson Bay and forced a main outlet across the Precambrian formation by the Nelson River. This outlet and its tributaries served as an entrance to the northwest from Hudson Bay. The advantages of the route were continually in evidence but were overcome temporarily by the canoe route under the French and under the English. With the use of the boat on this relatively short stretch the long line of the canoe route was cut in the centre, and after 1821 all goods for the West were taken in by York Factory, and the Fort William route was abandoned. For over half a century the York boat and Hudson Bay dominated the transport of western Canada. Brigades were organized throughout the Hudson Bay drainage basin and across to the Churchill, the Athabaska, the Peace, and the Mackenzie rivers.

Water transportation facilitated the exploitation of furs throughout the Precambrian area and beyond, but the efficiency of technique determined the routes to be used. The ocean ship to Quebec, the large boats to Montreal, the *canot de maître* to Fort William, and the *canot du nord* to the interior, assisted in the later period by the vessels on the lakes, proved unable to withstand the competition from the ocean ship to Nelson and the York boat to the interior.

The comparative ease with which the transport unit was borrowed and adapted, or devised to meet the demands of the water routes, gave the waterways a position of dominant importance in the moulding of types of economic and political structure. Rapid exploitation of the available staple product over a wide area was inevitable. Undoubtedly the character of the water routes was of fundamental importance in shifting the attention of Canada to the production of staple raw materials. It became necessary to concentrate energy on the transport of raw materials over long distances. The result was that the Canadian economic structure had the peculiar characteristics of areas dependent on staples—especially weakness in other lines of development, dependence on highly industrialized areas for markets and for supplies of manufactured goods, and the dangers of fluctuations in the staple commodity. It had the effect, however, of giving changes of technique a position of strategic importance in fluctuations in economic activity. In one year transport to the west shifted from Montreal to Hudson Bay. The St. Lawrence basin flourished with the opening of trade to the west and languished when it was cut off. The legacy of the fur trade has been an organized transport over wide areas especially adapted for handling heavy manufactured goods going to the interior and for bringing out a light, valuable commodity. The heavy one-way traffic made the trade discouraging to settlement, and in turn made the trade a heavy drain on settlement. The main routes had been well organized to handle trade over vast areas.

The disappearance of fur from the St. Lawrence basin was accompanied by the rise of lumber as a staple export.[6] The economy built up in relation to fur and water transport was shifted to the second product available on a large scale chiefly from the Precambrian area. Lumber in contrast to fur was a heavy, bulky commodity whether in the form of square timber, logs, deals, planks, or boards, and consequently its transport on a large scale was confined to the larger tributaries and the main St. Lawrence route. The Ottawa and upper St. Lawrence and Lake Ontario drained the most favourable areas for the growth of the large coniferous species, especially white pine. Rapid exploitation was limited to the softwoods which had a low specific gravity and could be floated down the rivers to Quebec. Lumber supplied its own method of conveyance, and the evolution of rafts suitable to running the rapids of the lower Ottawa in 1806, and the rapids of the St. Lawrence at a later date, and finally the introduction of slides for the upper Ottawa, solved the problem of technique. Square timber was floated down the lower St. Lawrence to be stored along the tidal beach at Quebec in preparation for loading on wooden ships for the protected markets of England.

The effects, on the economic development of the St. Lawrence basin, of dependence on lumber as a staple product, were the opposite of the effects of dependence on fur. Whereas fur involved a heavy incoming cargo, lumber favoured a large return cargo and consequently provided a stimulus to immigration and settlement. The coffin ships of the lumber trade made an important contribution to the movement of immigrants which became prominent after 1820. The trade created a demand for labour and for agricultural products. As in the case of fur it also created violent fluctuations in the economic activity of the colony, and its position as a raw material for construction made the St. Lawrence basin susceptible to an unusual extent to the effects of the business cycle.

The increase in settlement in Upper Canada after 1783 and the decline of the fur trade in 1821 raised serious problems for transportation above the Niagara Peninsula and on Lake Ontario. As early as 1801 a Kentucky boat with 350 barrels of flour was sent down the St. Lawrence rapids with success,7 and boats were used to an increasing extent to overcome the drawbacks of the route. A satisfactory outlet was obtained for goods going downstream, but upstream traffic continued a serious problem.

The limitations of the St. Lawrence route were accentuated with the introduction of steam. The industrial revolution and its effects on transportation were destined to have a far-reaching influence on the economic history of Canada. Application of the new technique to a transport system adapted to the handling of raw materials on the existing waterways accentuated the influence of the waterways on the later development. The steamship was adapted first to the stretch of river between Montreal and Quebec and continued in operation after 1809. It served as a complement to the lumber trade, and immigrants were taken upstream from Quebec without the inconvenience of a long upstream pull. The pressure from improved transportation to Montreal became evident in the increasing seriousness of the handicaps of the St. Lawrence rapids and the Great Lakes. Steamship communication on Lake Ontario was limited by the rapids of the St. Lawrence. Under these handicaps the competition of the Erie Canal at Buffalo above Niagara, and of the Oswego route above the St. Lawrence rapids, became important. An attempt to draw traffic from the upper lakes to the St. Lawrence River was made in the building of the Welland Canal, with eight-foot depth, completed in 1833. This improvement made increasingly necessary the improvement of the final link of the St. Lawrence rapids to Montreal. Eventually pressure from Upper Canada resulting from the handicap of high costs on the upstream traffic of manufactured goods contributed in part to the Rebellion of 1837, to the Durham *Report*, to the Act of Union, and to a determined effort to build the St. Lawrence canals. These canals were completed to nine feet in the forties, and lake steamers were able to go down regularly to Montreal after 1848.

It is important to emphasize at this point the relationship between the beginnings of the industrial revolution as seen in the application of steam to the St. Lawrence route, first from Quebec to Montreal, and later on the upper lakes, and the consequent pressure which led to the building of canals. These developments involved essential dependence on the government as seen in the Act of Union and the energetic canal policy of the first ten years. The Welland Canal was begun as a private enterprise, but inadequate supplies of cheap capital necessitated purchase by the government.[8] The relation between governmental activity and water transportation became an important factor in later developments.

The completion of the St. Lawrence route, and the stimulus to settlement, industry, and trade which it occasioned, intensified other limitations of the route. Moreover the delay in opening the route was responsible for rapid depreciation through obsolescence. Attempts to improve the St. Lawrence and compete with the Erie Canal, and to attract the export trade of the Middle West, were defeated by the construction of American railways.[9] The problem of offsetting the handicaps of the route by land transport began at an early date. In 1727 complaints were made that contrary winds were a serious cause of delay on the journey between Montreal and Quebec, and by 1736 a road had been built along the north shore. Stage roads became necessary above Montreal and along the north shore of Lake Ontario to Toronto and west to Dundas and western Upper Canada. The numerous ports along Lake Ontario became termini for roads to the back country.

This form of land transport, however, was far from adequate to meet the demands of trade and industry. Consequently the Grand Trunk was completed from Sarnia to Montreal in 1858. The old road from Toronto to Georgian Bay was abandoned with the completion of the Northern Railway from Toronto to Collingwood in 1854.

Chicago and Lake Michigan traffic was captured by this route, and traffic was developed on Lake Superior by the Sault Ste Marie Canal completed in 1855. Finally the handicap of closed seasons for navigation on the lower St. Lawrence disappeared with the completion of a short line through the Eastern Townships to Portland (1853), and of the Victoria Bridge (1859). By 1860 the St. Lawrence had been amply supplemented by a network of railways. After 1863 the trials of the Allan line on the St. Lawrence route in the fifties were overcome and the ocean steamship became an increasingly powerful factor in the development of the route.[10] Unfortunately the location of the Grand Trunk as a line supplementary to the St. Lawrence route left it exposed to competition from that route and it was brought to the verge of bankruptcy in 1857. The overwhelming importance of water transport was shown in the route followed by the Grand Trunk in tapping traffic areas built up on the St. Lawrence. The completion of these early railways marked the beginning of the amphibian stage of transport history....

Fiscal policy became involved not only in the improvement of transportation ... but also in developing manufactures, trade, and traffic. The development of industry contributed in turn to the growth of centres of large population and to an increase in traffic, a decrease in deficits, and a lighter burden for the government. The demands of transportation improvements were reflected directly and indirectly in fiscal policy. The fixed charges involved, especially in canals and the improvement of water transportation and in railways, led to a demand for new markets in the East and in the West. Expansion eastward and westward involved Confederation. The debates of the period suggest that the Intercolonial was not commercially feasible and that it was undertaken as a political measure, but it is difficult to conceive of its construction without reference to the demands for new markets. In any case, the results were evident. An excellent line was built at heavy initial cost, as is the custom with government undertakings, heavy interest charges followed, the line was operated at a loss, and goods were carried at unremunerative rates from the larger industrial centre to the Maritimes. The industrial area of central Canada strengthened its position with cheap water transport and access to the coal of the United States and Nova Scotia, and new markets were found in the Maritimes.

Sir Edward Watkin of the Grand Trunk regarded expansion to

the West as the solution of its difficulties.[11] The interest of Sir Hugh Allan in the early plans for expansion westward, which occasioned the Pacific Scandal, is significant of the continued importance attached to the development of traffic to the West in relation to the St. Lawrence route. The opening of the Intercolonial in 1876 gave the Allan line a Canadian winter port at Halifax, and the deepening of the St. Lawrence ship channel from seventeen and a half feet in 1860 to twenty-two feet in 1878 and to twenty-seven and a half feet in 1887 completed an efficient ocean steamship connection to Montreal in summer and to Halifax in winter. The immediate effects were evident in such divergent results as the rapid growth of the livestock industry in central Canada, the rapid decline of the wooden sailing vessel, the displacement of Quebec by Montreal, and the substitution of square timber by sawn lumber.

But of more striking importance was the demand for more rapid expansion westward to open markets for improved transport. From the standpoint of fiscal policy the outlay of capital in these improvements of transportation in canals and railroads contributed to the difficulties of the Mackenzie Administration and its free-trade policy in the depression of the seventies. The slow development of transportation to the West which followed from this policy was finally speeded up with the National Policy, which provided a guarantee of earnings on traffic carried within Canadian territory in case of success in keeping out goods and protecting the manufacturer, and a guarantee of revenue in case of failure to keep out goods with which to pay the deficit due to loss of traffic. The double-barrelled effectiveness of the policy was enhanced by recovery from the depression and the energetic construction of the Canadian Pacific Railway. Subsidies in money and in land and further protection of east-west traffic by the monopoly clause hastened the early completion of the line in 1885. It is only necessary to refer briefly to such additional developments as the establishment of the Pacific Ocean Services and the improvement of the line by the short line to Saint John in 1890 and the construction of the Crow's Nest Pass Railway after 1897.

The depression of the nineties was in part responsible for the delay in expected results, but the final expansion after 1900 was undoubtedly dependent on the deepening of the Sault Ste Marie Canal to nineteen feet in 1895, of the Welland Canal to fourteen feet in 1887, of the St. Lawrence canals to the same depth by 1901, and the St. Lawrence ship channel to thirty feet by 1906. The efficient transport system built up around the St. Lawrence basin for the handling of wheat hastened the industrial development of eastern Canada, including the iron and steel industry of the Maritimes, and contributed to the development of minerals, lumber, and fish in British Columbia. Eastern Canada lost her position as an exporter of dairy products to England and became a producer largely for rapidly increasing urban population in the home market. Improved transportation, followed by the opening of the West, was responsible for the period of marked prosperity from 1900 to 1914.

An important result of the dependence of staple products on transportation has been the suddenness of the changes which followed. The St. Lawrence canals were not available until the last lock had been built, and then the whole route was opened. Again the rapidity of construction of the railway from Skagway to Whitehorse revolutionized the placer mining of the Yukon. These sudden and unpredictable results were particularly important in the rapid accumulation of revenue from the tariff after 1900 and in the unexpected profitableness of Canadian Pacific Railway operations. These developments contributed in turn to the construction of two other transcontinental lines, the Canadian Northern Railway by guaranteed government bonds, and the Grand Trunk Pacific by the construction of the National Transcontinental Railway. The results included bankruptcy, the Drayton-Acworth report of 1917, and the Canadian National Railways and its problems.

The railway network has spread beyond the St. Lawrence basin but no one can deny the pull of the Great Lakes in the failure of wheat to move over the National Transcontinental Railway to Quebec. Canada has become to an increasing extent amphibian, but is still powerfully affected by the St. Lawrence basin. Nevertheless there are signs that the immense physical plant involved in transcontinental railways is beginning to have effects similar to those of the Northwest Company at the peak of its activities. The decline in importance of virgin natural resources has tended, with the railways as with the Northwest Company, to favour independent lines of growth. The Hudson Bay Railway, the opening of the Panama Canal and the growth of trade through Vancouver to the Orient parallel the independent development of the Pacific coast and the supremacy of the Hudson Bay route in the fur trade. Even with the support of the industrial revolution there are signs in the growth of regionalism that the second unity of Canada is beginning to drift in the direction of the first and that the control of the St. Lawrence waterway is slightly but definitely on the ebb. The increasing strength of the provinces in contrast to the Dominion parallels the increasing importance of railroads and the staples dependent on railroads—minerals, pulp, and paper. The seasonal fluctuations which characterize dependence on water transport tend to become less important with the continuous operation of industries linked to the railroads. The revolution which has followed the use of the gasoline engine as seen in the automobile, the truck, the tractor, the aeroplane, and the motor boat, and the opening of the north, appears to point in the same direction. We have been able to change the winter to the open season, and with electricity the sources of early difficulties to transportation have been converted into sources of power. All these tendencies point to an emergence from the amphibian to the land stage.

It is difficult to summarize the importance of transportation as a factor in Canadian economic history. We can suggest, however, the overwhelming significance of the waterways and especially of the St. Lawrence. Cheap water transportation favoured the rapid exploitation of staples and dependence on more highly industrialized countries for finished products. It favoured the position of Canada as an exporter of staples to more highly industrialized areas in terms of fur, lumber, and finally wheat, pulp and paper, and minerals. The St. Lawrence was important in the establishment of British power in Canada by its possibilities from a naval and military point of view, but even more from the standpoint of providing a basis for the economic growth of the Empire in the export of staple raw materials and the import of manufactured goods. We cannot in this paper describe the economic effects of dependence on these staple products other than to indicate the drain which they made in transportation costs on the energy of the community. We can suggest that each in its turn had its peculiar type of development and that each left its stamp on Canadian economic history. We can suggest that changes in technique, improvements in the waterways and in types of boats were responsible for rather violent fluctuations in economic development through the dependence on staple raw materials. It is scarcely necessary to describe the effects of dependence on water transportation on problems of finance involved in heavy expenditures which led ultimately to subsidies and government ownership. Water transportation and dependence on staples have been responsible for a variety of heavy overhead costs. Dependence on staple products and the difficulties of the waterway probably delayed improvement of transportation on the one hand and hastened it on the other by permitting the borrowing of mature technique from the United States. Railroads built at a later stage of development were completed more rapidly and the Canadian Pacific Railway was able to draw heavily on American experience in its early stage of development. Moreover, depreciation through obsolescence in American transportation hastened Canadian development, and steamboats, captains, and pilots, displaced on the Mississippi by railroads, moved up to the Red River, and the Saskatchewan, and the Fraser, as they did in turn in Canada from the Saskatchewan and the Fraser to the Mackenzie and the Yukon. The arrival of the first steamboat down the Red River to Winnipeg is surely the most dramatic event in Canadian economic history.

We have traced the evolution of transport in the fur trade, which reached its height in the expansion from the St. Lawrence following the development of vessels on the Great Lakes in combination with canoes on the rivers. This transport system disappeared with competition from the York boat from Hudson Bay. The disappearance of the fur trade from the St. Lawrence was followed by the rise of the lumber trade. Lumber tended to emphasize the efficiency of downstream traffic on the large rivers, whereas fur tended to emphasize the efficiency of upstream traffic on smaller rivers. The growth of settlement which accompanied the development of the lumber trade led to a demand for efficient upstream transport. This demand became more effective with the introduction of steamboats on the St. Lawrence from Quebec to Montreal, and on Lake Ontario and the upper lakes, especially after the completion of the Welland Canal. Pressure from Upper Canada for improved upstream traffic led to the completion of the St. Lawrence canals by 1850.

The St. Lawrence route, as improved by canals, was further strengthened by the completion of the Grand Trunk Railway and its connections with the seaboard in the following decade. These developments were in turn responsible for the completion of the

Intercolonial to Halifax in 1876, and the deepening of the St. Lawrence to Montreal to twenty-two feet in 1878, and for the construction of the Canadian Pacific Railway completed in 1885. Finally the deepening of the Sault Ste Marie, the Welland, and the St. Lawrence canals, and the St. Lawrence ship channel paved the way for the opening of the West, the export of wheat, and the addition of two transcontinental railways.

Again, we have suggested the relationship between the importance of the St. Lawrence waterway and Canadian fiscal policy. The Act of Union was a prerequisite to the financial support adequate to completion of the St. Lawrence canals, and in turn Confederation was essential to the financial support necessary to round out the policy inaugurated in canals and supplementary railways, by further improvements and extensions to the east with the Intercolonial Railway and to the west with the Canadian Pacific Railway. The policy necessary to provide financial support was outlined by [Alexander] Galt, and whether or not his explanation was one of rationalization after the fact, or of original theoretical analysis, reliance on the customs was undoubtedly the only solution. In the main this policy provided the basis for the elaboration under the National Policy of 1878. According to Galt's argument, the payment of duties actually reduced protection in so far as they were employed in reducing the cost of transportation on imports and exports. But the growing importance of railways, after the construction of the Intercolonial Railway, favoured the addition of the protection argument as a means of increasing traffic, especially in manufactured products. The National Policy was designed not only to increase revenue from customs from the standpoint of the waterways but also to increase revenue from traffic from the standpoint of railways. The increasing importance of railways has tended to emphasize the position of protection rather than revenue.

We can trace in direct descent from the introduction of steam on the St. Lawrence waterways, the Act of Union, the completion of the St. Lawrence canals, the Grand Trunk, Galt's statement, Confederation, the Intercolonial, the National Policy, the Canadian Pacific Railway, improved St. Lawrence canals, the new transcontinentals, and the drift toward protection. The overwhelming importance of the St. Lawrence waterways[12] has emphasized the production and export of raw materials, and in the case of wheat the extraordinary effects of a protective tariff during a period of expansion contributed to the construction of two new transcontinentals, and to the emergence of Canadian National Railways. The problem of the railways is essentially one of traffic to enable them to increase earnings without excessive cost to the producers of exports. The problem of protection is therefore that of increasing the traffic of manufactured goods and thereby increasing earnings, with the result that railroad costs may be decreased to the producers of raw materials to an amount equal to or more than the rise in the price of manufactured goods as a result of protection. Dependence on the application of mature technique, especially in transport, to virgin natural resources must steadily recede in importance as a basis for the tariff. It will become increasingly difficult to wield the tariff as the crude but effective weapon by which we have been able to obtain a share of our natural resources.

NOTES

1 See S.A. Cudmore, *History of the World's Commerce with Special Relation to Canada* (Toronto, 1929).
2 H.P. Biggar, *Early Trading Companies of New France* (Toronto, 1901); H.A. Innis, "The Rise and Fall of the Spanish Fishery in Newfoundland," *Transactions of the Royal Society of Canada*, third series, vol. XXV (1931), Section II, 51-70.
3 M.I. Newbigin, *Canada: The Great River, the Lands and the Men* (New York, 1926).
4 Champlain in 1608 went from Tadoussac to Quebec in pinnaces.
5 In 1932 as a result of construction of the railway to James Bay, the voyage conducted annually for over two and a half centuries through Hudson Straits to Charlton Island was abandoned.
6 See A.R.M. Lower, "Lumbering in Eastern Canada," doctoral thesis, Harvard University, 1929.
7 Milo M. Quaife, ed., *John Askin Papers*, II (Detroit, 1931), p. 343, also H.A. Innis and A.R.M. Lower, eds., *Select Documents in Canadian Economic History, 1783–1885* (Toronto, 1933), pp. 138ff.
8 The Lachine Canal was also begun as a private enterprise. See J.L. McDougall, "The Welland Canal to 1841," master's thesis, University of Toronto, 1923.
9 D.A. MacGibbon, *Railway Rates and the Canadian Railway Commission* (Boston, 1917).
10 William Smith, *History of the British Post Office in British North America, 1639–1870* (Cambridge, 1920), chaps. xvii-xviii.
11 Sir E.W. Watkin, *Canada and the States* (London, 1887).
12 The proposed improvement of the St. Lawrence waterways has not been given adequate consideration from the standpoint of the position of the St. Lawrence in the economic development of Canada. The valuable work done by antagonists and proponents of the scheme in terms of neatly calculated estimates has in the main tended to leave out of account the historical background and various incalculable items. This paper cannot undertake a detailed analysis but it does suggest that the tremendous investments of capital built up around the St. Lawrence system in terms

of ships, canals, terminal facilities, harbours, and railroads, from the standpoint of the export of wheat from the West will suffer materially from drains in other directions. Improvement of the St. Lawrence will contribute toward reducing the overhead costs of these tremendous investments. The strains of the political and economic structure built up largely in relation to the St. Lawrence would be lessened accordingly.

FURTHER READING

Innis's early seminal works include *The Fur Trade in Canada: An Introduction to Canadian Economic History* (New Haven: Yale University Press, 1930) and *The Cod Fisheries: The History of an International Economy* (New Haven: Yale University Press, 1940); while his most important later works include *Empire and Communications* (Oxford: Clarendon Press, 1950) and *The Bias of Communication* (Toronto: University of Toronto Press, 1951). Innis's early work inspired works of dependency theory, including Mel Watkins's "A staple theory of economic growth," in *The Canadian Journal of Economics and Political Science* 29 (1963): 141-58; his later ideas influenced Marshall McLuhan's *The Gutenberg Galaxy* (Toronto: University of Toronto Press, 1962). A good critique of Innis's economic theories is Robin Neill's *A New Theory of Value: The Canadian Economics of H.A. Innis* (Toronto: University of Toronto Press, 1972), and the best biography of his life is Donald Creighton's *Harold Adam Innis: Portrait of a Scholar* (Toronto: University of Toronto, 1957).

THE SECOND WAVE

(1950s–1970s)

A

SOCIAL JUSTICE

6   C.B. MACPHERSON

INTRODUCTION

The main project of C.B. Macpherson (1911–87) has been to understand the ways in which private property has affected and distorted the practice of democracy. In his most famous work, *The Political Theory of Possessive Individualism* (1962), he argues that the early liberal theories of Hobbes and Locke served primarily "to make the world safe for capitalism." In *Democracy in Alberta*, Macpherson explains how the experiments in new forms of democracy manifest in early prairie populism were unsuccessful because they would not challenge the system of private property underlying the exploitation of independent agricultural producers by "eastern imperialism." It is interesting to note that Macpherson's depiction of Alberta as a "quasi-party" system still seems remarkably relevant at the beginning of the twenty-first century.

DEMOCRACY IN ALBERTA: SOCIAL CREDIT AND THE PARTY SYSTEM (1953)

1. The Deterioration of Albertan Democracy

The same *petit-bourgeois* attributes of the agrarian outlook we have taken to explain the oscillation between radicalism and orthodoxy help to explain also the persistent rejection of the party system in favour of a one-party or non-party arrangement, and the deterioration in the quality of democracy which we have described as the trend from delegate to plebiscitarian democracy.

We have already seen how the early rejection of the party system grew out of the small-producer quasi-colonial position. Party was not needed to represent differences of interest within a fairly homogeneous economy. And, to protect their independence, the farmers did need a system of politics by which they could resist colonial subordination. The pioneer Albertans won their formal provincial independence in 1905 without having developed a party system of their own. When federal parties were introduced as the mechanism of provincial politics, they soon proved to be too closely identified with the eastern interests to be adequate for western needs.

Agrarian leaders, seeing this very clearly, deepened their perception into a critique of the party system as such. Not only was it a means of keeping the western producers subordinate to the eastern business interests; it was also a means of maintaining a class society, by dividing and ruling. This further perception strengthened the farmers' resistance to party: the crusade against the party system was justified not only by the interests of the western producers but also by the interests of humanity. The resistance to party, generated by colonial consciousness, was thus heightened by *petit-bourgeois* consciousness of the common subordination of the mass of "little men." From then on, to succeed as a party, it was necessary to attack the party system, and those who could do so most effectively got such support that they were in fact able to establish something approaching a nonparty system. The quality and effectiveness of the subsequent nonparty systems reflected their *petit-bourgeois* inspiration.

The first, and to the independent producer the most natural, alternative to the party system was the U.F.A. scheme by which cabinet rule was to give way to non-party "business government," parties were to be replaced by occupational group organizations, and delegate accountability was to be enforced throughout the political structure. "Group government," as such, never amounted to anything in practice, for no substantial groups other than farmers appeared on the political scene. The idea of "business government," however, persisted, and was indeed the *raison d'être* of the U.F.A.'s delegate democracy.

"When we learn to trade right we will have largely learned to live right," Henry Wise Wood had said in 1922. Democratic politics was to be a way of ensuring that people "traded right." Democratic organization as Wood conceived it, faithfully enough to the farmers' vision, was to be in the first instance, the means of protecting themselves from the wrongful trading of others—the monopolists, the manufacturers' association, the tariff lobby, and the rest of the "special interests." Ultimately it was to lead to a new society where everybody traded right and all was harmonious. How this was to come about was never well explained or well understood. But it was always clear that it was to ensure that the government would cleave to the farmers' trading interests that strict delegate control was demanded.

The U.F.A. concept of delegate democracy was thus permeated with the assumption that politics is trade. It was a peculiarly *petit-bourgeois* concept of trade: it distinguished between good trade and bad trade, and dreamed that good trade could drive out bad. Politics was seen as a means of doing this; political organization was to be designed for this purpose. This is the basic meaning of the delegate democracy of the U.F.A. The germ of its deterioration into the later plebiscitarian democracy was carried in the assumptions on which it was built. For trading assumptions in their pure form are appropriate to, and are the strength of, the party system. In their idealized *petit-bourgeois* form they lead to the rejection of party but at the same time vitiate the non-party alternative, delegate democracy.

The central weakness in the U.F.A. scheme was the attempt to replace monopolistic competition by a fully democratic system, while retaining the assumptions of competitive individualism. The farmers' movement accepted the liberal ethics of individual competition, while rejecting the ethics of monopolistic competition. The impossibility of rejecting the one while accepting the other was implicit from the outset. The farmers' insight that the party system was a case of monopolistic competition led them to reject party as a democratic instrument. Yet the only alternative they could adopt was a method of political organization designed to bring them more strenuously into monopolistic competition. Business government and delegate accountability were conceived primarily as means of strengthening the position of the farmers in the monopolistic competitive order, with only an ill-defined ultimate view to transcending it.

These devices served well enough as long as they were expected to do no more than strengthen the agrarian competitive position. But when they were called upon to transcend the monopolistic competitive order by popular sovereignty they failed. In the early 1930s, when popular sovereignty would have produced a direct attack on vested property rights, the divergence between business government and delegate democracy became acute, and delegate democracy succumbed. Wood's fundamentally liberal economic ideas and accompanying individualist theory of society could provide an alternative to the party system only as long as the alternative stayed within the same assumptions as the party system, the assumptions of a competitive capitalist order.

The limitations of the business analogue as a basis for popular democracy can be seen in another respect. Both the government of the province and the government of the U.F.A. were to be in effect boards of directors furthering the common interests of the shareholders. The shareholders were to participate actively and continuously, not by taking sides for and against rival groups of candidates for directorships, but by keeping an eye on the directors whom they had chosen for their business ability, and when necessary correcting their policies by instruction. The image was that of an old-fashioned business corporation, in which the shareholders had a personal knowledge of the business. Hence the insistence of the U.F.A., manifested in the "closed-door" policy, that the occupational group was the only truly effective basis of democratic political organization. Hence also the attempt to keep the elected legislative members free of cabinet control and responsible to constituency associations, and to make the annual delegate convention supreme. By keeping the elected member independent of cabinet and party, the farmers would secure their own independence.

As an instrument for ensuring that a farmer government adhered to the wants of the farmer group, delegate democracy was fairly effective, for the farmers did have a close knowledge of the business. But it was effective only in so far as those wants did not collide with the requirements of the mature Canadian capitalist economy, of which the independent commodity producers were a subordinate part. As those requirements made themselves felt, with varying intensity from 1921 to 1935, delegate democracy was subordinated to cabinet supremacy, the more readily because its assumptions were fundamentally the same as those of the Canadian economy.

The limits of *petit-bourgeois* liberalism were reached in the early 1930s with the U.F.A.'s failure to implement the popular will when it had come into conflict with property institutions. There was no question then of the people returning to the orthodox liberalism of the old party system; that would have been to submit again to the outside forces the havoc of whose operations they were determined to resist. On the other hand, as independent producers they were not greatly interested in any socialist transformation of society or socialist vision of democracy. The remaining possibility was some other form of *petit-bourgeois* democracy. The only forms left were various kinds of plebiscitary schemes. So, in reaction against the apparent failure of delegate democracy, they swung to what is in fact the other extreme (though it always presents itself in the guise of a stronger dose of popular sovereignty)—the plebiscitary democracy in which the people give up their right of decision, criticism, and proposal, in return for the promise that everything will be done to implement the general will. From then on, the deterioration was rapid.

The Social Crediters, too, conceived democracy in the image of a business system, but, more up to date than the U.F.A., their image was that of a giant corporation, in which the shareholders are atomized, their voices reduced to proxies, and their effective rights reduced to the one right of receiving a dividend. The corporate affairs being too complex for their understanding, they could have no effective control of policies. The directors and the experts would have a free hand; the shareholders retained only a paper sovereignty: the right to change directors and experts. Freedom for the individual was freedom to give or withhold his proxy.

In the later stages of Social Credit thinking, even the model of the business corporation was discarded as savouring too much of majority rule, only to be replaced by another commercial image, the relation of seller and buyer in the retail market—an even more fragmented relation than that of directors and shareholders. "Freedom within society simply means the right of the individual to choose or refuse any proposition placed before him without interfering with the same right of every other person."[1] The relations of the market were supposed to provide the ultimate in both individual freedom and popular sovereignty.

The individualism of Social Credit thinking, the apotheosis of a business civilization, thus passes into its opposite. Democracy is defined as the freedom of individuals, separately, not collectively, to take leave what is offered to them. The supposed union of all voters' wills into a mass will for general results reduces each will to nullity. The individual voter has no say as to what is to be offered for him to take or leave; that is arranged for him by those who preside over the general will. Political responsibility, supposed to be restored to the individual, is taken out of his reach. Democracy is denied while it is most vehemently asserted.

The plebiscitary democracy of Social Credit has obvious attraction for a community of independent producers who have reached the limits of genuine delegate democracy. The connection between acceptance of the social credit monetary panacea and acceptance of plebiscitarian democracy is not accidental. In circumstances of desperation the one is followed naturally by the other. Products of the same assumptions, they are equally false solutions of the *petit-bourgeois* predicament....

In historical perspective, the social credit theory is part of a long succession of utopian systems whose authors have denounced with varying degrees of insight the evils of business civilization, and have sought to remove them without altering the essential economic relationships by which they had been produced. It is not clear whether Major Douglas realized to what extent he was following the footsteps of the nineteenth-century utopians. That he was aware of their work is suggested by his assertion in 1931 that the present generation cannot take credit for discovering the cause of the trouble, as it had been discovered several times before, notably about a hundred years ago and in every case suppressed.[2] There was no indication to what thinkers this referred, but some resemblances are obvious.

There is in the social credit theory much of Fourier, with his rejection of the work fetish, his belief that the cause of poverty was the abundance of goods, his fascination with the laws of gravity, and his catalogue of waste. There is something of Saint-Simon, with his faith in "les industriels" who actually operate the productive and distributive system, his belief that "government" would be replaced by "administration," and his assurance that diffusion of credit would save the world. Even more striking is the similarity to the ideas of Proudhon,[3] the archetype of *petit-bourgeois* radicalism. Like Douglas, Proudhon explained the source of profit as the "increment of association," and the emergence of profit as a result of a miscalculation. Like Douglas he explained poverty as due to the depredation of industry by finance, which made it impossible for those who produced everything to buy back their own products; and found the solution in a scheme of free credit for producers, along with price-fixing. Like Douglas, he found that the handing over of the nation's credit to the national bank had elevated finance to the position of an occult power enslaving the whole country. Like Douglas, he held that the destruction of power by credit reform would remove oppression and misery without altering the labour-capital relationship; competition and private property would remain. Like Douglas, he denounced majority and popular sovereignty, holding that progress was always accomplished not by the people but by an *elite*. Like Douglas, he hated bureaucracy and the omnipotent state for their repression of individual liberty. His theoretical anarchism, being a rejection not of all coercive power but only of absolute state power, is essentially similar to the social credit position. Like Douglas, Proudhon was scornful of political parties, and saw a Jewish conspiracy dominating the press and government.

In the end Proudhon's false individualism led him to conclude in favour of the dictatorship of a leader who could prevail on the masses to give him power: Proudhon became a champion of the plebiscitarian dictatorship of Louis Bonaparte. From Proudhon to Hitler, doctrines which have singled out finance as the source of social evil have led to the plebiscitary state. And not without reason, for by seeking (or pretending) to remove the evils of which they complain by credit reform alone, they fail to resolve the class tension which, if not moderated by the democratic party system, can only be covered over by the devices of a plebiscitarian state.

In Alberta, of course, the class tension was not internal; it was a tension between the independent producers within, and the pressures of the other classes outside, the provincial economy. It is not suggested that the present Social Credit administration is a Bonapartist dictatorship. Whether it would have become one, had not the new-found wealth from the oil fields enabled the demands of the whole community to be met on an ample scale, must remain a speculation.

Manning's rejection of the later Douglas theory was of course not a rejection of the plebiscitarian notion of the general will. His attempt to distinguish between the principles of social credit and "the private views of Major Douglas," so as to reject the later and obviously democratic Douglas ideas while continuing to associate his government with social credit, was well meant. Genuine detestation of anti-Semitism, as well as recognition of its inappropriateness in Alberta led Manning to purge the "Douglasites" from the Alberta movement and government. But to jettison "Douglasism" was really to complete the rejection of all the principles that were uniquely social credit; all that was left was the plebiscitarian heritage. The Manning forces, who called themselves the "realists," in opposition to the Douglasites, were, in view of their failure to introduce social credit in practice, truly realist in abandoning social credit principles. But this kind of realism required also that they should continue to assert the principles. It is the realism of plebiscitarian leadership.

As long as the independent commodity producers retain their preponderance in Alberta, the plebiscitarian quality of Alberta politics is likely to persist. That preponderance is decreasing, and may continue to do so; but if, before such a trend should become decisive, the Social Credit administration should be displaced by another reform movement, the resulting system (a non-party one, of course) would not easily depart from the plebiscitarian pattern. The C.C.F. (the more likely contender) treasures the principle of delegate democracy as much as the U.F.A. did, but if it came to office in Alberta on the basis of yet another farmer revolt against renewed economic pressure from outside it would not be long before the limits of provincial popular sovereignty and delegate democracy would again be reached. No party which takes office as the provincial champion of the independent producer is likely to be able to transcend these limits, unless indeed it is prepared and able to do away with the capitalist basis of the whole national economy. And once the limits are reached, to the inevitable disappointment of the rank and file, there is no way to hold office but by something approaching a plebiscitarian system. The most that could be expected in these circumstances would be a swing away from plebiscitarian to delegate democracy in the first few years of the new regime.

We may conclude that deterioration in the quality of substitutes for the party system is a highly probable result of the needs and outlook of a community of independent commodity producers which forms a subordinate part of a maturing or mature capitalist economy. The deterioration is not constant; the quality of non-party democracy may achieve relative stability, with only brief deviations, for an indefinite period. Deterioration follows from the persistence of the independent producers' demands beyond the point which their governments can satisfy within the limits set by an outside economy which is yet fundamentally acceptable to them. If, owing to changes in the outside economy, the limits recede, a period of relative stability may set in; the system of government can settle down at whatever level of delegate or plebiscitary democracy it has reached. Or, without the limits receding, there may be an increasing recognition by the independent producers that the limits confronting their demands are implicit in an economic system which they do not wish to destroy. In this way stability may result from reconciliation to the limits, whose acceptance in the last resort is inherent in the *petit-bourgeois* outlook.

2. The General Theory

The analysis just concluded has indicated that the most probable course of political organization in Alberta is a continued rejection of the orthodox party system and the maintenance of a fairly stable system of plebiscitarian democracy, possibly with excursions into more active delegate democracy. It suggests also that a new species of political system has come to stay. Before considering the possibilities and limits of the system it will be well to establish the usefulness of introducing the new term "quasi-party system" to describe it.

It is clear that what has prevailed in Alberta for at least thirty years is not the party system of the orthodox liberal-democratic tradition. Government has not been conducted, nor have policies been decided, by continual competition between two main parties for the support of the majority of the electorate. Nor can the reality be fitted to the orthodox pattern by treating either the U.F.A. or Social Credit as third parties. While they resemble, in structure and outlook, popular movements which elsewhere have entered into a regular party system as third parties, they have not done so. Neither of them was ever third, nor did either, starting third, become one of two fairly equal contenders; each came at one stroke to such predominance as almost to displace all others. Needless to say, there is no approximation, either, to the multi-party system typical of continental western European nations. The party system, then, in any of its usual senses, is a misnomer for what has been in existence for more than three decades in Alberta.

To describe what has actually prevailed we have been using, with or without qualification, the terms "one-party" and "non-party" system. Yet it is apparent that these categories are not adequate, and it will be better now to discard them.

In the first place, what we have is not strictly a non-party system. It may be doubted whether any political structure is really non-party.

Parties, at least of a tenuous sort, are apt to be formed in any body which needs continuous government and in which the government is formally chosen by the governed. They may be found in business corporations, in trade unions, in religious congregations, and in all manner of voluntary associations. Yet the designation "non-party" may generally be allowed these, inasmuch as their governments are not elected or supported by means of regularly organized, identified, and opposed political machines, but are chosen for efficiency in administration of policies on which there is no deep and lasting division among the electorate. In this sense, Canadian local government is normally non-party. But Alberta government, except during the early Territorial period, does not qualify as a fully non-party system. Both the U.F.A. and Social Credit were parties, seeking the support of a majority of voters on a party programme, even though that programme included the aim of transcending party. They stood for certain principles and for certain specific policies in a way which makes their practice quite distinct from that of non-party municipal government. The Alberta system cannot therefore properly be described as a non-party system.

Nor can it be described with any accuracy as a one-party system. Other parties, although much reduced, continued to operate and to elect candidates in at least some constituencies. So complete was the predominance of the party in power that there was no need, from its own point of view, to attempt to proscribe other parties. Nor was there any inclination to do so. In spite of an occasional confusion between the functions of party and state in the Social Credit regime, there was no serious thought of establishing a totalitarian one-party rule. There was, indeed, no basis for an outright one-party dictatorship: such a system is only thrust up as part of revolutionary (or counter-revolutionary) transfer of power in a strongly class-divided society.

Nor is the Alberta system adequately to be understood as an imperfect or deviant form of a two- or three-party or non-party or one-party system. For one thing, it partakes too much of the character of all three to be considered an affinity of any one of them. It shares the attributes of the ordinary party system, at least to the extent that it operates by permanently organized and publicly identified electoral machines with some opposition from other machines. It shares the attributes of a non-party system in its emphasis on "business government," that is, on administration rather than policy formation as the function of government and as the government's main claim on the electorate. It shares, too, some of the qualities of a one-party system, especially in its rejection of the orthodox notion that party is beneficial, and in its belief in a general will of the community.

More important, it lacks an affinity in the other sense to any one of the three recognized types. There is nothing in its nature, or in the conditions which produced it, to lead us to expect that it will become more like any one of them. It is built distinctly on rejection of the two- or three-party system. It developed, as we have seen, out of a provincial non-party system which early proved insufficient. And there is no basis, in present circumstances at least, for it to become an outright one-party system.

For these reasons it is best considered to be *sui generis*. A distinct category requires a new term. "Quasi-party" will serve.

The quasi-party system, as it has emerged in Alberta, may be seen as a response to the problem of democratic government in a community mainly of independent producers which forms a subordinate part of a more mature capitalist economy. It appears as a middle way between an alternate-party system which has become unreal or harmful and a one-party state which would be unacceptable and for which there is not the requisite class basis. We must now inquire to what extent the quasi-party system can meet the problem of democratic government in such a community. We may also ask whether it is suitable beyond the one province in which we have seen it.

To ask these questions about the quasi-party system is to raise two prior questions. First, what is the central problem of democratic government, or, which is much the same thing, what are the essential functions of democratic government? Secondly, what part does the orthodox party system play in the performance of these functions?

On the first question there are, in the European-Anglo-American tradition, two quite different views. One, which goes back to the seventeenth century, is a class concept; the other, which is the prevalent liberal-democratic view in the twentieth century, is pluralistic.

In the first view, democracy is an affair of the presently unprivileged; it means government responsible to and infused with the will of the "common people," those whose claim to consideration is their common humanity rather than their estates, their life and labour rather than accumulated wealth or hereditary status. This is an old dream, expressed before the modern period in peasants' revolts. It becomes more articulate and pressing from the seventeenth century on through the nineteenth, being the demand at first of the small independent producers and later of an employed working class as well. Democracy, till well on in the nineteenth century, was a revolutionary or at least a radical reformist creed, abhorred and denounced, with a few exceptions, by politicians and political thinkers alike. But neither its advocates nor its opponents were in any doubt as to what it meant. This idea of democracy is of more than historical interest; although now supplanted in the orthodox canon, it has been repeatedly revived in popular reformist as well as revolutionary movements in the nineteenth and twentieth centuries, after the popular franchise had been attained and been found wanting.

Twentieth-century liberal-democratic thought, on the other hand, has submerged the class theory of democracy in a pluralistic theory. It has assumed that with the establishment of a popular suffrage the class function of democracy is no longer significant. The primary problem of democratic government is taken to be the representation and reconciliation of a multitude of diverse and conflicting group interests—regional, occupational, racial, religious, ethical— which cut across and blur class lines. In this view the machinery of government is, in itself, neutral; it has no inherent class content, but operates in response to the pressures of all the groups.

Orthodox twentieth-century political science has in effect neutralized democratic theory while still trying to uphold democratic values. By treating the demands and pressures of all the groups as the data of the science, it has put itself in the position of treating them all as ethically equal or neutral; all, that is, except demands which would bring democracy to an end. But because the theorists have so reduced the ethical content of democracy, they have found some difficulty in drawing even that line. To the extent that they reduce politics to a sort of market which measures and equates political supply and demand, they destroy the basis for any ethical criterion of demand. There is an obvious parallel between the transformation of political economy into economics after Ricardo and that of political thought or philosophy—the term was never precise—into political science after John Stuart Mill. The change came a little later (and is not yet as advanced) in political science, but it is the same change: the humanistic substance is taken out, supposedly in the interests of more refined scientific handling of the problems. In the case of political science the removal is commonly justified, if it is noticed, by the assumption that the class problem of democracy has been solved by the attainment of popular suffrage, or that what remains of the problem can now be adjusted by the free play of the political market.

This view, largely the product of the twentieth century, had some justification in the first few decades of the century, especially in America where class lines have been less distinct than in Europe. But even while it was reaching general academic acceptance, its inadequacy was being demonstrated by the emergence of class movements which, after some experience of orthodox politics with the new universal franchise, rejected the pluralist view and resorted to political action based on the older concept of democracy. Just when the pluralist theory was being received as a solution to (or a way of avoiding) the problem that had exercised English liberals in the nineteenth century—how to reconcile democracy with the individualism and property institutions of a maturing capitalist economy—it was being made apparent, by labour and socialist movements in England and Europe, and by labour and agrarian movements in America, that the problem of democracy had again to be restated, and in something like the old terms.

The fact that the older view of democracy keeps being rediscovered indicates that it corresponds to some reality which the pluralistic theory does not adequately comprehend. The achievement of universal suffrage and the flowering of voluntary associations as political pressure groups have not erased class lines, nor is there any reason to expect that they will do so. We may conclude, therefore, that in a mature capitalist world the problem of democracy is not only the pluralistic one of representing and reconciling the conflicts of multitudinous group interests, but also (and more fundamentally) one of expressing and containing the conflict of class interests.

Turning now to the second prior question—what is the role of the party system in performing the democratic function—we find again two distinct views, corresponding to the two concepts of democracy.

In the first view, party is distrusted and denounced as part of the apparatus of rule by the privileged class. Designed to pervert or cripple the will of the people, party can perform no democratic function. In its place may be put the direct democracy of the town meeting, the local assembly of all the citizens, or, as with the Jacobins, a single mass party which, by embracing all true democrats, transcends party. In other words, democracy requires a non-party or a one-party state. This view of party reappears, as we have seen, in agrarian reform movements in the twentieth century.

The second view of party, the orthodox twentieth-century rationale of the party system, has been built on the pluralistic view of democratic society. The party system is seen as having two main functions, both of which are held to be essential to democratic government. The first is, as a brokerage apparatus or entrepreneurial system—some such analogy from business is generally used—to sift and bring together into two or a few combinations the multitude of divergent group demands and equate them to the available supply of political goods, giving due weight to each without destroying any. The task is to produce at all times out of a very diverse series of minorities, a majority capable of supporting an effective government. On the pluralistic assumption that the really important interests of individuals are those which unite them in overlapping groups no one of which is a numerical majority, it is essential for continuous government, indeed for government of any kind, that they be brought together in political parties.

The second function is, to act as a safeguard against a permanent irresponsible oligarchy and as a check to abuse of power, by providing always an alternative body of occupants for the commanding positions. Without the agency of party to perform these functions, it is said, democratic government could not survive.

There is little question that these functions are performed more or less adequately by the party system wherever it exists, and that they must be performed if democracy is to be maintained in such societies. Whether the two functions can be performed in any modern society only by a party system, as is usually claimed, is more difficult to determine.

Whether the first of these functions can be performed only by party is a less important question than it may seem, because the first function is becoming relatively less important than it has been. If, as we have argued, the central problem of democratic government in a mature capitalist world is coming to be the moderation and containment of conflicting class interests rather than the entrepreneurial problem of sifting, weighing, and adjusting a multitude of sectional and group interests, it is evident that the entrepreneurial function of the party system is being replaced in importance by the function of moderating class tension.

The orthodox theory recognizes, of course, that the party system can operate only where class division in the society is not so strong as to prevent any class from accepting the verdict of the polls; in Lord Balfour's often-quoted phrase "our whole political machinery presupposes a people so fundamentally at one that they can safely afford to bicker."4 But this is to emphasize, characteristically, not the degree of class division that does exist—this is reduced to bickering—but the supposed fundamental oneness of the whole people. If we bring back into serious consideration the problem of class tension in a democracy, as we are compelled to do by the fact of its reassertion by radical movements in our own day, it appears that the function of the party system in maintaining democracy is not only to weigh and adjust a multitude of sectional and group interests and to provide against a permanent oligarchy, but also to moderate the conflict of class interests. The party system, wherever it prevails, does do all these things.

Its capacity for moderating class conflict, within limits, is evident in its history and in its design. This function can be performed either by a pair of parties which substantially represent different classes (as the English Conservative and Labour parties), or by a pair of parties which do not represent different classes (as the Democratic and Republican parties in the United States, or the Canadian Liberal and Conservative parties) but which private organizations representing class interests seek to control or to influence in their favour. It may also be performed by the continental European multi-party system, in which the government normally rests on the support of two or more of a series of several class parties, and is thereby compelled to continual and shifting compromise. This system has at least as great a claim to be considered democratic as has either of the types of alternate-party system, and in any full investigation of the claims of the party system it would demand thorough exploration. But since the multi-party system is neither indigenous nor easily transplanted to those countries in which a two-party system has been long established, we shall disregard it here. From now on we shall use the term "party system" or (where the context suggests it) "alternate-party system" to refer to the two- or three-party system of the British and American tradition; and "orthodox" theory to refer to the prevailing Anglo-American liberal-democratic theory.

Either of the two types of alternate-party system takes some of the strain out of the antagonism of class interests by providing, if not satisfaction for one class, at least continual hope of further satisfaction for both. Of the two types the American seems better designed for containing and moderating class tension. By cutting straight across class lines, with each party appealing to all classes, it rules out class parties almost completely. Once it is established, with appropriate electoral devices, it can shut out third parties from power while allowing them to function as a useful vent for discontent. The other type of two-party system, however, is not unsuccessful. Although there the two parties are drawn up along class lines, it is not long before the necessity, in a business civilization, of running politics like a business, gives over the direction of both parties to professional politicians. The professionalized party, in or out of office, then devotes itself to seeking votes from, by appealing to, all classes. Thus the tendency is for the class content of what were built as class parties to be reduced. In this way, as long as the hegemony of parties is accepted by the electorate, even class parties do moderate class opposition.

Either type of alternate-party system, then, is competent, within limits, to perform the function of containing class opposition. And in any long view this function is more continuously necessary than the pluralistic function of adjusting diverse group interests. Historically, the latter function appears as the primary task of the party system only in expanding societies in which the prevailing economic and political power relations are sufficiently accepted that there is no strong pressure to establish a new structure of economic class relations. Since the arrival of the democratic franchise, these conditions have existed in most cases only for a few decades in the late nineteenth and twentieth centuries, the decades in which the now orthodox theory was developed. When these conditions cease to prevail, the party system can still maintain democracy but does so by virtue of its ability to moderate class conflict rather than its ability to perform the brokerage function between a multitude of groups. The two functions, of course, are commonly found together, and can indeed only be separated in abstract analysis. But we appear to be moving into a period in which the class function is becoming the more important function of the party system.

We may conclude that the party system, or something like it, is essential to the maintenance of democracy in a class-divided society. Nothing else has been found which can moderate class conflict so successfully, either by partially satisfying or by confusing the interests of opposed classes. This, of course, was the burden of the U.F.A.'s complaint against the party system.

While the brokerage function of parties may thus be reduced to secondary importance, the other main function allotted to parties by the orthodox theory—the checking of arbitrary government— still remains fundamental in a class-divided society. Where there is a strong division of class interests there is a tendency toward a government representing one class or combination of classes exclusively and permanently, or yielding so far to the demands of one class as to jeopardize the position of the other. A flourishing party system is the most effective deterrent that has been found, and may thus be considered essential to the maintenance of democracy in such a society.

Whether the party system is needed in a less class-divided society for the prevention of arbitrary government is not so clear. The need of a party system for this purpose in *any* society can be shown if it is assumed that there is always a natural conflict between the government and the people. It may be said, however, that the more homogeneous a society is, the less likely is the government to be regarded as a natural enemy. At the theoretical extreme of a society without class division, and with popular franchise, the people would regard the state's purposes as their own and the party system would not be required for the maintenance of democracy. Only in such a society is it possible to think of a general will sustaining a democracy without alternate parties. This, of course, is the meaning of the claim made by Soviet Russia and the "new democracies" of eastern Europe for their systems as true democracy. With this claim we are not here concerned, for it is appropriate only to a society where class divisions in the Marxist sense have been or are being eliminated by the elimination of capitalist relations of production.

The society we have been examining is not a "classless society" in this sense. It may appear so, because it is more homogeneous than an advanced industrial society, but its homogeneity is that of a quasi-colonial community of independent producers who are a subordinate part of mature capitalist economy. In such a society a one-party state does not even theoretically meet the requirements of democracy; there is no more basis for it than for the alternate-party system. A one-party state will not arise unless there is a mass will for a fundamentally different society; one-party states have always been the outcome of a revolutionary dissolution of a previous class and property structure, or of a counter-revolutionary attempt to restore or maintain such a structure.

We need not venture the paradox that only a class-divided society requires a party system for the maintenance of democracy. All that is relevant to our problem here is that a class-divided society, to be a democracy, *does* require a party system, or a substitute which can perform the same functions, namely the moderation and containment of class opposition, and the provision of some safeguard against arbitrary government.

Our original question—whether the quasi-party system can meet the requirements of democracy—may now be restated in terms of its capacity to perform these functions. We now have grounds for concluding that, in the specific conditions (a quasi-colonial and largely *petit-bourgeois* society) which gave rise to the quasi-party system, it can perform the same functions as the regular party system, though in reduced degree, and that it is the only system that can do so.

Enough has been said already to show that in the specific conditions there is no basis for either a two- or three-party system, or a strictly one-party system, or a completely non-party system. It now appears that, given the unsuitability or impossibility of these systems, the quasi-party system can to a limited degree express and moderate the conflict of class interests in which such a society is involved.

The achievement of both the U.F.A. and Social Credit was to do just this. The peculiarity of a society which is at once quasi-colonial and mainly *petit-bourgeois* is that the conflict of class interests is not so much within the society as between that society and the forces of outside capital (and of organized labour). This does not mean, of course, that the conflict is expressed only in federal politics; the opposition of class interests is reflected back into provincial politics, as was clearly seen in, for instance, the U.F.A. debt legislation and the Social Credit monetary control legislation.

The record analysed in earlier chapters shows that the class conflict was expressed and contained by the Alberta radical movements, sufficiently to permit the maintenance of democratic government in greater or less degree. It suggests also, however, that there are limits to the possibility of maintaining democracy by a quasi-party system. In the Social Credit period it became possible to moderate the class tension only by a process of delusion. Whether it is thought that this was delusion of the people by the party leaders, or whether it is thought to have extended to self-delusion of the leaders is irrelevant here. The point is that the quasi-party system shifted from a genuinely democratic delegate basis to an inspirational plebiscitarian basis. A plebiscitarian system is a way of covering over class tension which can neither be adequately moderated by party nor be resolved short of an outright totalitarian one-party rule. Thus, the quasi-party system, to the extent that it cannot moderate class tension while expressing it, contains it by concealing it. The resulting system is at best an illusory democracy....

We may conclude that the quasi-party system is capable of performing one of the main functions of the regular party system—the moderation of class conflict—but that the circumstances which bring it into existence are liable to carry it into a plebiscitarian stage which cannot be considered fully democratic but which can maintain the form and some of the substance of democracy.

The other function of the regular party system—the prevention of arbitrary use of power—may also be performed, in reduced degree, by the quasi-party system. While it does not provide an ever ready alternative government, it does generally provide an opposition group in the legislature which, with some outside backing and some access to publicity, acts as a brake on arbitrary government. There is no reason to think that the existence of such opposition would prevent a descent into completely arbitrary rule, but, so long as the circumstances prevail which led to the quasi-party rather than a one-party system, the existence of a recognized opposition performs this democratic function in some degree....

From the example of Alberta, it appears that a quasi-party system tends to become plebiscitarian when it can no longer satisfy the economic demands of the electorate within the framework of a mature capitalist economy. It appears also that a quasi-party system can continue to maintain some of the substance of democracy if the economy enters an expansive phase (in the case of Alberta, post-war prosperity and oil) which enables the demands to be satisfied in larger measure than was possible when the shift to a plebiscitarian system took place. There is, however, no mechanical correspondence between the degree of economic expansiveness and the democratic quality of the quasi-party system. Once it has entered a plebiscitarian phase, no economic expansion is likely to restore it to a more fully democratic level, for the effect of prosperity will ordinarily be to strengthen the existing party's attractiveness without requiring it to change its ways....

NOTES

1 *Canadian Social Crediter,* Jan. 25, 1945.
2 C.H. Douglas, *Warning Democracy* (London, 1931); quoted in Philip Mairet, ed., *The Douglas Manual* (London, 1934), p. 146.
3 Douglas may have been acquainted with Proudhon's ideas indirectly through Gesell.
4 Introduction (1927) to Bagehot's *The English Constitution* (London, 1933), p. xxiv.

FURTHER READING

While his most famous book remains *The Political Theory of Possessive Individualism* (Oxford: Clarendon Press, 1962), Macpherson's most accessible works are *The Real World of Democracy* (Oxford: Clarendon Press, 1966), originally presented as a series of lectures for CBC radio, and *The Life and Times of Liberal Democracy* (Oxford: Oxford University Press, 1977). Commentaries on Macpherson include William Leiss, *C.B. Macpherson: Dilemmas of Liberalism and Socialism* (Montreal: New World Perspectives, 1968); Joseph Cairns, ed., *Democracy and Possessive Individualism: The Intellectual Legacy of C.B. Macpherson* (New York: SUNY Press, 1993); Peter Lindsay, *Creative Individualism: The Democratic Vision of C.B. Macpherson* (New York: SUNY Press, 1996); and Jules Townshend, *C.B. Macpherson and the Problem of Liberal Democracy* (Edinburgh: Edinburgh University Press, 2000). For a more historical account of agrarian populism, see W.L. Morton, *The Progressive Party in Canada* (Toronto: University of Toronto Press, 1950) or David Laycock, *Populism and Democratic Thought in the Canadian Prairies, 1910 to 1945* (Toronto: University of Toronto Press, 1990).

7 LESTER B. PEARSON

INTRODUCTION

While Lester B. Pearson (1897–1972) is known better for his political accomplishments than for a body of written work, Pearson's legacy of international multilateralism nonetheless remains a powerful political vision. Although he worked briefly as a professor of history at the University of Toronto, Pearson's true calling was in diplomacy. Working as a diplomat, an Ambassador, Secretary of State for External Affairs, and, finally, as Prime Minister, Pearson viewed an alliance of sovereign states working cooperatively as the best way to mitigate international conflict. In 1956, in response to Nassar's nationalization of the Suez Canal, Britain, France, and Israel attacked Egypt. To prevent Britain and France from facing censure by the United Nations, Pearson advocated the creation of a UN-led peace-keeping force to allay the conflict; and for this he was awarded the 1957 Nobel Peace Prize. Pearson gave the speech included here soon after receiving the award. In his address presentation, he discussed the need to address the Cold War from a multilateral perspective. Later, he would urge that the Americans avoid escalation in the Korean conflict and advise that the British accommodate the independence of Commonwealth states. Thus Pearson not only presented workable solutions to international problems but, more importantly, contributed to a way of thinking about managing international conflict.

WHERE DO WE GO FROM HERE? (1957)

... From time to time great divides appear that separate the stages in man's development, that make eras out of his history. Our own lifetime has seen two of these, though perhaps it would be more accurate to refer to them as two ridges of a single divide.

The conquest of outer space is the second of these in time, but first in the sudden and shattering nature of its impact, even though the ordinary mind is hardly able to grasp its full significance, except perhaps in terms of politics and security. Our first reaction to this stupendous leap forward by man—this is a sad commentary on our times—was not one of delight, but of chagrin that it was made by the wrong men. Our more considered conclusion can only be that for better or for worse a new dimension has been added to our vision and to our fears.

Russia's man-made moon would, however, not be circling our planet today if earlier in this century first Russian and then other Asian millions had not emerged into the age of power through technology. This process in some parts of Asia has hardly yet begun. In others it is far from completion. It has, however, gone so far in the Soviet Union that, in facing these new, enigmatic, and monstrous forces from the East, which we do not even yet fully understand, we will need all the courage, steadiness, and wisdom we can muster.

Out of Lenin's inflexible will, out of the days that shook the world in 1917, there has emerged a massive totalitarian society compounded of communism, czarism, and science; a society under iron despotic control and dedicated to the proposition that its tenets will conquer the earth in one way or another—peacefully, if that can be done, but if not, well, Russia now possesses instruments of annihilative assault through its achievements in the science of destruction and has not hesitated to threaten their use.

Nikita Khrushchev may have been perfectly sincere when he once assured me—as he has assured many others—that their Soviet system is inherently stronger than ours; that Marxist socialism, which he thinks the Russians have, is far superior to free enterprise, which he thinks we have; that the triumph of their system over ours in "competitive coexistence" is as inevitable as it can be peaceful.

One would get more comfort from this Communist conviction, as a factor which makes for at least an avoidance of open war, if it were not likely that Mr. Khrushchev—and other Communists—are also convinced that the capitalist leaders, faced with the inevitable deterioration and collapse of their own order in this competition, will, according to the laws of scientific Marxism, drag the world into war in one last desperate gamble. Believing this, and professing to find an abundance of contemporary evidence to support both our disintegration and our determination to stop it by imperialist wars and adventures, Khrushchev and his temporary colleagues who control Russia keep adding to the armed power of their state and trying to extend Communist influence. They also resist by any means required, including force, the efforts of their satellite states to extricate themselves from the thralldom of Moscow; and they carry with ever-increasing vigor the war of words into world forums such as the United Nations.

These Russian moves increase our own fears of open aggression, and even more of a miscalculation of events which may lead to the use of force. Therefore, we search for more power to defend ourselves. It is a vicious and it could be a fatal circle; nor does it do any good in trying to cut through it merely to assume that all is right on our side and wrong on the other, to wrap ourselves in a cloak of impeccable rectitude and diplomatic rigidity.

The triumph, at least temporarily, of Soviet communism in Russia and its penetration into other areas of the world are partly the cause and partly the result of the decline of Western Europe in strength and influence. In the nineteenth century European power was at its height. Even then, however, it was losing ground by divisive nationalist tendencies which were neutralizing the unifying influences of the French Revolution. The development of nation-states in Europe during the nineteenth century was both necessary and desirable. But unfortunately it took place under conditions which made for conflict rather than cooperation between those states. This culminated in Germany's effort to restore the European idea in the wrong way, by force and tyranny in 1914 and again in 1939.

The slaughter and destruction of those wars, the miseries and sufferings of their aftermath, brought to an end Europe's supremacy in the world. From a first force, however, it has not, and we should be grateful for this, become a third force. Rather it has become part of a new North Atlantic-Western European coalition. The new world of the United States has indeed, and with a vengeance, been called in to redress the balance of the old.

This has brought face to face, and it is the central political fact of our time, the totalitarian empire of Russia and the mighty democracy of the United States of America. The former, whether inspired by fear, by ambition, or by a crusading ideology, or, as I suspect, by all three, has been building up its power with ruthless determination to the point where in the last two or three months some of the manifestations of that power, with a superb sense of timing, have been spectacular indeed. They have delighted its own people, worried, to say the least, the West, and impressed the hundreds of millions who are uncommitted to either side. This Russian power is based on a state organization which subordinates every individual interest to a collective purpose; which controls every activity—or tries to—and can concentrate all the necessary resources and energy on any particular task; which organizes every aspect of life and is able to maintain a relatively low standard of living in the interest of a high standard of state achievement. I know this whole totalitarian concept is alien and contrary to everything we stand for. I know it means the negation of human values in the interest of a ruthless dictatorship. I know that it will not permanently work and that it does indeed bear within it the seeds of its own decay.

But I know also that in a material sense it has accomplished much for its people, that those people are comparing their lot, not with ours, but with that of Russians fifty years ago, as they have learned about it from their own propaganda and educational agencies. The great majority are no doubt satisfied with the comparison and are proud of their country's position in the world.

Somehow or other a strong, dynamic impulse for national creation has been created in the Soviet Union. Its citizens in recent years made great progress in many fields of human endeavor though at a price that we would not think of paying. If we have any tendency to regard them as Moujiks and lumpish proletarians we had better dismiss it at once. They have devoted and resourceful men who rank with our best in science, engineering, and technology and they intend to keep their standing in this field or improve it. Their education is in fact directed primarily to that end. As an incentive to excellence and accomplishment the outstanding scientist and engineer are put on a level of prestige and privilege which in our society is reserved for heroes of the stadium, the stage, or the screen.

So we had better awaken from our illusion of easy technical and material superiority which we have been cherishing because we have a car in every garage, frozen food in every electric refrigerator, and kissproof lipstick on every lip. These things will not bring us victoriously through competitive coexistence, however glamorously we display them in advertising copy.

What do we oppose to this controlled and centralized society? Too often, merely the well-worn cliches of the superiority of freedom and democracy and our "way of life." I don't want to be misunderstood. These things are superior to anything that Soviet communism can produce or will produce. The imposed order and the directed activity of the Russians may seem to give them at times a selective advantage over our free and competitive society, but in the long run there is no salvation, no hope, in their system because it enslaves the free thought and free soul of man to the dictates of a few irresponsible despots.

While that "long run," however, is taking place, there are some signs that our own social and economic and political institutions will not be equal to the challenges which face them, that these cliches which I have mentioned are too empty of content for too many.

Soviet life, Soviet policy, I know, are founded on compulsion, rather than consent. But are we sure that our own social purpose, derived from the right of the individual to make his own choice, is steady, strong, constructive, and based on enduring values?

Perhaps we should worry more about that, and not only about what is going on behind or over the iron curtain.

The very word "freedom" has now lost some of its earlier, angry meaning of stern and sturdy resistance to pressures and persecutions, from men or mass opinion. The current popularity of that awful expression "the organization man" and the vogue for dissecting our motivations and desires so that we may fit into a group, whether as executives of a corporation or as purchasers of soap, are depressing portents. Surely we are not going to escape total state control in order to seek security in the "big organization" type of social and economic conformity.

This would merely be getting the worst of both worlds. That venerable poet and rugged New Englander Robert Frost had more than the germ of a good idea when, the other day, he proposed to Mr. James Reston of the New York *Times* the banding together of all men and women who wished to stamp out "togetherness." He meant of course not the "togetherness" of a good company of free men but the "huddleness" of the lonely crowd. The glory of America, Frost added (and nowhere has that glory been better shown than in the West), has been its pioneers, who celebrated "separateness" and were not always seeking security.

There is, in fact, no tolerable substitute for a society of free individuals, refusing to be pushed around, but consecrated to a worthy
purpose and willing to accept the disciplines, the sacrifices, and
the concentrated effort necessary to achieve it. The Soviet system
can offer nothing to match the permanence and power of that kind
of free and responsible society. But are we gaining it, or are we
losing it?

Certainly, we will not achieve it if we permit our social values to
become debased; if "bread and circuses" become the end of life and
the policy of government; if the man who thinks deeply is derided
as an "egghead" while the demagogue who merely talks loudly is
followed as a leader; where the ball player or an oil promoter can
occupy a more important place in the community in terms of prestige and material reward than the teacher or the preacher.

When the headlines in a Milwaukee paper blazened a few weeks
ago that a new era had begun, it was referring, not to the launching
of the Russian satellite the day before—that was on an inside page—
but to the launching of the first game of the first World Series ever to
take place in that city. The Soviet leaders would have been encouraged by this evaluation of the relative importance of events. I have no
right to criticize it myself because I confess that at that time I read the
sports news out of Milwaukee or New York before I turned to news
from Washington or Moscow or Syria. I represent, therefore, at least
in this respect, these debilitating and dangerous tendencies which I
have been telling you to worry about!

Our cause for anxiety, however, does not spring from any single
source. It is from the general trend in the assessment of values, a
trend which encourages those who are opposed to us to believe
that the fiber of our society is weakening; that we are devoting most
of our energies, often in a wastefully competitive way, to things of
secondary importance; that freedom is no longer a source of
strength to us; that riches have made us fat and smug and soft.

All this gives the tough, implacable, and determined men who
are directing the Communist world more confidence than they
have a right to possess, and thereby adds to our problems and to
our dangers.

True and responsible freedom does mean strength. We know
that. We know also that we have to pay a price for it, and we are
glad to do so. But let us not by our own action, or inaction, make

that price any higher than necessary. Inevitably also we tend to advertise our weaknesses and our failures. They make news on the "man bites dog" theory. But surely a sense of responsibility in this regard should be dictated by the realization that this kind of ammunition—which we not only manufacture but fire from the biggest guns possible—is directed against ourselves by ourselves. The other side can sit back and chuckle over our success in fighting his battle.

Undoubtedly we of the West must accept some handicaps in the contest with the Communist world. I have mentioned a few. I have oversimplified and perhaps exaggerated those. Nor have I even attempted to catalogue our strong points. Perhaps that is not a serious omission because we know them so well. In any event, it is a time for soul searching, perhaps for soul shocking, rather than self-satisfaction as we face this new force of Soviet Communist imperialism armed with all the latest devices of a technology which we used to think peculiarly our own, and indeed possessing some that we have not yet acquired.

All this adds up to the fact that the strengthening of our own institutions, the putting of first things first at home, the acceptance of the necessary individual sacrifices for a good social objective, are the first and most important objectives of defense. It is the defense of values.

This thought was once put by William James in the following words:

"The deadliest enemies of nations are not their foreign foes, but those that dwell within their borders and from these internal enemies civilization is always in need of being saved. The nation blessed above all nations is she in whom the civic genius of the peoples does the saving day by day, by acts without external picturesqueness, by speaking, writing, voting reasonably, by smiting corruption swiftly, by good temper between parties, by the people knowing true men when they see them, and preferring them as leaders to rabid partisans or empty quacks."

There is, of course, another and more conventional aspect of defense which I should mention. It is the strengthening of the alliance of free nations, particularly in NATO—strengthening it militarily, economically, and politically.

This is a problem of immediate and pressing importance, for an alliance of this kind cannot stand still. It will go forward or it will disappear. If the latter, the primary aim of Russian foreign policy will be achieved: the detachment, the splitting off, of Western Europe from North America.

Believe me, there is a danger of this happening, with results which I think would be tragic for everyone but the Kremlin. At present, while real efforts are being exerted to make it otherwise, it would be idle to deny that the strongest element in the cement that holds the members of NATO together is fear. In maintaining the health of the alliance, a shot in the arm from Moscow is more effective than all the tonics prescribed in reports and resolutions at council meetings. In this respect, Khrushchev—as Stalin before him—has done more for NATO than any of its own "wise men" could possibly do.

There are signs, however, that this cement of fear, in spite of current shocks, is not as strong as it once was. This is not because of any evidence that the danger of aggression has been removed, but because of a growing feeling among certain of the European members that NATO, as such, no longer provides security against it; and also that the target of any aggression is now more likely to be over the air across the Atlantic. This questioning of the security value of NATO has been increased by the realization that the most effective military deterrent against all-out aggression by the Soviet on Western Europe is the ability of the United States, not NATO as such, to counterattack massively by air against Moscow, and the conviction in the Kremlin that such aggression would meet such retaliation.

This creates a sense of the futility of local defense as at present organized, and, therefore, of the folly of spending great sums of money on it. This feeling could possibly be changed if European countries had under their own command those tactical atomic weapons which could repel advancing masses from the East. Then they could themselves provide a deterrent against aggression without involving the use of bombs and missiles which would automatically convert what might be a limited war into global destruction.

As it happens, however, no continental European NATO country now has these atomic weapons under its own control or is manufacturing them. The ability of the United States to make them freely available is limited by legislation. All this is a serious weakening of the principle and practice of collective defense. Surely, in an alliance of this kind, every aspect of defense must be fully collective and cooperative, whether strategic or merely tactical considerations are involved; and all weapons must be shared. The time has come, I think, when security risks—if there is much risk now in view of what the Russians know—must be subordinated to the greater risk of the alliance weakening and disappearing.

Indeed if NATO cannot continue on the widest possible basis of pooling and partnership, it is not likely to continue at all, at least as an effective organization.

If there are dangers ahead for collective action for defense, the situation is even more disturbing in the field of political and economic cooperation. Here again at intervals the Russians make an aggressive move which shocks us into appeals for greater unity and closer cooperation. Then the crisis passes and too often also our noble resolve to work more closely together.

There has recently been some emphatic talk that the NATO countries should not only pool weapons but also their experience and their resources in the field of science and technology, should avoid wasteful duplication and provide for full exchange of information and know-how in this field. This admirable idea seems to have been given a sudden impetus by a heightened appreciation of Soviet scientific progress brought about by the startling realization that Sputnik has been scurrying around our world every few minutes and sending signals back to Moscow. But scientific pooling is no new idea. Indeed a proposal to convene a special conference to do something about it was put forward to the NATO Council on December 1, 1956, in the Report of the Committee of Three on non-military cooperation. There is nothing to indicate that this recommendation caused at that time very much interest among the governments most concerned.

It is the same with political cooperation generally. Every NATO member, including the Canadian, becomes eloquent on appropriate occasions over the virtues of the closest kind of such cooperation and consultation. But there is a steady reluctance, especially among the more powerful members, to take the necessary measures to make it effective. That would mean perhaps too much interference with the sacred cow of national sovereignty, would impose too great a limitation on the freedom of national action—and national legislatures.

We have, then, if I may sum up, two duties in the West, first to protect our institutions within the city walls from deterioration and decay, and then to defend the walls themselves.

There is, however, a third and even more important duty: to bring about a state of affairs in the world where no one will wish to attack us at all—or we, them; where eventually walls themselves will be as much of an anachronism as trenches, barbed wire, and forts on the United States-Canadian border.

This is the supreme obligation of all men in all nations—the extension of the area of peace with law and justice and freedom. We cannot be sure, of course, that all other nations will cooperate with us in that task. So we must maintain means for our own defense while taking every possible step, and making every possible effort, to remove any fear in others that our force, military and diplomatic, will ever be used for any aggressive and unworthy purpose.

Our insistence on the primacy of this task of making peace by international negotiation, our seizure of every political opportunity to this end, does not mean that we should or need contemplate agreements which would betray either our friends or our principles. Indeed, peace on such terms would be false and any arrangements made would be worthless. I know that there are those who look with suspicion on every move which is made that implies a desire or even a willingness to negotiate; who call it "appeasement"—one of those words debased by polemics—or softness toward communism. Such critics forget that if total and unremitting hatred of communism were the only test of loyalty to democratic ideals, Hitler would be the greatest democrat of all time.

Ignoring the voices of passionate, if often sincere, prejudice and unreason, we should, I think, as the most important move in this third phase of defense policy, go on seeking, patiently and persistently, a basis for negotiation and agreement with the other side. In the process we should refuse to adopt the rough, crude tactics which may be used against us, or allow our own attitudes, even more our own policies, to be determined by such tactics. This is not a sign of weakness on our part but of confidence and strength. Hence, we should refuse to get too elated over our successes or too downcast by our setbacks, too optimistic over peaceful promises or too alarmed over exaggerated threats.

I quite realize that the easiest, and in some quarters the most popular, attitude that we could adopt in the cold war would be a relentless and immovable stand on a platform of inveterate and inflexible hostility to Soviet Russia and determined opposition to every move she makes or tries to make any place, any time. The corollary to this means taking steps to counter and defeat every such move in the hope that Russia will eventually accept without conditions our terms for ending the cold war and withdraw—actually and ideologically—behind her old czarist boundaries. I myself see no prospect of any easing of tension, and, ultimately, of international peace and security, if we base our policy and diplomacy on any such thesis.

Such a policy is simply one of political "unconditional surrender." It means limiting our diplomacy and foreign policy to that requirement. It means, also, of course, remaining armed to the teeth, and at a time when it is equally useful to be armed to the brain. I have already emphasized that whatever we do we have to be well armed for defense in all its aspects. I'm not suggesting that we throw away any elements of our military forces except some antediluvian weapons and ideas. I accept the fact that no matter how enlightened and flexible our policy, we cannot safely allow it to result in a weakening of what the military call our defense posture. If, however, we allow an exaggerated and provocative posture to be brought about by the cold war calisthenics of an "unconditional surrender" type of diplomacy, we make the establishment of peace through tolerable arrangements even more difficult than it already is.

What I suggest is that without throwing away any of our necessary arms we refuse to allow our policy to be determined too much by purely military considerations, or our diplomacy either to be frozen by fear or weakened by illusions.

An ostrich may stupidly try to escape the consequences of its fears by burying its head in the sand. But rushing about in a panic is equally ineffective.

I am not naive enough to think that if we only follow steadily these principles of policy, satisfactory solutions will soon emerge for the international problems that divide and bedevil the world. Certainly my own experience makes me more than skeptical about finding in the present political climate any such solutions based on friendship or understanding or mutual trust between Communists and non-Communists. That is certainly not possible. My hopes are no higher than that some accommodations may be brought about step by step, point by point, on a basis of mutual tolerance and self-interest; and certainly without betrayal of any principle on our side. It may be that we cannot achieve even this. That does not mean, however, that we should not try, and make sure that if failure comes it will be through no fault of ours. As the Bible says, "It must needs be that offences come; but woe to that man by whom the offence cometh!"

In following the course I have outlined, we can take hope from the knowledge that no society, certainly no Russian Communist society, remains static. There is a ferment of freedom ever at work, even in Russia; for freedom, as the tragic epic of Hungary has shown, cannot be rooted out of the human mind by force or by fraud. Signs of this evolution which is taking place in Russia have been noticeable in the last few years. This gives us reason to hope that one day in a different Russia settlements can be made which will have stronger foundations than any which are possible now.

There is also in Russia a continual and implacable struggle for power going on within the Kremlin walls. This struggle, in addition to the light that it throws on the conspiratorial and shifting nature of Russian power, often reflects itself in the violence of a position that may be taken and expressed by Russia on some international issue at the United Nations or elsewhere. What may often seem to be an indication of brute strength and confidence at New York or at a Moscow cocktail party may conceal weakness and division in the Kremlin. In this kind of discord, the forces of reason which exist among the Russian people have a chance to become stronger.

Such an evolution, however, will be held back, perhaps indefinitely, if we now take fixed and final positions in opposition to every Russian move. As I see it, if and when Russia has a legitimate interest in some area or some development, we would be foolish to act as if that interest can either be ignored or destroyed. Such an attitude, of course, plays right into the hands of the worst elements inside the Kremlin. It also weakens our position in those nations that have no love for communism but refuse, for reasons which seem perfectly good to them, to take sides in the cold war. There are situations in the world today that do not admit of any permanent solution which will bring about stability without Russian participation in, or at least acceptance of, that solution. We might as well admit that hard fact.

In short, I think that if we wish to go forward from where we now are to something better, not only must we keep our domestic institutions strong, free, and healthy, our defensive coalition firm in its collective will and power, but we should take full advantage of every opportunity to negotiate, indeed create opportunities to negotiate differences with those whom we have had and still have good reason to fear.

In that course, followed steadily and not by spasms, with positive actions rather than panic reactions, based on a strength which is more than military, lies our best hope for a peace with law and order; a peace which will be endurable and perhaps, therefore, enduring....

FURTHER READING

Pearson's autobiography, in three volumes, is simply entitled *Mike* (Toronto: University of Toronto Press, 1973); shorter biographies include Robert Bothwell's *Pearson: His Life and World* (Toronto: McGraw Hill Ryerson, 1978) and John English, *Shadow of Heaven: The Life of Lester Pearson* (Toronto: Lester & Orphen Dennys, 1989). A critical collection of essays on Pearson's political thought is *Pearson: The Unlikely Gladiator*, edited by Norman Hillman (Montreal: McGill-Queen's University Press, 1999). For a more general overview of multilateralism, see Tom Keating's *Canada and World Order: The Multilateralist Tradition in Canadian Foreign Policy* (Toronto: McClelland and Stewart, 1993).

CHAPTER

8

TOMMY DOUGLAS

INTRODUCTION

While Thomas Clement Douglas (1904-86) was not an academic
thinker, his social vision for Canada has had a tremendous impact on
Canadian political values. Douglas went to Ottawa in 1935 under the
banner of the new CCF party; but his lasting influence was as Premier
of Saskatchewan from 1944 to 1961. Standing at the helm of the first
social democratic government in North America, Douglas introduced
not only universal medical insurance but also public automobile insurance, rural development, and unionization of the public service. In
this selection, a speech made in the Saskatchewan legislature in 1961,
Douglas defends his party's decision to introduce their medical insurance plan. His is perhaps the most articulate account of the Canadian
belief that medical care "is something to which people are entitled,
by virtue of belonging to a civilized community."

MEDICARE: THE TIME TO TAKE A STAND (1961)

I think it is significant that in his address yesterday the Leader of
the Opposition said nothing about the basic principles of medical
care. His only references to a medical care program were those
which were designed to throw cold water on the idea. First he said,
"Why don't we wait for a national plan?" Well, Mr. Speaker, I am
sure there were a lot of people in Saskatchewan who heard that
and who said to themselves, "How long are we supposed to wait?"
The Liberal party at its national convention in 1919 promised a
national comprehensive health insurance program. They were in
office from 1921 to 1930 and from 1935 to 1957. In 1945, during
the election immediately following the war, Liberal candidates went
up and down the country waving a copy of the Heagerty Report
and waving a copy of the bill which was never put into law, and

saying, "You elect us now that the war is over and we're going to have comprehensive health insurance." It's true we had a Hospital Insurance Act. But it was a Hospital Insurance Act which contained within it a "joker," whereby we couldn't get a national health insurance plan until at least Ontario or Quebec along with four other provinces were willing to come into the plan. The Liberal party left office without having contributed one five-cent piece to a national hospital insurance plan.

The Conservatives then came into office. Let it be said to their everlasting credit that one of the first things they did was to take the joker out of the Act, and to make national hospital insurance available to whatever provinces were prepared to proceed with such a plan. But they had promised in 1957 that if they were elected they would not only take the joker out of the Act, but they would extend hospital insurance to cover all hospital cases. This they haven't done. They promised to make hospital insurance applicable to mental hospital patients, and to tuberculosis sanitoria, and this they haven't done. The result is that hospital insurance in Canada today covers only 50 percent of the hospital beds in Canada. We haven't got complete hospital insurance yet. Someone has said that we should wait for the report of the Royal Commission on Medical Care which has been set up by the Government of Canada. Well, first of all, most of us have had some experience about waiting for action to be taken on the reports of Royal Commissions, and if one looks at the terms of reference of that commission, one can see that it is not specifically beamed at dealing with the problem of setting up a comprehensive health insurance program. Therefore, Mr. Speaker, to say that we should wait for a national plan, is to ask the people of Saskatchewan to drag along and wait, as they have waited for thirty or forty years, for the federal government to act and knowing full well that they are not likely to act unless some province leads the way.

The other thing the Leader of the Opposition said about the medical care program was, "What's the hurry?" He said the government is just hurrying this plan through, for the publicity effect in a federal election. Yet, I remember at the last regular session of the legislature, that at least two or three members opposite asked the government when were we going to get on with the medical care plan. They pointed out that the government had promised it in the election of 1960. They wanted to know what we were waiting for—how long was the medical advisory committee going to take to get a report down—what was holding us up? Mr. Speaker, this is surely a disorganized army. The rank and file are saying forward, and the leader is saying retreat. They had better make up their minds. Does the Liberal party believe we should have a medical care plan? Do they believe we should have it now? Do they want to postpone it? They can't be "forwards-backwards" all the time. They've got to take a stand. I think all the people of this province have a right to know where they stand on this question. When the House votes on this matter they'll have a chance to see, and their constituents will have a chance to see what they think about a medical care plan.

There was one statement made by the Leader of the Opposition about medical care which astonished me. He said, "There's not a shred of evidence to show that any person in the province has been unable to get medical attention." Surely if ever a comment indicated that an individual was out of touch with people, it is that remark. It is like Marie Antoinette at the time of the French Revolution when the people were crying for bread, saying, "Why don't they eat cake?" To say that there is no evidence to show that any person in the province has been unable to get medical attention, is to fly in the face of all the facts.

The Canadian Sickness Report, 1951, conducted by the Government of Canada, shows clearly that the lower income groups in the period under study had more illness and more days of disability than did the higher income groups. It shows, conversely, that the volume of medical care received by the low income groups is much less than that received by higher income groups. The low income groups, because of poor diet, poor housing conditions, and harder working conditions, have more illness and more disability. Yet the records show that they are the people who get the least medical care. The Canadian Sickness Report shows that the low income groups spent on an average $58.10 per family, whereas the higher income groups spent on an average $158.70 per family. The higher income groups spent almost three times as much per family on medical care as did the low income groups, despite the fact that the low income groups had more sickness and more disability.

If my hon. friend would take the trouble to turn to page 58 of the Interim Report of the Advisory Committee on Medical Care he could see there a table which shows that in the year 1959, 120,941 persons or families in Saskatchewan had incomes of less that $2500 per year. Forty-eight percent of the income earners of this province had an income of less than $2500. The same report shows thirty-five percent of the income earners in this province didn't earn enough to pay income tax. They didn't earn $2000 a year if they were married with no dependent children. Those figures can be duplicated right across Canada as the recent survey will show. It is sheer nonsense therefore to say that there is no evidence that people are not able to get the medical attention they require.

Now I readily grant that no doctor has turned patients away. No doctor could do so without violating his Hippocratic oath. But what happens? First of all, patients are reluctant to go to the doctor if they know they can't pay. People fail to seek medical counsel and medical advice when they should get it and they often time leave it until the situation is serious and even dangerous. The second fact is that many people who do go to doctors incur bills and debts which cripple them for years to come, and this does not just apply to poor people. There are thousands of people in Saskatchewan and across Canada living on reasonably comfortable incomes who are able to make the payments on their houses and their cars and on their television sets and who can get by providing two things: firstly, they don't lose their jobs; and secondly, that the breadwinner doesn't get seriously ill. For such people, doctor bills amounting to large sums of money can put that family in a serious financial predicament for years to come.

The Leader of the Opposition yesterday spent a good deal of time talking about the terrible costs which this would place upon the taxpayers of this province. I thought some of his sentences were gems. He said, "The Liberals believe in a medical care plan if it can be done without hardship to the taxpayer." Now, which taxpayer is he worried about—the ones that are going to be paying less under the plan than they pay now, or the ones that are going to be paying more? Which is he worried about? He goes on and says, "Many people wonder if we can afford $20,000,000 at a time like this for a medical care plan." Many people wonder! Is he one of them? Are the members opposite among those who wonder if we can afford $20,000,000 for a medical care plan? Let them say so.

The *Leader-Post* for three months has been writing editorials telling the people of Saskatchewan they cannot afford a medical care plan.

Is the Liberal press speaking for the Liberal party? It is time the Liberal party got off the fence and took a stand. The Leader of the Opposition says the people cannot stand more taxes. He says that land taxes are too high. Mr. Speaker, of course land taxes are too high. I want to point out two things. The CCF government doesn't impose any land taxes. There is no provincial land tax. There was a provincial land tax when we took office, and it was put there by a Liberal government. The CCF government took it off. It was a tax of two mills on every bit of land in Saskatchewan.

I want to remind you, moreover, that by gradually increasing school grants and giving additional help to municipalities for roads, we have saved the municipalities a great deal of money which they would otherwise have had to get by levying land taxes. If we had continued to pay school grants, not in the same amounts, but in the same percentage of the total cost of education that the Liberal party gave, and if we gave assistance for roads to municipalities on the same basis that the Liberal party gave them, the municipalities of this province—rural and urban—would have had to impose another 17.5 mills on every bit of land in the province of Saskatchewan. The generous help the municipalities have had from the government has enabled them to keep the land taxes from going any higher than they are now.

I want to point out, Mr. Speaker, that the cost of a medical care plan is not a new cost to the people of Saskatchewan. The people of this province now are spending $18 million to $20 million a year for medical care. This is not a new cost. It is a different distribution of the cost—that is all. This money had to be paid before. Doctors of this province had to be paid. Everything has had to be paid for— their staff, X-ray technicians, lab technicians, these things all had to be paid for. But they have been paid for by those who were unfortunate enough to be ill. We are now saying they should be paid for by spreading the cost over all the people. We propose that the family tax, which we admit is a regressive tax, since there is a flat rate on every family, and therefore bears no relationship to ability to pay, should be kept as small as possible. We propose that the balance of the cost—probably two-thirds of the cost—ought to be raised by factors which have a measure of ability to pay.

Maybe this is why the Liberal press have been so vehement in their attacks on this plan. It may be that some of them begin to suspect that they are going to have to pay a part of the medical bill of some other people who are not able to pay their own.

Yesterday the Leader of the Opposition sneered at the idea of "I am my brother's keeper." He said, "There isn't much cream in Saskatchewan." I want to suggest that the *Leader-Post* and the *Star-Phoenix,* the Sifton interests and the Leader of the Opposition have fattened quite a bit during the term of the CCF government in office, and it will certainly not hurt them at all to make some contribution towards the medical care for those less fortunate than themselves.

The Leader of the Opposition when he began his remarks on Wednesday said, "The member for Regina doesn't know what this medical care plan will cost," and "I doubt if the government knows." This is strange. It's strange in the first place the government would-n't know what it is going to cost, when the Leader of the Opposition has been going up and down the length and breadth of this province, saying that he knows what it's going to cost because he has the government's secret documents.

If the government has a secret document saying what it is going to cost and the Leader of the Opposition says he's got a copy of it, how can he say the government doesn't know what it's going to cost?

When the Leader of the Opposition says that the government doesn't know the cost, and he doesn't know the cost, I wonder if he read a copy of the *Interim Report of the Advisory Planning Committee on Medical Care.* This was sent to him the very day it was released to the press. He will find that on page 85 estimates are given. They say it will cost between $19,970,000 and $20,570,000. If you add to that the administrative costs, which they estimate at $1 million, this means somewhere between $21 million and $21.5 million, and if a utiliza-tion fee is charged, you can subtract $1,800,000 from these amounts. There isn't much doubt as to what the cost will be. We're talking about a sum of money in the neighbourhood of $20 million—more if you don't impose utilization fees, and slightly less if you do.

It seems to me to be begging the question to be talking about whether or not the people of this province, or the people of Canada can afford a plan to spread the cost of sickness over the entire popu-lation. This is not a new principle. This has existed in nearly all the countries of western Europe—many of them for a quarter of a century. It has been in Great Britain since 1948; it has been in New Zealand since 1935; it has been in Australia. The little state of Israel

that only came into existence in 1948 has today the most comprehensive health insurance plan in the world. It has more doctors,
and nurses and dentists per thousand of its population than any
other industrialized country or any country for which we can get
statistics.

It is not a new principle. To me it seems to be sheer nonsense to
suggest that medical care is something which ought to be measured just in dollars. When we're talking about medical care we're
talking about our sense of values. Do we think human life is important? Do we think that the best medical care which is available is
something to which people are entitled, by virtue of belonging to
a civilized community? I looked up the figures, and I found that,
in 1959, the people of Canada spent $1,555 million, or eight
percent of their personal expenditures on alcohol and tobacco. I
would be the last person to argue that people do not have the right,
if they want to, to spend part of their income for either alcohol or
tobacco or entertainment, or anything else. But in the same period
of time, the people of Canada spent $944 million for medical and
dental care, or four and one-half percent of their income expenses.
In other words, in the year 1959 we spent almost twice as much on
luxuries such as tobacco and alcohol as we spent on providing
ourselves and our families with the medical and dental care which
they require.

If we can afford large sums of money for other such things as
horse-racing, and many other things, and we do—I'm not arguing
against them—then I say we ought to have sufficient sense of values
to say that health is more important than these things, and if we
can find money for relatively non-essential things, we can find the
money to give our people good health.

The Liberal press in this province have been running editorials
regularly for months now against the welfare state, particularly attacking the welfare state in the United Kingdom. The other day they
pointed out that the British government was spending more on the
welfare state than they were spending on national defence. Well,
this to me is not a crushing criticism. As a matter of fact, Mr. Speaker,
it shows that the Parliament of Great Britain recognizes that giving
people security, giving people good health, giving people the feeling of well-being, is the most important defence there is against
communism. Communities where people have security and where

care is taken of the needy and unfortunate have the kind of society into which Communism has never been able to infiltrate. They published the figures on what this welfare state is costing the British taxpayer. They quoted them as $2.5 billion and that is approximately correct. But there are 55 million people in Great Britain. If you divide 55 million people into $2.5 billion, this works out at less than $50 per person.

Mr. Speaker, $50 per capita gives every man, woman and child in Great Britain security from the cradle to the grave. It takes care of their doctor bills, dental bills, hospital bills, optometric care and appliances. The only thing for which there is a deterrent fee is drugs, and that is very small. It gives them unemployment insurance, baby bonuses, and pensions when they are physically disabled. It provides benefits in the event of death, and it provides adequate pensions for widows and their children. I say that if any government, of any country, can give its people that kind of security for less than $50 per capita, then it is worth the price, and many times over.

The fact is, Mr. Speaker, that a medical care plan can only be financed out of one or two sources of revenue. The first one is from taxes. Everyone knows you have to pay taxes if you want services. Many people under this plan will pay less than they are paying now if they belong to a private plan. Other people will pay more, because if some of the money is collected on a basis of ability to pay, and if they are in the higher income groups, they may be paying a little more. The important thing for the government to ensure is that the part which must be collected from taxes is collected as equitably as possible in order to distribute the burden as equitably as possible.

The other source from which the government can get money, of course, is resource development. I want to remind you that this government has collected probably $100 for every dollar which a Liberal government ever collected from resource development in this province. Yesterday the Leader of the Opposition again made a sweeping statement. He said that the crown corporations cost the people of this province millions of dollars. The fact is, of course, that the last financial statement showed conclusively that after providing for the losses on the woollen mill and the shoe factory and the tannery, the smaller crown corporations—not including gas and power and telephones—have accumulated over $12 million in surpluses. If you include power, gas, and telephones, the surpluses are over $53 million—$53,804,067 to be exact. The crown corporations have paid into the government treasury in royalties some $7,870,000; they paid to the municipality in lieu of taxes $3,609,000 and have paid out in wages over $181 million.

I believe, Mr. Speaker, that the people of this province want health security. I think hospital insurance proves that. In spite of all the criticism we had when hospital insurance was set up, and in spite of the protest of the Liberal party that we should allow it to be handled by the municipalities, the fact is that today no one in this province in their right mind would suggest abolishing hospital insurance. On the contrary, our pioneering in hospital insurance proved so successful that today our example has been followed in every other province in this Dominion.

I believe that the great bulk of the people of this province support the idea of the medical care plan. I believe they will indicate they are willing to pay for it, providing the cost is spread equitably on the basis of ability to pay. The only ones who are likely to oppose it are those who fear that they will have to help those less fortunate than themselves.

Mr. Speaker, you will note in the Speech from the Throne it says that this medical care plan is to be a province-wide plan, with universal coverage. This was an important decision for the Advisory Planning Committee on Medical Care to make. They had before them briefs from the doctors of the province, and from the Chamber of Commerce, which advocated a partial medical care plan. In very brief terms the recommendation was that the great bulk of the people who were self-supporting would ensure themselves by joining the private plan of their choice, and that the remainder should have an extra premium paid on their behalf to the private plan, providing they could show that they were in need. Private plans ordinarily do not take people who have congenital illnesses. But if these people are in need and if an extra premium is paid on their behalf private plans would accept them. Similarly, people who were over 65 who are not accepted by private plans, if they can show they are in need, and if an extra premium was paid on their behalf by the government, they would get medical care from private plans. Those people generally who, because of low incomes, were not able to pay the private plan premium would also be covered by the private plans if they could show they were in need and if the government would pay their premium.

It was said by those submitting this plan that this could be done for some $3,600,000. This would be so much cheaper than a general plan. Well, the majority report of the Advisory Planning Committee on Medical Care showed that the rest of the Committee were very dubious about this $3,600,000. It also showed that they were convinced the people of Saskatchewan in the aggregate would pay much more to private plans than they are going to pay under a government-sponsored plan.

There are two basic weaknesses in the proposals which were put forward by those who wanted a limited coverage for medical care. The first is the private plans bear no relationship to ability to pay. I want to make it abundantly clear, Mr. Speaker, that the private plans such as Medical Services Incorporated, and Group Medical Services have rendered a marvellous service to the people of Saskatchewan. In the absence of a government plan I have advised people through-out the years, if they can possibly afford it, to join these private plans. They have been well operated, and I hope that much of their experience and their facilities and staff may be made available to those who will be managing the government-sponsored medical care plan. But a private medical care plan can only raise money in one way, and that is by putting a flat premium on every family irrespective of whether the family's income is $20,000 a year or $10,000. They have no way of graduating premiums on the basis of ability to pay. Only the government is in a position to say that those who have less will pay less, and those who have more will pay more. This is why, in my opinion, and in the opinion, apparently, of the majority of the Committee, the idea of partial coverage was dropped.

The other weakness in the proposal of a partial coverage medical care program is that a great many groups in the province would only get coverage if they could prove need. This means imposing a means test; this means probing into people's affairs, and this is a pretty serious thing to do.

I want to say that the time is surely past when people should have to depend on proving need in order to get services that should be the inalienable right of every citizen of a good society.

It is all very well for some people to say that there is no stigma or humiliation connected with having to prove need. This is always said by people who know that they are in no danger of having to prove need. I am very glad that the Committee recommended and the government decided that there will be no such stigma and that there will be no means test. Every person in the province who is self-supporting and able to pay a relatively small per capita tax, will be eligible for care and those who are not self-supporting will be covered by other programs.

I want to say that I think there is a value in having every family and every individual make some individual contribution. I think it has psychological value. I think it keeps the public aware of the cost and gives the people a sense of personal responsibility. I would say to the members of this House that even if we could finance the plan without a per capita tax, I personally would strongly advise against it. I would like to see the per capita tax so low that it is merely a nominal tax, but I think there is a psychological value in people paying something for their cards. It is something which they have bought; it entitles them to certain services. We should have the constant realization that if those services are abused and costs get out of hand, then of course the cost of the medical care is bound to go up.

I believe, Mr. Speaker, that if this medical care insurance program is successful, and I think it will be, it will prove to be the forerunner of a national medical care insurance plan. It will become the nucleus around which Canada will ultimately build a comprehensive health insurance program which will cover all health services—not just hospital and medical care—but eventually dental care, optometric care, drugs and all the other health services which people require. I believe such a plan operated by the federal and provincial governments jointly will ultimately come in Canada. But I don't think it will come unless we lead the way. I want to say that when the history of our time is written, it may well be recorded that in October 1961, the Saskatchewan legislature and the Saskatchewan people pioneered in this field and took a first step towards ultimately establishing a system of medical care insurance for all the people of Canada....

The government believes that health is too important to be left to the chance that the average family will have the necessary money to buy health services. I believe that if we put this health plan into operation it will have the same history as the Hospital Insurance Plan. I am convinced that inside two or three years both the doctors who provide the service and the people who receive the service will be so completely satisfied with it that no government will dare to take it away.

FURTHER READING

The classic works on prairie socialism are Seymour Martin Lipsett's *Agrarian Socialism: The Co-operative Commonwealth Federation in Saskatchewan* (Berkeley: University of California Press, 1971) and Walter D. Young's *Democracy and Discontent: Progressivism, Socialism, and Social Credit in the Canadian West* (Toronto: Ryerson Press, 1969); two more recent accounts are A.W. Johnson's *Dream No Little Dreams: A Biography of the Douglas Government of Saskatchewan, 1944–61* (Toronto: University of Toronto Press, 2004) and John Warnock's *Saskatchewan: The Roots of Discontent and Protest* (Montreal: Black Rose Books, 2004). A detailed history of the development of the health care system in Canada can be found in C. David Naylor's *Health Care and the State: A Century of Evolution* (Montreal: McGill-Queen's University Press, 1992).

CHAPTER 9

KARI LEVITT

INTRODUCTION

It was concern for the rapidly increasing level of foreign ownership in the Canadian economy that led Kari Levitt (b. 1923) to publish her study of American multinational corporations in Canada. She argued that control of the Canadian economy was being ceded to American interests and that this would mean a loss of political decision-making ability for Canadians. Levitt's work was a rallying point for the "Waffle Movement," a left-nationalist splinter of the New Democratic Party that existed between 1969 and 1974. This movement was a prophetic prototype for contemporary anti-globalization organizations, which argue, again, that American economic domination has a detrimental effect upon the sovereignty of states throughout the world.

SILENT SURRENDER: THE MULTINATIONAL CORPORATION IN CANADA (1970)

The dominant institution in the peripheral economy in the contemporary period is the foreign affiliate or branch plant of the great modern corporation. In *The New Industrial State*, Professor John Galbraith has given a name to that part of the American economy which is characterized by a few hundred technically dynamic, massively capitalized and highly organized corporations. He calls it the "Industrial System." What is important here is not the particular name Galbraith has chosen to distinguish the phenomenon, but that he perceives so clearly the way in which a system characterized by very large corporations is qualitatively different in its processes from a system comprised of an infinite number of small enterprises.[1] These differences are crucial in understanding the impact of the expansion of the metropolitan corporation on the hinterlands, the peripheral fringes and margins of its domain.

In summary, the argument runs as follows: the imperatives of modern technology increase both the amount of capital committed and the time for which it is committed. Further, the commitment of time and money tends to be ever more specific to a given task. This sets up requirements for specialized manpower and the inevitable counterpart of specialization, which is organization. In the interest of securing stable and growing profits and of reducing risk and uncertainty, the firm is motivated to engage in planning. It may be added here, in anticipation, that risk is not so much eliminated, as shifted to small-scale entrepreneurs and to the peripheral or hinterland economies.

The "Industrial System," and the New Industrial State which is its political counterpart, entails a massive concentration of power in the hands of the corporate elite, or "technostructure." The commitment of time and money inherent in contemporary technology means that the needs of consumers must be anticipated by months or years. The modern corporation engages in systematic and comprehensive planning, ruthlessly efficient and responsible only to its own requirements of survival.

> In addition to deciding what the consumer will want and will pay, the firm must take every feasible step to see that what it decides to produce is wanted by the consumer at a remunerative price. It must see that the labour, materials and equipment that it needs will be available at a cost consistent with the price it will receive. It must exercise control over what is sold. It must exercise control over what is supplied. It must replace the market with planning.[2]

Contrary to the postulates of economic doctrine, it follows that the initiative in deciding what is produced comes not from the sovereign consumer who issues instructions to the market which bend the productive mechanism to his will, but rather from the great producing organization which reaches forward to control the markets that it presumes to serve. In this process, it is the corporation that bends the consumer to its needs, and in so doing deeply influences his values and beliefs.

The economic calculus whereby the corporation acts to shape

consumer tastes and needs is central to the argument. The creation of particular tastes for particular products largely determines the technology to be used, the parts, supplies and capital goods required, the complementary goods demanded, the professional skills used, and the channels of distribution through which inputs and outputs flow. Metropolitan demands are transferred to hinterlands as the more privileged strata of the population there attain higher income levels and aspirations approximating those of the metropolitan countries. The phenomenon has variously been labelled the "demonstration effect," "the "trickle-down effect," and "Cocacolonization."

For the hinterlands, the significance of the accretion of control and power in the head offices of the multinational corporations lies in their increasing dependence on entrepreneurial initiatives originating in the metropoles. The hinterlands are the countries in which subsidiaries are located to supply the corporations with their inputs of raw materials and to dispose of their output of consumer, intermediate and capital goods. They may be older metropolitan centres, such as those of Western Europe, or they may be peripheral economies in which foreign subsidiaries and branch plants have always been the dominant economic institutions. Canada lies somewhere along this spectrum of dependence. For the hinterlands the result is the re-creation of certain patterns of the old mercantilism and the fragmentation and destruction of national economies and associated national political systems in states such as Canada and some of the Latin American countries. Present conditions are particularly unfavourable to national economic and political integration in the many new states established in the postwar period. Thus we are witnessing a simultaneous process of de-colonization and re-colonization.

In pursuit of security, the corporation is driven to minimize uncertainty by converting market transactions into internal allocative decisions. Increasingly, the market is replaced by corporate planning. Thus a steady flow of raw material at predictable cost can be secured by direct control over extractive operations; while the sale of output can be assured by control over marketing and distribution facilities. In this way the play of market forces on strategic cost factors is minimized by an extension of corporate planning.[3]

It follows that the most obvious requirement for effective corporate planning is size. There is virtually no limit on the size of the corporation. Size is not, as economists generally believe, determined by the requirements of economies of large-scale production; nor is it determined simply by the desire to exercise monopoly power in markets. The typical corporation is large enough to afford a score of production units of optimum technical size, and typically extends into the production of a large diversity of goods. As for market power associated with monopoly, the threat of competition requires a constant stream of product-innovations designed to capture markets by want-creation and product-differentiation.4

The strategy of eliminating market uncertainty by eliminating the market is not confined to the procurement of supplies and the disposition of outputs. The capital market has also been severely restricted. The control of the supply of savings is strategic for industrial planning. No form of market uncertainty is so serious as that involving the terms and conditions on which capital is obtained. Insofar as the corporation can rely on self-financing, the decision on what will be saved and what will be invested has largely been converted into an internal decision.5 By and large the big corporation no longer faces the risk of the capital market. According to Galbraith, it has full control over its rate of expansion, over the nature of that expansion, and over decisions between products, plants and processes. No banker can impose conditions as to how retained earnings are to be used.

It is well known that personal savings are a relatively unimportant source of finance compared with the internal savings of business. In 1965, for instance, in the United States savings by individuals, much of it institutional, amounted to $25 billion, while business savings was $84 billion. The decisions which supply the bulk of the community's supply of savings are made not by individuals but by the managements of a few hundred corporations. The decisions as to what will be invested are made by the same set of large firms. The decision to save is not made by the individual earner of income—the corporation does not give him the choice.

> The individual serves the industrial system, not by supplying it with savings and the resulting capital; he serves it by consuming its products. On no other matter, religious, political or moral, is he so elaborately and skilfully and expensively instructed.6

Sovereign Corporation, Captive Consumer

The shaping of consumer tastes is central to the strategy of profit-maximization of the large corporation. Seen in this light it is the corporation which is sovereign; the consumer is captive. The savings of the corporation arise from the sale of goods produced by persons who as consumers have been conditioned to need *paquotille*. Galbraith reminds us that, in the olden days, commodities such as tobacco, alcohol, and opium which involved a physical and progressive addiction were considered useful trade goods. Nowadays,

> in all underdeveloped countries, the effort inspired by the introduction of modern consumer goods—cosmetics, motor scooters, transistor radios, canned foods, bicycles, phonograph records, movies, American cigarettes—is recognized to be of the highest importance in the strategy of development?7

It is becoming clear that this strategy of economic development is really the strategy of long-term profit maximization of the international corporation.

The success of the large corporation is reflected by a fact which has been little noticed: they do not lose money. In 1957 for instance, which was a year of recession, not one of the hundred largest U.S. corporations failed to turn in a profit. Only one of the largest two hundred finished the year in the red.

It follows from all this that the summing of the market value of goods and services produced or consumed cannot logically be accepted as a measure of economic welfare. G.N.P.-fixation may be regarded as the projection onto the national and international level of the requirements of the corporation for continuously expanding markets and sales.8 It is discouraging to note that the elevation of the rate of growth of output of material goods and services to the prime social goal is not confined to countries dominated by corporate capitalism.

Galbraith reminds us that no other test of social success has such nearly unanimous acceptance as the annual increase in Gross National Product. And this is true of all countries, developed or underdeveloped, communist, socialist or capitalist. It is now agreed that ancient cultures—India, China and Persia—should measure their progress towards civilization by their percentage increase in G.N.P. Their own scholars are the most insistent of all.9

Because economies of scale in research, design and technology are realized by spreading costs over total output, the global profitability of the international corporation is assisted by every influence which eliminates cultural resistance to the consumption patterns of the metropolis. The corporation thus has a vested interest in the destruction of cultural differences and in a homogenized way of life the world over.10 In a deep insight into the "internationalism" of the modern corporation, George Grant has observed that "corporation capitalism and liberalism go together in the nature of things," and that "liberalism is the ideological means whereby individual cultures are homogenized."11 Further, he observed that "at the heart of modern liberalism lies the desire to homogenize the world. Today's natural and social sciences are consciously produced as instruments to this end." In this context it appears that the economists are the high priests of corporate capitalism—they have elevated the rate of increase of consumption of goods and services to the ultimate criterion of social good.

For the corporation, there is no shortage of capital—only a shortage of homogenized consumers. The corporation has institutionalized capital accumulation within the framework of its organization. The process is self-sustaining and self-financing so long as new products can be devised and new markets created. In the words of Neil McElroy, chairman of the board of directors of the Procter and Gamble Company: "Our problem is not access to capital and I believe this is true of most American companies. Our problem is the development of ideas that will justify the investment of capital."12

Galbraith's model of the New Industrial State is largely drawn from the experience of the United States and focuses attention on the role of the American corporation within the domestic economy. But his insights are particularly helpful in understanding the operations of the corporation in the international economy. They illuminate the processes which have created an "overseas economy" of the United States corporations whose annual sales had reached $90 million by 1964—almost four times the total value of U.S. commodity exports.

Entrepreneurial vs. Managerial Decisions

The executives of branch plants are managers, not entrepreneurs. They dispose of funds, equipment and personnel within the means allocated to them. They do not formulate policy, they administer it. The decisions they make are routine in the sense that they are constrained by budgetary allocation made at head office. While some have more scope than others, every subsidiary is of necessity an instrument of its parent company. An economy composed of branch-plant industry must of necessity lack the self-generating force which characterizes successful entrepreneurship. To the degree that Canadian business has opted to exchange its entrepreneurial role for a managerial and rentier status, Canada has regressed to a rich hinterland with an emasculated, if comfortable, business elite.

In a fascinating study of the strategy and structure of industrial enterprise Professor Alfred D. Chandler defines entrepreneurial decisions as those which concern the allocation of resources for the enterprise as a whole. They are the domain of the executive.[13] Operating decisions, in contrast, refer to decisions by managers within the means allocated to them. Executives operate from the general office and deal with several industries, or with one industry operating in several geographic regions of countries. Their business horizons range over national and international economies. The executive determines the long-term basic goals and objectives of an enterprise. Decisions to set up distant plants, to move into new functions (vertical integration), develop new products (diversification), are examples of entrepreneurial or strategic decisions.[14]

Managers on the other hand make decisions about prices charged on specific products, about design and quality of the existing products and the development of new ones, about more immediate markets and marketing, about probable sources of supply, about technological improvements and about the flow of product from supplier to consumer. But these decisions are made within the framework set by the policy guides and financial budgets through which the general executives determine the present and future allocation of the resources of the enterprise as a whole.[15]

It follows from this that, protestations notwithstanding, the executive of Canadian and other foreign operations of American companies are managers, not entrepreneurs. They do not make the guiding decisions concerning the global goals of the enterprise or the allocation of money; they operate within guide-lines set down by the general office. The role of the management of a branch plant is perhaps best described by a man who was director and vice-president of a large prestigious Canadian subsidiary of a well-known multinational corporation: "Clearly any subsidiary is always the chosen instrument of its parent company. Its very reason for existence is to carry out the functions of the parent in its designated sphere of activity, and it must recognize this relationship in all its actions...."[16]

The general executive as described by Professor Chandler is Schumpeter's entrepreneur. The active role which Schumpeter ascribed to his entrepreneur was, if anything, an understatement of the degree to which the exercise of corporate decision-making power affects the economic and social environment in the scores of countries in which the great multinational corporations operate.

The successful corporation creates the market for its products and creates the financial resources required to sustain perpetual expansion. It is an entrepreneurial operation geared to the "development of ideas that will justify the investment of capital." Success is assured to the enterprise which can keep its resources effectively employed. Of these resources trained personnel, with manufacturing, engineering, scientific and managerial skill often becomes more important than warehouses, plants, offices and other physical facilities.

With increased emphasis on "know-how" rather than hardware, competitive advantage accrues to enterprises whose resources of men and equipment are transferable in the sense they are geared to handle a range of technology rather than a specific set of end products or of raw materials. Thus, as Chandler points out, in the chemical, electrical, electronic and power machinery industries the same personnel, using much the same raw materials, were able to develop synthetic fibres, new films and plastics, new electrical and electronic devices, and new machines and new household articles. Increasingly large amounts of total resources were invested in research and development and these resources became less and less tied to any specific product line. Continued growth and accumulation of resources typically came in new product lines which the companies had themselves developed. It should be noted that this account accords well with the findings of investigations into patterns of international trade which proceed from the "product cycle" hypothesis and emphasize the competitive advantage of the American firm in R and D resources and product-innovation.

The Direct Investment Decision

Efforts to apply traditional equilibrium analysis to incremental capital expansion by means of direct investment fly in the face of the observed fact that direct investment is not particularly sensitive to earning differentials; nor does it move to those sectors and countries where, by the aggregative reckoning of textbook economics, capital is the scarce factor and profit rates allegedly highest. Indeed the "lending" aspect of direct investment is in an important way incidental to the purposes of the operation.

Thus the National Conference Board Study by Polk, Meister and Veit found that a differential profit rate was unlikely to induce a company to establish production facilities abroad and even less to suggest that a company would, because of the disappearance of this differential, discontinue the investment support needed for its marketing position. They found that even a continual decline in a market may provoke rather than discourage further investment, depending on the company's opinion of what is required to safeguard its larger-range financial interests.[17]

They concluded that direct investment is the response of the individual corporation to the requirements of competitive survival and that market strategy is clearly the dominant element in the investment decision. To stand still is to lose:

> Normally investment, even when it appears new or expansionary, is necessary to maintain competitiveness and is made to strengthen the continued earning ability of the enterprise as a whole, not just to produce additional profits.... Growth is organic and not incremental and can be arrested only at the expense of viability.[18]

Since the borrowing subsidiary and the lending parent are of course the same corporation, the "loan" implied in direct investment is best regarded as an accounting fiction. Behind it lies a real transfer of corporate resources, an extension of the corporation's productive apparatus and the creation or strengthening of an organic connection between the productive structures of the two countries concerned.[19]

Exporting from the metropolis and the setting up of production facilities abroad are complementary rather than competitive activities, being firm investments in the strategy market expansion:

> In the producers' view, the familiar course of marketing on the usual basis of producing at lowest achievable cost for any potential market demand, is first to export to a market, next to produce abroad as directed by local circumstances abroad (of which cost is only one), then to export more as market opportunities are established, then to produce more—and so on in a sequence alterable by changing circumstances but always in accordance with the principle of meeting market opportunities in the most suitable competitive manner.[20]

When the corporation undertakes direct investment, the market expansion involved enables it to maintain and extend its technological and marketing initiative in research, design and taste-formation and promotion. Increased sales permit the spreading of a larger volume of output over committed costs and with that bring larger profits out of which to finance further expenditures on further expansion. Even if in the corporate economy the individual entrepreneur has been replaced by a faceless bureaucracy, it is more than ever Schumpeter's world: the rewards accrue to managerial and technological initiative and innovation. In this dynamic world the fixed element in costs is not the physical hardware of plant and equipment, which have traditionally preoccupied economists. These have, indeed, become a relatively variable item of cost; the most "fixed" element is the specialized managerial, financial, marketing and innovative capacity of the corporation.

The motivations and mechanisms of U.S. direct investment abroad do not differ substantially from those which guided American business in its earlier expansion within the domestic market. The competitive techniques perfected in the domestic environment have now been transferred to the world scene.[21] Subsidiaries and branch plants, take-overs and mergers, are innovative techniques of competition. The obstacles placed in the way of corporate expansion by trust-busting legislation and by the fragmented and localized character of the American banking system may have been contributing factors in breeding a particularly resilient and self-contained form of business enterprise. Whatever the explanation, there is no doubt that the identity of interest and the single-focus decision-making involved in the American corporation was a superior device to its European counterpart, the business arrangement or cartel.[22] The following summary of the characteristic behaviour of the modern corporation is based principally, but by no means exclusively, on an article by Professor Raymond F. Mikesell:[23]

1. The typical management-controlled firm is motivated mainly by the desire to grow. Considerations of short and long term market conditions are paramount in all strategic decisions and in innovation, including innovation in internal organization. Growth is necessary for the survival of the corporation as a collective entity.

2. Profits are regarded by management more as a means of growth than as ends in themselves. They provide resources to be disposed of by internal decision and direction and they strengthen the credit position of the firm on the capital market. The paid-out portion of profit keeps shareholders quiet and in effect transforms them into rentiers.

3. Because of the exigencies of competitive strategies, firms tend to take a long-run view towards profit and are normally willing to sacrifice higher immediate profits for the opportunity to enter a market with a large growth potential.

4. Growth and profits are primarily a function of the internal resources of the firm, in terms of managerial ability and experience and initiative to bring to fruition new profitable areas of activity which must in turn increase the internal resources of the firm for further growth.

5. The large and even the medium-sized firm is not confined to expansion of any particular product line, or to any one regional or national market. Managerial ability and technical experience can be transferred and extended to new products and new markets.

6. Expansion frequently takes the form of the acquisition of existing firms rather than starting from scratch to build new plant or develop a wholly new market. Such acquisitions also bring into the firm new managerial and technical talent which constitutes the most important source for growth.

7. Parent companies have a strong preference for 100 per cent control over subsidiaries. Concentration of legal ownership claims in the stock of the parent company maximizes the flexibility of the administration in deploying the total resources of the firm.
8. Because the strategy of the firm is global, differences in profit rates at home and abroad do not provide a satisfactory explanation of the movement of American direct investment abroad, just as differences in profit rates do not provide an adequate explanation of the movement of investment among different industries within the United States.

The Parent-Subsidiary Relationship

It is evident that the contribution of the subsidiary to the parent is evaluated with respect to its effect on the profit rate of the corporation as a global financial unit. The subsidiary is an instrument to be used within the context of the total operation. Conflicts of interest would be inevitable if the subsidiary were an independent financial unit. As Mr. Frank S. Capon, director and vice-president of the Dupont Company of Canada, put it:

> ... often it is impractical to sell equity shares at anything like the per unit value to the parent company because of initial loss periods or because the chief impact of the subsidiary is on the incremental earnings of the parent, rather than any direct profit in the subsidiary.[24]

This explains the well-established reluctance of parent companies to permit direct shareholding in subsidiaries, and their many statements to the effect that subsidiaries are frequently not operating at a profit.

The attitude of the typical multinational corporation to minority shareholding in subsidiaries is illustrated by the resounding negative response to a three-year campaign by the Montreal Stock Exchange to encourage American companies to sell a part of the equity of their subsidiaries to the Canadian public. Ninety-four of the largest fully-owned subsidiaries were approached by the Montreal Stock Exchange in the early 1960s. Sixty-four replied, only one of which said it planned to issue minority shares.

From the scores of replies received by the president of [the] Montreal Stock Exchange we select three:[25]

We have been represented in Canada for many years by wholly-owned subsidiaries. As a matter of fact we do business through wholly-owned subsidiaries in some twenty-two countries throughout the world. A change to public ownership of any one of these companies would represent a substantial departure from the pattern in which we are geared to do business and at the moment we do not feel we are prepared to undertake a change of this kind.

All operations outside the United States are handled by wholly-owned subsidiaries. The Canadian company represents one of —— foreign subsidiaries all of which are wholly-owned. To date we have found this method of operations has been very beneficial to our customers and employees as well as to our stockholders, throughout the world.

At the present time we have no plans for outside financing at all so we do not contemplate any sale of any stock. At present the stock of —— is listed on the New York Stock Exchange and is available to investors, and an investor has the opportunity for investment in the entire scope of operations. *We consider this preferable from an investor's point of view, since the broader scope of the investment should make for increased stability of the investment.* [Our emphasis.]

Some of the replies were more explicit in explaining why the parent corporations did not wish to have stockholders in subsidiaries. Where the subsidiaries were engaged in extracting raw materials for use by the parent company, obvious conflicts of interest could arise over the selling price and the degree of processing, if parent company control were not assured.

Thus, a U.S. steel producer with iron ore mining operations in Canada, explained its position as follows:

As you no doubt realize, the only subsidiary functions which we have in Canada are related to iron ore operations. *We do not construe this operation as an independent function but rather as one of several essential functions of an integrated steel manufacturer.* We have never felt that this type of venture was appropriate for public participation in the United States and this viewpoint also holds with respect to Canada. [Our emphasis.]

Another United States corporation with wholly-owned Canadian mines explicitly refers to the conflict of interest which would result from minority stockholding:

> In our case, the overwhelmingly important Canadian operation from a financial standpoint is that of mining—the mines produce raw material for factories in the United States and Canada—but of course, on account of the difference of population, the United States factories consume by far the larger part. This makes the mine an integrated part of our entire production scheme. If we had minority stockholders in the mine itself with our parent company's stockholders therefore owning only part of the mine, we *would have two conflicting interests within the company regarding a single integrated process. This fact has always caused us to reject the idea of selling a minority interest.* [Our emphasis.]

It is implicit in the above statements that the raw materials supplied by the subsidiary to its parent are under-valued as an export from the hinterland. Indeed, there are good reasons why it serves the interests of an integrated corporation to under-value raw materials. One of these is that the output of small independent producers can be purchased at a depressed price. Another is that to show unduly large profits might result in the reduction or withdrawal of concessions, or in increases in taxation. Then again, low valuation of exports of staples reduces the exchange risk to the companies where hinterland governments find themselves in revenue or balance of payments difficulties and might seek to prevent the repatriation of profit. Considerations of corporate security thus point towards pricing policies which provide the parent companies with cheap inputs.

Ultimate control over the ability of marginal or new producers to sell to independent users, however, is assured only when processing facilities are tightly controlled by the existing big companies. Corporate resistance to minority shareholding in the raw material sector is, therefore, also a defence against demands for local processing installations.

Interestingly, it is no longer enough for a raw material producer to control smelting and refining facilities. The new trend is to vertical integration forward towards final manufacturing. This is in the service of both corporate security and profits to be made from technological advance in manufacturing. An interesting example of this trend is provided by the aluminum industry, which experienced serious over-expansion of ingot capacity in the 1950s.

> All through the world aluminum industry, the jostling is still going on to align smelter capacity with fabricating mills and markets for sheet and shapes. More and more, the big producers are going vertical and farther into technically-oriented products—because that's where the profits lie. An ingot producer can't live alone these days. He's murdered on the open markets.[26]

Where subsidiaries are engaged in manufacturing or assembly and constitute market outlets, there is an equal desire for full control over operations. In this connection the following comments by Mr. Eric Kierans when he was Minister of Revenue of Quebec are interesting:

> The purpose of investment in subsidiaries is not simply to earn a profit. In the parent-affiliate relationship, a profit on inter-company transactions may be taken at either end, but is normally taken by the parent. Thus, a subsidiary could lose money and still make a net contribution to the parent company's income by the profit on purchases of raw materials and component parts from the parent, by patents, royalties and fees for management, advertising and research services. In fact, the primary purpose of investment in overseas markets is to earn a profit for the parent by the control of markets for the export of parts, components and raw material concentrates. It is not essential that the affiliate show a profit.[27]

Here too, the low profitability of subsidiaries was frequently offered as a reason why it would not be feasible for multinational corporates to sell minority stock of subsidiaries. Insofar as the costs of these subsidiaries include management fees and charges for similar services supplied by the parent company as well as expenditures on commodity inputs, it is difficult to know whether the profit margins of Canadian subsidiaries are really as low as they are reported to be. These subsidiaries are integrated units of a manufacturing complex and there is an obvious conceptual difficulty in establishing profit rates for them.

Low profit margins of subsidiaries, however, become important when we consider the difficulties experienced by independent firms in competing with branch plants. The former cannot charge back losses against profitable parent companies. The parent company can offset losses against profits earned on exports to subsidiaries, royalties and fees received, and so justify the continuance of the branch plant, even where the accounting profit of the individual subsidiary is small or negative. If the independent firm, however, can make only a small profit or if it makes a loss it cannot long survive.

In these conditions of branch-plant industrialization there is a tendency to over-expansion of capacity. The manufacturing sector becomes both inefficient and highly competitive, in the sense that too many competing but slightly different products are produced. This has been named the "miniature replica" effect.[28] It is most dramatically illustrated in Canada, where the variety of products produced and assembled can only be explained in terms of the economics of the international manufacturing corporation. Because there exists a market for each of these products created by the spill-over of the taste pattern of the American consumer, it pays the multinational corporation to produce a great variety of products in Canadian subsidiaries. Inefficiency, which is usually laid at the door of protective tariffs, is in fact the result of a combination of two circumstances—the tariff and the entry of numerous branch plants.

In the decade 1950 to 1960 direct investment in manufacturing subsidiaries in Canada was very heavy. The total number of companies engaged in manufacturing in Canada rose from ten thousand to seventeen thousand. The percentage of manufacturing output controlled by foreigners rose from 50 per cent to 60 per cent over the decade. The percentage of loss companies rose from 26 per cent to 31 per cent. The rate of profit after tax fell from 9.5 per cent to 4 per cent.

While low profitability is the reason corporations advance for refusing to issue equity stock in subsidiaries, the truth is probably that their financial strength permits them to expand to the margin and beyond the margin of profitability. We must, however, draw attention to the fact, already mentioned, that the profits shown in statements of subsidiaries must be added to the contributions they make to the profits of the parent by their purchase of goods and services.

An important effect of the tendency to take the profit at the metropolitan end of the parent-affiliate relationship is the assured and substantial increase in the earnings of the parent company.

Shareholders in the parent company can be shown highly satisfactory and secure earnings, in hard and familiar currency. This enables management to set limits to the rate of dividend pay-out in the parent concern. The shareholders know that they can, if they wish, realize capital gains by selling their stock which appreciates to the extent that investment is financed from internal savings. Management stresses the advantages of holding shares in the parent company and discourages shareholding in subsidiaries. To the extent that it succeeds, it is faced by only one set of shareholders, who themselves are, in a way, "insiders," insofar as the corporation goes to the market only for marginal financing.

A number of countries have legislated to force corporations to entertain local participation. The companies appear to regard compliance as a concession to be made in particular circumstances and to be opposed as a matter of general policy. An example:

We have characterized our ... operations as a "Free-World Enterprise," based in the United States. We have manufacturing plants in 18 foreign countries and our products are available in more than 80 countries of the free world. We consider each of our branches and subsidiaries as part of a unified whole, with a large degree of inter-dependence. We believe that less than full ownership usually presents problems and complications that tend to limit the activities of the subsidiary to a particular product or group of products. Nevertheless, in some cases we have taken in local partners.

In deciding initially, or giving consideration to a change in organizational structure, some of the key points we consider are:

(a) The contribution that local participation can make including financial, marketing, and general operating knowhow, and public, government and employee relations;
(b) The Government Attitude.
(c) The possibilities of conflict of interests between ... and local interests on the basic and operating philosophy of the company, research policy, product line and product promotion, managements and personal policies, and dividend policies.[29]

Local participation is thus found where legislation forces it, where a subsidiary is acquired by buying interests in an established concern, where local people can supply access to marketing and operating know-how, or where public relations indicate the advisability of selling subsidiary stock to nationals. The need to obtain funds does not appear to motivate companies to issue equity stock in foreign subsidiaries. Where additional local funds are required it is more likely that they will be sought in the form of bank loans or longer-term debt borrowing. Safarian speculated that the reason why a number of firms revert to the parent rather than seek local resources probably reflects the relative ease and cheapness of funds from this source, particularly where the parent is generating surplus funds itself or has easy access to low-cost sources of financing itself in more highly developed money markets.[30] While this may provide part of the explanation, it does not explain why subsidiaries borrow by bank loan and bond issues in hinterland countries. The chief reason is probably to be sought in the reluctance of the companies to dilute monopolistic quasi-rents by increasing the number of stockholders, particularly stockholders in subsidiaries whose interests may conflict with that of the global enterprise.

NOTES

[1] John Kenneth Galbraith, *The New Industrial State* (Boston: Houghton Mifflin Co., 1967), p. 9.

[2] *Ibid.*, pp. 23, 24.

[3] *Ibid.*, pp. 27, 28.

[4] "The size of General Motors is in the service not of monopoly, or the economies of scale but of planning. And for this planning-control of supply, control of demand, provision of capital, minimisation of risk—there is no clear upper limit to the desirable size. It could be that 'the bigger the better.' The corporate form accommodates to this need. Quite clearly it allows the firm to be very, very large." *Ibid.*, p. 76.

[5] *Ibid.*, Chapter 4.

[6] *Ibid.*, p.38.

[7] *Ibid.*, p.271.

[8] "The belief that increased production is a worthy social goal is very nearly absolute." "That social progress is identical with a rising standard of living has an aspect of faith ... it is important to the technostructure that technological change of whatever kind be accorded a high value." *Ibid.*, p. 164.

[9] *Ibid.*, p.173.

[10] See comments on the "product cycle" below.

[11] George Grant, *Lament For A Nation* (Toronto: McClelland and Stewart, 1965).

[12] Hon. Neil McElroy, to the House of Representatives, Committee of Ways and Means, 87th Congress, Sessions on Tax Recommendations, pp. 2921–2938.

[13] Alfred D. Chandler, *Strategy and Structure, Chapters in the History of the Industrial Enterprise* (M.I.T. Press, Cambridge, Mass., 1962). I wish to express my thanks to Professor Stephen Hymer for drawing this book to my attention.

CHAPTER 9: Kari Levitt | 143

[14] Quoted by Chandler, *ibid.*, pp. 310–11.

[15] *Ibid.*, p. 302.

[16] Frank S. Capon, director and vice-president of the Dupont Company of Canada, *Problems of Canadian Subsidiaries: Seminar on Canadian-American Relations*, University of Windsor, November 1961, p.108.

[17] Judd Polk, Irene Meister and Lawrence Veit, *U.S. Production Abroad and the Balance of Payments, A Survey of Corporate Investment Experience* (N.Y., National Industrial Conference Board, 1966), p. 61.

[18] *Ibid.*, p. 59.

[19] A.E. Safarian, *Foreign Ownership of Canadian Industry* (McGraw-Hill Company of Canada Ltd., 1966), p. 188.

[20] Polk *et al, op. cit.*, p. 19.

[21] *Ibid.*, p. 55.

[22] C. Kindleberger, "The International Firm and the International Capital Market," *The Southern Economic Journal*, Oct. 1967, p. 228.

[23] Raymond F. Mikesell, "Decisive Factors in the Flow of American Direct Investment to Europe," *Economic Internazionale*, August 1967, p. 447. Revision of a paper prepared for the "Colloque sur la politique industrielle de l'Europe integree et rapport des capitaux exterieurs," organized by Professors Maurice Bye and Andre Marchal of the University of Paris, May 1966.

[24] Frank S. Capon, *op. cit.*, p. 108.

[25] Material prepared by the Hon. Eric Kierans, formerly president of the Montreal Stock Exchange, as 'Appendix B' to "The Economic Effects of the Guidelines," an address to the Toronto Society of Financial Analysts, Feb. 1, 1966 (mimeo). All subsequent extracts from replies to the M.S.E. enquiry are from the same source.

[26] *Montreal Star*, Feb. 20, 1968.

[27] Eric Kierans, "The Economic Effect of the Guidelines." See note 25 above.

[28] H. Edward English, *Industrial Structure in Canada's International Competitive Position*, Canadian Trade Committee, Private Planning Association of Canada, June 1964, p. 40. Professor English argues that the Canadian tariff is the primary cause of the excessive number of products produced and assembled in Canada. There is no doubt that the tariff has induced Canadian branch-plant production by U.S. firms. There is no reason to suppose, however, that a tariff without foreign investment in manufacturing would have resulted in "the miniature replica" effect. Furthermore, a considerable number of branch plants would have located in Canada even if there had been no tariff. It is the combination of Canadian protective commercial policy with heavy direct investment that has resulted in excessive numbers of products being produced in quantities insufficient to realize economies of scale.

[29] Another reply to the M.S.E. enquiry produced this comment:

To move from the general to the particular, we have very flexible policies with regard to local equity situations. In a Latin American Company where we have recently applied for a license to ... , we have decided that the best course is to create a joint venture company with considerable local participation.

In our Canadian situation it is our view that the operation's size and fluctuating fortunes do not warrant changing our present equity situation.

A number of large American corporations in the recent past have expressed the view that the long range solution to internationalizing one's shareholder base and broadening the foundations of the private enterprise system *lies not so much in the sale of local equities—with its many potential conflicts of interests*—but rather with making it easier and more attractive for the local investor to purchase common shares of the parent U.S. corporation and thus, of course, share in the world wide profits. [Our emphasis.]

[30] A.E. Safarian, *op. cit.*, pp. 243–44.

FURTHER READING

A large body of work exists by those who were involved in or influenced by the Waffle Movement in the early 1970s. These individuals include Mel Watkins, James Laxer, Mel Hurtig, Duncan Cameron, and Cy Gonick. Paul Kellogg has more recently written many reflective articles discussing the nature and future of left nationalism in Canada: see, for example, "After left nationalism," *Marxism* 2 (2004): 21–31.

10   GEORGE WOODCOCK

INTRODUCTION

Anarchism seems, on the face of it, to be both obsolete and irrelevant to modern politics. To the contrary, anarchism has had a very strong impact upon twenty-first century politics. Although anarchism defies clear definition, and is characterized by numerous categories (such as anarcho-syndicalism, communist anarchism, or eco-feminist anarchism), the overarching concept underlying anarchy is a strong dislike of hierarchical authority, usually (but not exclusively) in the form of the State. Like liberalism and libertarianism, anarchism's focus is on the individual; but anarchists see a much greater role for social cooperation and believe that this can best be achieved through minimal intrusion from "top-down" institutions. The following selection by Woodcock (1912–95) reflects this position well.

In a contemporary context, anarchism informs much of the anti-globalization protest directed at suprastate organization (such as the World Trade Organization). It also informs the "civil society" strategy underlying attempts at both foreign development and domestic re-engagement. Civil society literature holds that positive substantive change in political behaviour must be achieved "from the grassroots up," through the active participation in all individuals within the community.

REFLECTIONS ON DECENTRALISM (1972)

I was asked to write on decentralism in history, and I find myself looking into shadows where small lights shine as fire-flies do, endure a little, vanish, and then reappear like Auden's messages of the just. The history of decentralism has to be written largely in negative, in winters and twilights as well as springs and dawns, for it is a history which, like that of libertarian beliefs in general, is not observed in progressive terms. It is not the history of a movement, an evolution. It is the history of something that, like grass, has been with us from the human beginning, something that may go to earth, like bulbs in winter, and yet be there always, in the dark soil of human society, to break forth in unexpected places and at undisciplined times.

Palaeolithic man, food-gatherer and hunter, was a decentralist by necessity, because the earth did not provide enough wild food to allow crowding, and in modern remotenesses that were too wild or unproductive for civilized men to penetrate, men still lived until very recently in primitive decentralism; Australian aborigines, Papuan inland villagers, Eskimos in far northern Canada. Such men developed, before history touched them, their own complex techniques and cultures to defend a primitive and precarious way of life; they often developed remarkable artistic traditions as well, such as those of the Indians of the Pacific rain forests and some groups of Eskimos. But, since their world was one where concentration meant scarcity and death, they did not develop political life that allowed the formation of authoritarian structures nor did they make an institution out of war. They practised mutual aid for survival, but this did not make them angels; they practised infanticide and the abandonment of elders for the same reason.

I think with feeling of those recently living decentralist societies because I have just returned from the Canadian Arctic where the last phase of traditional Eskimo life began as recently as a decade ago. Now, the old nomadic society, in which people moved about in extended families rather than in tribes, is at an end, with all its skills abandoned, its traditions, songs and dances fading in the memory. Last year cariboo-hunting Eskimos probably built their last igloo; now they are herded together into communities ruled by white men, where they live in groups of four to six hundred people, in imitation white men's houses and with guaranteed welfare hand-outs when they cannot earn money by summer construction work. Their children are being taught by people who know no Eskimo, their young men are losing the skills of the hunt; power elites are beginning to appear in their crowded little northern slums, among a people who never knew what power meant, and the diminishing dog teams (now less than one family in four owns dogs and only about one family in twenty goes on extended hunting or trapping journeys) are symbolic of the loss of freedom among a people who have become physically and mentally dependent on the centralized, bureaucrat-ridden world which the Canadian Government has built since it set out a few years ago to rescue the peoples of the North from "barbarism" and insecurity.

The fate of the Eskimo, and that of so many other primitive cultures during the past quarter of a century, shows that the old, primal decentralism of Stone Age man is doomed even when it has survived into the modern world. From now on, man will be decentralist by intent and experience, because he has known the evils of centralization and rejected them.

Centralization began when men settled on the land and cultivated it. Farmers joined together to protect their herds and fields from the other men who still remained nomadic wanderers; to conserve and share out the precious waters; to placate the deities who held the gifts of fertility, the priests who served the deities, and the kings who later usurped the roles of priest and god alike. The little realms of local priest-kings grew into the great valley empires of Egypt and Mesopotamia, and overtowering these emerged the first attempt at a world empire, that of the Achaemenian Kings of Persia, who established an administrative colossus which was the prototype of the centralized state, imitated by the despots of Northern India, the Hellenistic god-kings, and the divine Caesars of Rome.

We have little knowledge how men clung to their local loyalties and personal lives, how simple people tried to keep control of the affairs and things that concerned them most, in that age when writing recorded the deeds of kings and priests and had little to say about common men. But if we can judge from the highly traditional and at least partly autonomous village societies which still existed in India when the Moghuls arrived, and which had probably survived the centuries of political chaos and strife that lay between Moghuls and Guptas, it seems likely that the farther men in those ages lived away from the centres of power, the more they established and defended rights to use the land and govern their own local affairs, so long as the lord's tribute was paid. It was, after all, on the village communities that had survived through native and Moghul and British empires that Gandhi based his hopes of *panchayat raj*, a society based on autonomous peasant communes.

In Europe the Dark Ages after the Roman Empire were regarded by Victorian historians as a historical waste land ravaged by barbarian hordes and baronial bandits. But these ages were also in fact an interlude during which, in the absence of powerful centralized authorities, the decentralist urge appeared again, and village communes established forms of autonomy which in remoter areas, like the Pyrenees, the Alps and the Appenines, have survived into the present. To the same "Dark" Ages belong the earliest free city republics of medieval Europe, which arose at first for mutual protection in the ages of disorder, and which in Italy and Germany remained for centuries the homes of European learning and art and of such freedom as existed in the world of their time.

Out of such village communes and such cities arose, in Switzerland, the world's first political federation, based on the shared protection of local freedoms against feudal monarchs and renaissance despots.

Some of these ancient communes exist to this day, the Canton of Appenzell still acts as a direct democracy in which every citizen takes part in the annual voting on laws; the Italian city state of San Marino still retains its mountaintop independence in a world of great states. But these are rare survivals, due mainly to geographic inaccessibility in the days before modern transport. As national states began to form at the end of the Middle Ages, the attack on decentralism was led not merely by the monarchs and dictators who established highly organized states like Bourbon France and Cromwellian England, but also by the Church and particularly by the larger monastic orders who in their houses established rules of uniform behaviour and rigid timekeeping that anticipated the next great assault on local and independent freedoms and on the practice of mutual aid; this happened when the villages of Britain and later of other European countries were depopulated in the Agricultural Revolution of the eighteenth century, and their homeless people drifted into the disciplined factories and suffered the alienation produced by the new industrial towns, where all traditional bonds were broken, and all the participation in common works that belonged to the medieval villages became irrelevant.

It was these developments, the establishment of the centralized state in the seventeenth century and of industrial centralization in the eighteenth and nineteenth centuries, that made men for the first time consciously aware of the necessity of decentralism to save them from the soulless world that was developing around them.

Against Cromwell's military state, Gerrard Winstanley and the original Diggers opposed their idea and practice of establishing new communes of landworkers on the waste lands of England, communes which would renounce overlords and extended participation and equality to men, women and even children.

When the French Revolution took the way of centralism, establishing a more rigidly bureaucratic state than the Bourbons and introducing universal conscription for the first time, men like Jacques Roux and his fellow enragés protested in the name of the local communes of Paris, which they regarded as the bases of democratic administration, and at the same time in England William Godwin, the first of the philosophic anarchists, recognized the perils of forms of government which left decision making in the hands of men gathered at the top and centre of society. In his *Political Justice* Godwin envisaged countries in which assemblies of delegates would meet— seldom—to discuss matters of urgent common concern, in which no permanent organs of central government would be allowed to continue, and in which each local parish would decide its own affairs by free agreement (and not by majority vote) and matters of dispute would be settled by ad hoc juries of arbitration.

The British and French Utopian socialists of the early nineteenth century, as distinct from the Marxists and the revolutionary socialists led by Auguste Blanqui, were inspired by their revulsion against monolithic industrial and political organization to base the realization of their theories on small communal units which they believed could be established even before the existing society had been destroyed. At that period the American frontier lay still in the valley of the Mississippi, and there was a tendency—which existed until the end of the pioneering days— for the small pioneer societies of trappers and traders, miners and farmers, to organize themselves in largely autonomous communities that managed their own affairs and in many senses of the word took the law into their own hands. In this society, where men responded to frontier conditions by ad hoc participatory and decentralist organization, the European and American Utopian socialists, as well as various groups of Christian communities set up self-governing communes which would be the cells of the new fraternal world. The followers of Cabet and Fourier, of Robert Owen and Josiah Warren, all played their part in a movement which produced hundreds of communities and lasted almost a century; its last wave ebbed on the Pacific coast in the Edwardian era, when a large Finnish socialist community was established on the remote island of Sointula off the coast of British Columbia. Only the religious communities of this era, which had a purpose outside mere social theory, survived; even today some of the Mennonite communities of Canada keep so closely to their ideals of communitarian autonomy that they are leaving the country to find in South America a region where they can be free to educate their children as they wish. The secular communities all vanished; the main lesson their failure taught was that decentralist organization must reach down to the roots of the present, to the needs of the actual human beings who participate, and not upward into the collapsing dream structures of a Utopian future.

Other great crises in the human situation have followed the industrial revolution, and every one has produced its decentralist movements in which men and women have turned away from the nightmares of megapolitics to the radical realities of human relationships. The crisis of the Indian struggle for independence caused Gandhi to preach the need to build society upon the foundation of the village. The bitter repressions of Tsarist Russia led Peter Kropotkin to develop his theories of a decentralized society integrating industry and agriculture, manual and mental skills. World War II led to considerable community movements among both British and American pacifists, seeking to create cells of sane living in the interstices of a belligerent world, and an even larger movement of decentralization and communitarianism has risen in North America in contradiction to the society that can wage a war like that in Vietnam. Today it is likely that more people than ever before are consciously engaged in some kind of decentralist venture which expresses not merely rebellion against monolithic authoritarianism, but also faith in the possibility of a new, cellular kind of society in which at every level the participation in decision making envisaged by nineteenth-century anarchists like Proudhon and Kropotkin will be developed.

As the monstrous and fatal flaws of modern economic and political centralism become more evident, as the State is revealed ever more convincingly as the enemy of all human love, the advocacy and practice of decentralism will spread more widely, if only because the necessity for it will become constantly more urgent. The less decentralist action is tied to rigid social and political theories, and especially to antediluvian ones like those of the Marxists, the more penetrating and durable its effects will be. The soils most favourable to the spread of decentralism are probably countries like India, where rural living still predominates, countries like Japan where the decentralization of factories and the integration of agricultural and industrial economies has already been recognized as a necessity for survival, and the places in our western world where the social rot has run deepest and the decentralists can penetrate like white ants. The moribund centres of the cities; the decaying marginal farmlands; these are the places which centralist governments using bankers' criteria of efficiency cannot possibly revivify, because the profit would not be financial but human. In such areas the small and flexible cell of workers, serving the needs of local people, can survive and continue simultaneously the tasks of quiet destruction and cellular building. But not all the work can be done in the shadows. There will still be the need for theoreticians to carry on the work which Kropotkin and Geddes and Mumford began in the past, of demonstrating the ultimately self-destructive character of political and industrial centralism, and showing how society as a whole, and not merely the lost corners of it, can be brought back to health and peace by breaking down the pyramids of authority, so that men can be given to eat the bread of brotherly love, and not the stones of power—of any power.

FURTHER READING

Like the British writers (including Aldous Huxley, George Orwell, and T.S. Eliot) with whom he socialized before emigrating to Canada, George Woodcock was strongly influenced by the radical politics of his day, including the Spanish anarchist movement of 1936–37. In 1949, Woodcock came to Canada, writing in a desultory manner for a wide variety of sources. A champion of Canadian literature, Woodcock's literary output was enormous, although he is best known for his works on anarchism, including *Anarchism: A History of Libertarian Ideas and Movements* (Cleveland: Meridian Books, 1962); *The Anarchist Reader* (Glasgow: Fontana/Collins,

1977); and *Anarchism and Anarchists: Essays* (Kingston: Quarry Press, 1992). Peter Hughes published his biography *George Woodcock* in 1972 (Toronto: McClelland and Stewart); and contemporary theoretical analyses of anarchism include Daniel Guérin's *Anarchism: From Theory to Practice* (New York: Monthly Review Press, 1970) and Alan Ritter's *Anarchism: A Theoretical Analysis* (Cambridge and New York: Cambridge University Press, 1980).

B

NATION AND IDENTITY

11 PIERRE ELLIOTT TRUDEAU

INTRODUCTION

Strongly influenced by the autocratic rule of Quebec premier Maurice Duplessis, Pierre Elliott Trudeau (1919–2000) began his career in direct opposition to what he saw as a corrupt elite of reactionary nationalists controlling the future of Quebec. Demanding "democracy before ideology," Trudeau's thought is consistently characterized by his suspicion of rhetoric before reason, his dislike of blind nationalism in place of tolerance and balance, and his belief in egalitarianism over privilege. Thus he supported multiculturalism in place of cultural nationalism, and he spoke passionately about the need for reason in politics. Trudeau's intellectual belief in individualism, rationality, and democracy is well reflected in his political achievements, including universal health care, liberal divorce reforms, privacy laws, and regional development. His pre-eminent political legacy is perhaps the repatriation of the Canadian Constitution in 1982, including the creation of an entrenched Charter of Rights and Freedoms. In this classic essay, Trudeau argues that cultural nationalism is an unpersuasive, and ultimately destructive, basis for a modern state; and that the collective "will," or thoughtful reason, of a people, moderated by federalism (which, he states, "is by its very essence a compromise and a pact") is a far superior basis for a contemporary nation-state.

FEDERALISM, NATIONALISM, AND REASON* (1964)

State and Nation

The concept of federalism with which I will deal in this paper is that

* I wish to thank my friends Albert Breton, Fernand Cadieux, Pierre Carignan, Eugene

of a particular system of government applicable within a sovereign state; it flows from my understanding of state and nation. Hence I find it necessary to discuss these two notions in part I of this paper, but I need only do so from the point of view of territory and population. Essentially, the question to which I would seek an answer is: what section of the world's population occupying what segment of the world's surface should fall under the authority of a given state?

Until the middle of the eighteenth century, the answer was largely arrived at without regard to the people themselves. Of course in much earlier times, population pressures guided by accidents of geography and climate had determined the course of the migrations which were to spill across the earth's surface. But by the end of the Middle Ages, such migrations had run their course in most of Europe. The existence of certain peoples inhabiting certain land areas, speaking certain languages or dialects, and practising certain customs, was generally taken as data—*choses données* —by the European states which arose to establish their authority over them.

It was not the population who decided by what states they would be governed; it was the states which, by wars (but not "people's wars"), by alliances, by dynastic arrangements, by marriages, by inheritance, and by chance, determined the area of territory over which they would govern. And for that reason they could be called territorial states. Except in the particular case of newly discovered lands, the population came with the territory; and except in the unusual case of deportations, very little was to be done about it.

Political philosophers, asking questions about the authority of the state, did not inquire why a certain population fell within the territorial jurisdiction of a certain state rather than of another; for the philosophers, too, territory and population were just data; their philosophies were mainly concerned with discovering the foundations of authority over a *given* territory and the sources of obedience of a *given* population.

In other words, the purpose of Locke and Rousseau, not unlike that of the medieval philosophers and of the ancient Stoics, was to

Forsey, and James Mallory, who read the manuscript and helped me clarify several ideas. Since the paper was read, on June 11, 1964, other friends have been very helpful with their comments; I dare not acknowledge them by name until I have had time to work their suggestions into this paper.

explain the origins and justify the existence of political authority *per se*, the theories of contract which they derived from natural law or reason were meant to ensure that within a given state bad governments could readily be replaced by good ones, but not that one territorial state could be superseded by another.

Such then was the significance of social contract and popular sovereignty in the minds of the men who made the Glorious Revolution, and such it was in the minds of those who prepared the events of 1776 in America and 1789 in France. As things went, however, the two latter "events" turned out to be momentous revolutions, and the ideas which had been put into them emerged with an immensely enhanced significance.

In America, it became necessary for the people not merely to replace a poor government by a better one, but to switch their allegiance from one territorial state to another, and in their own words, to

> declare, that these United Colonies, are, and of right ought to be, free and independent states; that they are absolved from all allegiance to the British crown, and that all political connection, between them and the state of Great Britain, is and ought to be totally dissolved; and that, as free and independent states, they have full power to levy war, conclude peace, contract alliances, establish commerce, and to do all other acts and things which independent states may of right do.

Here then was a theory of government by consent which took on a radically new meaning. Since sovereignty belonged to the people, it appeared to follow that any given body of people could at will transfer their allegiance from one existing state to another, or indeed to a completely new state of their own creation. In other words, the consent of the population was required not merely for a social contract, which was to be the foundation of civil society, or for a choice of responsible rulers, which was the essence of self-government; consent was also required for adherence to one territorial state rather than to another, which was the beginning of national self-determination.

Why the theory of consent underwent such a transformation at this particular time is no doubt a matter for historical and philosophical conjecture. Perhaps the prerequisites had never been brought together before: a population (1) whose political traditions were sufficiently advanced to include the ideology of consent, (2) subject to a modern unitary state the centre of which was very remote, and (3) inhabiting a territory which was reasonably self-contained.

Be that as it may, it appears to be at this juncture in history that the word "nation" became charged with a new potential. In the past, the *word* had meant many things, from Machiavelli's "Ghibelline nation" to Montesquieu's "pietistic nation"; its broadest meaning seems to have been reached by the *Encyclopédistes* who understood thereby "une quantité considérable de peuple, qui habite une certaine étendue de pays, renfermée dans de certaines limites, et qui obéit au même gouvernement." The *idea* of nation also had roots which plunged deep in history;[1] and a sentiment akin to nationalism had sometimes inspired political action, as when French rulers reacted against Italian popes. But the idea, like the word, only took on its modern meaning during the last quarter of the eighteenth century.

Consequently, it might be said that in the past the (territorial) state had defined its territorial limits which had defined the people or nation living within. But henceforth it was to be the people who first defined themselves as a nation, who then declared which territory belonged to them as of right, and who finally proceeded to give their allegiance to a state of their own choosing or invention which would exercise authority over that nation and that territory. Hence the expression "nation-state." As I see it, the important transition was from the *territorial state* to the *nation-state*. But once the latter was born, the idea of the national *state* was bound to follow, it being little more than a nation-state with an ethnic flavour added. With it the idea of self-determination became the principle of nationalities.

Self-determination did not necessarily proceed from or lead to self-government. Whereas self-government was based on reason and proposed to introduce liberal forms of government into existing states, self-determination was based on will and proposed to challenge the legitimacy and the very existence of the territorial states.

Self-determination, or the principle of nationalities (I am talking of the doctrine, for the expressions became current only later) was bound to dissolve whatever order and balance existed in the society of states prevailing towards the end of the eighteenth century.

But no matter; for it was surmised that a new order would arise, free from wars and inequities. As each of the peoples of the world became conscious of its identity as a collectivity bound together by natural affinities, it would define itself as a nation and govern itself as a state. An international order of nation-states, since it would be founded on the free will of free people, would necessarily be more lasting and just than one which rested on a hodgepodge of despotic empires, dynastic kingdoms, and aristocratic republics. In May 1790, the Constituent Assembly had proclaimed: "La nation française renonce à entreprendre aucune guerre dans un but de conquête et n'emploiera jamais de forces contre la liberté d'aucun peuple."

Unfortunately, things did not work out quite that way. The French Revolution, which had begun as an attempt to replace a bad government by a good one, soon overreached itself by replacing a territorial state by a nation-state, whose territory incidentally was considerably enlarged. In 1789, the *Déclaration des droits de l'homme et du citoyen* had stated: "Le principe de toute souveraineté réside essentiellement dans la Nation. Nul corps, nul individu ne peut exercer d'autorité qui n'en émane expressément." But who was to be included in the nation? Danton having pointed out in 1793 that the frontiers of France were designated by Nature,[2] the French nation willed itself into possession of that part of Europe which spread between the Rhine, the Pyrenees, the Atlantic Ocean, and the Alps.

France was indeed fortunate, in that her natural frontiers thus enabled her to correct the disadvantage which might have arisen in Alsace, for example, from a will based on linguistic frontiers. Fortunately for German-speaking peoples, however, Fichte was soon to discover that the natural frontiers were in reality the linguistic ones; thus the German nation could will itself towards its proper size, provided of course that the language principle be sometimes corrected by that of historical possession, in order for instance to include Bohemia. Other nations, such as Poland, enlightened their will by greater reliance on the historical principle, corrected when necessary by the linguistic one. Then finally there were nations who, spurning such frivolous guide-lines as geography, history, and language, were favoured by direct communication with the Holy Ghost; such was the privilege of the United States of America who saw the annexation of Texas, California, and eventually Canada as—in the words of O'Sullivan—"the fulfillment of our manifest destiny to overspread the continent alloted by Providence for the free development of our yearly multiplying millions."3

The political history of Europe and of the Americas in the nineteenth century and that of Asia and Africa in the twentieth are histories of nations labouring, conspiring, blackmailing, warring, revolutionizing, and generally willing their way towards statehood. It is, of course, impossible to know whether there has ensued therefrom for humanity more peace and justice than would have been the case if some other principle than self-determination had held sway. In theory, the arrangement of boundaries in such a way that no important national group be included by force in the territorial limits of a state which was mainly the expression of the will of another group, was to be conducive to peaceful international order. In practice, state boundaries continued to be established and maintained largely by the threat of or the use of force. The concept of right in international relations became, if anything, even more a function of might. And the question whether a national minority was "important" enough to be entitled to independence remained unanswerable except in terms of the political and physical power that could be wielded in its favour. Why did Libya become a country in 1951 and not the Saar in 1935, with a population almost as great? Why should Norway be independent and not Brittany? Why Ireland and not Scotland? Why Nicaragua and not Quebec?

As we ask ourselves these questions, it becomes apparent that more than language and culture, more than history and geography, even more than force and power, the foundation of the nation is will.4 For there is no power without will. The Rocky Mountains are higher than the Pyrenees but they are not a watershed between countries. The Irish Sea and the Straits of Florida are much narrower than the Pacific Ocean between Hawaii and California, yet they are more important factors in determining nationhood. Language or race do not provide, in Switzerland or Brazil, the divisive force they are at present providing in Belgium or the United States.

Looking at the foregoing examples, and at many others, we are bound to conclude that the frontiers of nation-states are in reality nearly as arbitrary as those of the former territorial states. For all their anthropologists, linguists, geographers, and historians, the nations of today cannot justify their frontiers with noticeably more rationality than the kings of two centuries ago; a greater reliance on general staffs than on princesses' dowries does not necessarily spell a triumph of reason. Consequently, a present-day definition of the word "nation" in its juristic sense would fit quite readily upon the population of the territorial states which existed before the French and American revolutions. A nation (as in the expressions: the French nation, the Swiss nation, the United Nations, the President's speech to the nation) is no more and no less than the entire population of a sovereign state. (Except when otherwise obvious, I shall try to adhere to that juristic sense in the rest of this paper.) Because no country has an absolutely homogeneous population, all the so-called nation-states of today are also territorial states. And the converse is probably also true. The distinction between a nation-state, a multi-national state, and a territorial state may well be valid in reference to historical origins; but it has very little foundation in law or fact today and is mainly indicative of political value judgments.

Of course, the word "nation" can also be used in a sociological sense, as when we speak of the Scottish nation, or the Jewish nation. As Humpty Dumpty once told Alice, a word means just what one chooses it to mean. It would indeed be helpful if we could make up our minds. Either the juristic sense would be rejected, and the word "people" used instead (the people of the Soviet Union, the people of the United States; but what word would replace "national"? People's? Popular?); in that case "nation" would be restricted to its sociological meaning, which is also closer to its etymological and historical ones. Or the latter sense would be rejected, and words like "linguistic," "ethnic," or "cultural group" be used instead. But lawyers and political scientists cannot remake the language to suit their convenience; they will just have to hope that "the context makes it tolerably clear which of the two [senses] we mean."[5]

However, for some people one meaning is meant to flow into the other. The ambiguity is intentional and the user is conveying something which is at the back of his mind—and sometimes not very far back. In such cases the use of the word "nation" is not only confusing, it is disruptive of political stability. Thus, when a tightly knit minority within a state begins to define itself forcefully and consistently as a nation, it is triggering a mechanism which will tend to propel it towards full statehood.[6]

That, of course, is not merely due to the magic of words, but to a much more dynamic process which I will now attempt to explain.

When the erstwhile territorial state, held together by divine right, tradition, and force, gave way to the nation-state, based on the will of the people, a new glue had to be invented which would bind the nation together on a durable basis. For very few nations—if any— could rely on a cohesiveness based entirely on "natural" identity, and so most of them were faced with a terrible paradox: the principle of national self-determination which had justified their birth could just as easily justify their death. Nationhood being little more than a state of mind, and every sociologically distinct group within the nation having a contingent right of secession, the will of the people was in constant danger of dividing up—unless it were transformed into a lasting consensus.

The formation of such a consensus is a mysterious process which takes in many elements, such as language, communication, association, geographical proximity, tribal origins, common interests and history, external pressures, and even foreign intervention, none of which, however, is a determinant by itself. A consensus can be said to exist when no group within the nation feels that its vital interests and particular characteristics could be better preserved by withdrawing from the nation than by remaining within.

A (modern) state needs to develop and preserve this consensus as its very life. It must continually persuade the generality of the people that it is in their best interest to continue as a state. And since it is physically and intellectually difficult to persuade continually through reason alone, the state is tempted to reach out for whatever emotional support it can find. Ever since history fell under the ideological shadow of the nation-state, the most convenient support has obviously been the idea of nationalism. It becomes morally "right," a matter of "dignity and honour," to preserve the integrity of the nation. Hence, from the emotional appeal called nationalism is derived a psychological inclination to obey the constitution of the state.

To say that the state uses nationalism to preserve its identity is not to say that the state is the inventor of nationalism. The feeling called nationalism is secreted by the nation (in whatever sense we use the word) in much the same way as the family engenders family ties, and the clan generates clannishness. And just like clannishness, tribalism, and even feudalism, nationalism will probably fade away by itself at whatever time in history the nation has outworn its utility: that is to say, when the particular values protected by the idea of nation are no longer counted as important, or when those values no longer need to be embodied in a nation to survive.7

But that time is not yet; we have not yet emerged from the era of the nation-state when it seemed perfectly normal for the state to rely heavily, for the preservation of the national consensus, on the gum called nationalism, a natural secretion of the nation. In so doing, the state (or the political agents who desired a state) transformed the feeling into a political doctrine or principle of government. Nationalism, as defined by history, is a doctrine which claims to supply a formula for determining what section of the world's population occupying what segment of the world's surface *should* fall under the authority of a given state; briefly stated, the formula holds that the optimum size of the sovereign state (in terms of authority and territory) is derived from the size of the nation (in terms of language, history, destiny, law, and so forth).8

It might be remarked here that history is not always logic; and in the case of nationalism it has embarked upon a type of circular reasoning which leaves the mind uneasy. The idea of nation which is at the origin of a new type of state does not refer to a "biological" reality (as does, for instance, the family); consequently the nation has constantly and artificially to be reborn from the very state to which it gave birth! In other words, the nation first decides what the state should be; but then the state has to decide what the nation should remain.

I should add that some people who call themselves nationalists would not accept this line of reasoning. Nationalism to them has remained a mere feeling of belonging to the nation (in a sociological or cultural sense); they liken it to a dream which inspires the individual and motivates his actions, perhaps irrationally but not necessarily negatively. I cannot, of course, quarrel with people merely because they wish to drain two centuries of history out of a definition. I can only say that it is not about *their* nationalism that I am writing in this paper; it is only fair to remind them, however, that their "dreams" are being converted by others into a principle of government.

Let us then proceed to see what happens when the state relies on nationalism to develop and preserve the consensus on which it rests.

Nationalism and Federalism

Many of the nations which were formed into states over the past century or two included peoples who were set apart geographically (like East and West Pakistan, or Great Britain and Northern Ireland), historically (like the United States or Czechoslovakia), linguistically (like Switzerland or Belgium), racially (like the Soviet Union or Algeria). Half of the aforesaid countries undertook to form the national consensus within the framework of a unitary state; the other half found it expedient to develop a system of government called federalism. The process of consensus-formation is not the same in both cases.

It is obviously impossible, as well as undesirable, to reach unanimity on all things. Even unitary states find it wise to respect elements of diversity, for instance by administrative decentralization as in Great Britain,9 or by language guarantees as in Belgium; but such limited securities having been given, a consensus is obtained which recognizes the state as the sole source of coercive authority within the national boundaries. The federal state proceeds differently; it deliberately reduces the national consensus to the greatest common denominator between the various groups composing the nation. Coercive authority over the entire territory remains a monopoly of the (central) state, but this authority is limited to certain subjects of jurisdiction; on other subjects, and within well-defined territorial regions, other coercive authorities exist. In other words, the exercise of sovereignty is divided between a central government and regional ones.

Federalism is by its very essence a compromise and a pact. It is a compromise in the sense that when national consensus on *all* things is not desirable or cannot readily obtain, the area of consensus is reduced in order that consensus on *some* things be reached. It is a pact or quasi-treaty in the sense that the terms of that compromise cannot be changed unilaterally. That is not to say that the terms are fixed forever; but only that in changing them, every effort must be made not to destroy the consensus on which the federated nation rests. For what Ernest Renan said about the nation is even truer about the federated nation: "L'existence d'une nation est ... un plébiscite de tous les jours."10 This obviously did not mean that such a plebiscite could or should be held every day, the result of which could only be total anarchy; the real implication is clear:

the nation is based on a social contract, the terms of which each new generation of citizens is free to accept tacitly, or to reject openly.

Federalism was an inescapable product of an age which recognized the principle of self-determination. For on the one hand, a sense of national identity and singularity was bound to be generated in a great many groups of people, who would insist on their right to distinct statehood. But on the other hand, the insuperable difficulties of living alone and the practical necessity of sharing the state with neighbouring groups were in many cases such as to make distinct statehood unattractive or unattainable. For those who recognized that the first law of politics is to start from the facts rather than from historical "might-have-been's," the federal compromise thus became imperative.

But by a paradox I have already noted in regard to the nation-state, the principle of self-determination which makes federalism necessary makes it also rather unstable. If the heavy paste of nationalism is relied upon to keep a unitary nation-state together, much more nationalism would appear to be required in the case of a federal nation-state. Yet if nationalism is encouraged as a rightful doctrine and noble passion, what is to prevent it from being used by some group, region, or province within the nation? If "nation algérienne" was a valid battle cry against France, how can the Algerian Arabs object to the cry of "nation kabyle" now being used against them?

The answer, of course, is that no amount of logic can prevent such an escalation. The only way out of the dilemma is to render what is logically defensible actually undesirable. The advantages *to the minority group* of staying integrated in the whole must on balance be greater than the gain to be reaped from separating. This can easily be the case when there is no real alternative for the separatists, either because they are met with force (as in the case of the U.S. Civil War), or because they are met with laughter (as in the case of the *Bretons bretonnisants*). But when there is a real alternative, it is not so easy. And the greater the advantages and possibilities of separatism, the more difficult it is to maintain an unwavering consensus within the whole state.

One way of offsetting the appeal of separatism is by investing tremendous amounts of time, energy, and money in nationalism, *at the federal level*. A national image must be created that will have such an appeal as to make any image of a separatist group unattractive.

Resources must be diverted into such things as national flags, anthems, education, arts councils, broadcasting corporations, film boards; the territory must be bound together by a network of railways, highways, airlines; the national culture and the national economy must be protected by taxes and tariffs; ownership of resources and industry by nationals must be made a matter of policy. In short, the whole of the citizenry must be made to feel that it is only within the framework of the federal state that their language, culture, institutions, sacred traditions, and standard of living can be protected from external attack and internal strife.

It is, of course, obvious that a national consensus will be developed in this way only if the nationalism is emotionally acceptable to all important groups within the nation. Only blind men could expect a consensus to be lasting if the national flag or the national image is merely the reflection of one part of the nation, if the sum of values to be protected is not defined so as to include the language or the cultural heritage of some very large and tightly knit minority, if the identity to be arrived at is shattered by a colour-bar. The advantage as well as the peril of federalism is that it permits the development of a regional consensus based on regional values; so federalism is ultimately bound to fail if the nationalism it cultivates is unable to generate a national image which has immensely more appeal than the regional ones.

Moreover, this national consensus—to be lasting—must be a living thing. There is no greater pitfall for federal nations than to take the consensus for granted, as though it were reached once and for all. The compromise of federalism is generally reached under a very particular set of circumstances. As time goes by these circumstances change; the external menace recedes, the economy flourishes, mobility increases, industrialization and urbanization proceed; and also the federated groups grow, sometimes at uneven paces, their cultures mature, sometimes in divergent directions. To meet these changes, the terms of the federative pact must be altered, and this is done as smoothly as possible by administrative practice, by judicial decision, and by constitutional amendment, giving a little more regional autonomy here, a bit more centralization there, but at all times taking great care to preserve the delicate balance upon which the national consensus rests.

Such care must increase in direct proportion to the strength of the alternatives which present themselves to the federated groups. Thus, when a large cohesive minority believes it can transfer its allegiance to a neighbouring state, or make a go of total independence, it will be inclined to dissociate itself from a consensus the terms of which have been altered in its disfavour. On the other hand, such a minority may be tempted to use its bargaining strength to obtain advantages which are so costly to the majority as to reduce to naught the advantages to the latter of remaining federated. Thus, a critical point can be reached in either direction beyond which separatism takes place, or a civil war is fought.

When such a critical point has been reached or is in sight, no amount, however great, of nationalism can save the federation. Any expenditure of emotional appeal (flags, professions of faith, calls to dignity, expressions of brotherly love) at the national level will only serve to justify similar appeals at the regional level, where they are just as likely to be effective. Thus the great moment of truth arrives when it is realized that *in the last resort* the mainspring of federalism cannot be emotion but must be reason.

To be sure, federalism found its greatest development in the time of the nation-states, founded on the principle of self-determination, and cemented together by the emotion of nationalism. Federal states have themselves made use of this nationalism over periods long enough to make its inner contradictions go unnoticed. Thus, in a neighbouring country, Manifest Destiny, the Monroe Doctrine, the Hun, the Red Scourge, the Yellow Peril, and Senator McCarthy have all provided glue for the American Way of Life; but it is apparent that the Cuban "menace" has not been able to prevent the American Negro from obtaining a renegotiation of the terms of the American national consensus. The Black Muslims were the answer to the argument of the Cuban menace; the only answer to both is the voice of reason.

It is now becoming obvious that federalism has all along been a product of reason in politics. It was born of a decision by pragmatic politicians to face facts as they are, particularly the fact of the heterogeneity of the world's population. It is an attempt to find a rational compromise between the divergent interest-groups which history has thrown together; but it is a compromise based on the will of the people.

Looking at events in retrospect, it would seem that the French Revolution attempted to delineate national territories according to the will of the people, without reference to rationality; the Congress of Vienna claimed to draw state boundaries according to reason, without reference to the will of the people; and federalism arose as an empirical effort to base a country's frontiers on both reason and the will of the people.

I am not heralding the impending advent of reason as the prime mover in politics, for nationalism is too cheap and too powerful a tool to be soon discarded by politicians of all countries; the rising *bourgeoisies* in particular have too large a vested interest in nationalism to let it die out unattended.[11] Nor am I arguing that as important an area of human conduct as politics could or should be governed without any reference to human emotions. But I would like to see emotionalism channelled into a less sterile direction than nationalism. And I am saying that within sufficiently advanced federal countries, the auto-destructiveness of nationalism is bound to become more and more apparent, and reason may yet reveal itself even to ambitious politicians as the more assured road to success. This may also be the trend in unitary states, since they all have to deal with some kind of regionalism or other. Simultaneously in the world of international relations, it is becoming more obvious that the Austinian concept of sovereignty could only be thoroughly applied in a world crippled by the ideology of the nation-state and sustained by the heady stimulant of nationalism. In the world of today, when whole groups of so-called sovereign states are experimenting with rational forms of integration, the exercise of sovereignty will not only be divided within federal states; it will have to be further divided between the states and the communities of states. If this tendency is accentuated the very idea of national sovereignty will recede and, with it, the need for an emotional justification such as nationalism. International law will no longer be explained away as so much "positive international morality," it will be recognized as true law, a "coercive order ... for the promotion of peace."[12]

Thus there is some hope that in advanced societies, the glue of nationalism will become as obsolete as the divine right of kings; the title of the state to govern and the extent of its authority will be conditional upon rational justification; a people's consensus based on reason will supply the cohesive force that societies require; and politics both within and without the state will follow a much more functional approach to the problems of government. If politicians must bring emotions into the act, let them get emotional about functionalism!

The rise of reason in politics is an advance of law; for is not law an attempt to regulate the conduct of men in society rationally rather than emotionally? It appears then that a political order based on federalism is an order based on law. And there will flow more good than evil from the present tribulations of federalism if they serve to equip lawyers, social scientists, and politicians with the tools required to build societies of men ordered by reason.

Who knows? humanity may yet be spared the ignominy of seeing its destinies guided by some new and broader emotion based, for example, on continentalism.

Canadian Federalism: The Past and the Present

Earlier in this paper, when discussing the concept of national consensus, I pointed out that it was not something to be forever taken for granted. In present-day Canada, an observation such as that need not proceed from very great insight. Still, I will start from there to examine some aspects of Canadian federalism.

Though, technically speaking, national self-determination only became a reality in Canada in 1931, it is no distortion of political reality to say that the Canadian nation dates from 1867, give or take a few years. The consensus of what is known today as the Canadian nation took shape in those years; and it is the will of that nation which is the foundation of the state which today exercises its jurisdiction over the whole of the Canadian territory.

Of course, the will of the Canadian nation was subjected to certain constraints, not least of which was the reality of the British Empire. But, except once again in a technical sense, this did not mean very much more than that Canada, like every other nation, was not born in a vacuum, but had to recognize the historical as well as all other data which surrounded its birth.

I suppose we can safely assume that the men who drew up the terms of the Canadian federal compromise had heard something of the ideology of nationalism which had been spreading revolutions for seventy-five years. It is likely too that they knew about the Civil War in the United States, the rebellions of 1837-8 in Canada, the Annexation Manifesto, and the unsatisfactory results of double majorities. Certainly they assessed the centrifugal forces that the constitution would have to overcome if the Canadian state was to be a durable one: first, the linguistic and other cultural differences between the two major founding groups, and secondly the attraction of regionalisms, which were not likely to decrease in a country the size of Canada.

Given these data, I am inclined to believe that the authors of the Canadian federation arrived at as wise a compromise and drew up as sensible a constitution as any group of men anywhere could have done. Reading that document today, one is struck by its absence of principles, ideals, or other frills; even the regional safeguards and minority guarantees are pragmatically presented, here and there, rather than proclaimed as a thrilling bill of rights. It has been said that the binding force of the United States of America was the idea of liberty,[13] and certainly none of the relevant constitutional documents let us forget it. By comparison, the Canadian nation seems founded on the common sense of empirical politicians who had wanted to establish some law and order over a disjointed half-continent. If reason be the governing virtue of federalism, it would seem that Canada got off to a good start.

Like everything else, the Canadian nation had to move with the times. Many of the necessary adjustments were guided by rational deliberation: such was the case, for instance, with most of our constitutional amendments, and with the general direction imparted to Canadian law by the Privy Council decisions. It has long been a custom in English Canada to denounce the Privy Council for its provincial bias; but it should perhaps be considered that if the law lords had not leaned in that direction, Quebec separatism might not be a threat today: it might be an accomplished fact. From the point of view of the damage done to Quebec's understanding of the original federal compromise, there were certainly some disappointing—even if legally sound—judgments (like the New Brunswick, Manitoba, and Ontario separate school cases) and some unwise amendments (like the B.N.A. No. 2 Act, 1949); but on balance, it would seem that constitutional amendment and judicial interpretation would not by themselves have permanently damaged the fabric of the Canadian consensus if they had not been compounded with a certain type of adjustment through administrative centralization.

Faced with provinces at very different stages of economic and political development, it was natural for the central government to assume as much power as it could to make the country as a whole a going concern. Whether this centralization was always necessary, or whether it was not sometimes the product of bureaucratic and political empire-builders acting beyond the call of duty,[14] are no doubt debatable questions, but they are irrelevant to the present inquiry. The point is that over the years the central administrative functions tended to develop rather more rapidly than the provincial ones; and if the national consensus was to be preserved some new factor would have to be thrown into the balance. This was done in three ways.

First, a countervailing regionalism was allowed and even fostered in matters which were indifferent to Canada's economic growth. For instance, there was no federal action when Manitoba flouted the constitution and abolished the use of the French language in the legislature;[15] and there was no effective federal intervention[16] under paragraphs 3 and 4 of Section 93 (B.N.A. Act) or under paragraphs 2 and 3 of Section 22 (Manitoba Act) when New Brunswick, Ontario, and Manitoba legislated in a way which was offensive to the linguistic or religious aspirations of their French-speaking populations.

Second, a representative bureaucracy at the central level was developed in such a way as to make the regions feel that their interests were well represented in Ottawa. A great administrative machine was created, in which "the under-representation of Quebec can be considered an ethnic and educational factor rather than a regional one."[17] It was this efficient bureaucracy, by the way, which was unable to convert the machinery of government to the production of bilingual cheques and letter-heads, during the forty years it took to debate the subject in Parliament; then suddenly the reform took place in five minutes without help even from the cabinet. But such are the miracles of automation!

Third, tremendous reserves of nationalism were expended, in order to make everyone good, clean, unhyphenated Canadians. Riel was neatly hanged, as an example to all who would exploit petty regional differences. The Boer War was fought, as proof that Canadians could overlook their narrow provincialisms when the fate of the Empire was at stake. Conscription was imposed in two world wars, to show that in the face of death all Canadians were on an equal footing. And lest nationalism be in danger of waning, during the intervals between the above events Union Jacks were waved, Royalty was shown around, and immigration laws were loaded in favour of the British Isles.

Need I point out that in those three new factors, French Canadians found little to reconcile themselves with centralization? First, regionalism as condoned by Ottawa meant that the French Canadians could feel at home in no province save Quebec. Second, representative bureaucracy for the central government meant that regional safeguards would be entrusted to a civil service somewhat dominated by white Anglo-Saxon Protestants. And third, nationalism as conceived in Ottawa was essentially predicated on the desirability of uniting the various parts of the nation around one language (English) and one flag (the Union Jack).

I readily admit that there are elements of oversimplification in the four preceding paragraphs. But I am prepared to defend quite strenuously the implications which are contained therein: that the rational compromise upon which the nation rested in 1867 was gradually replaced by an emotional sop; and that this sop calmly assumed away the existence of one-third of the nation. In other words, the French-Canadian denizens of a Quebec ghetto, stripped of power by centralization, were expected to recognize themselves in a national image which had hardly any French traits, and were asked to have the utmost confidence in a central state where French Canada's influence was mainly measured by its not inconsiderable nuisance value.

Under such circumstances, Canadian nationalism—even after it ceased looking towards the Empire, which took quite some time— could hardly provide the basis for a lasting consensus. So time and time again, counter-nationalist movements arose in Quebec which quite logically argued that if Canada was to be the nation-state of the English-speaking Canadians, Quebec should be the nation-state of the French Canadians. But these warning signals were never taken seriously; for they were hoisted in years when Quebec had nowhere to go, and it obviously could not form an independent state of its own. But a time was bound to come—"Je suis un chien qui ronge l'os"—when French-Canadian national self-determination could no longer be laughed out of court; a time when the frightened Quebec and Ottawa governments (albeit in obvious contempt of their respective constitutional mandates) found sense in making "scientific" studies of separatism.[18]

In short, during several generations, the stability of the Canadian consensus was due to Quebec's inability to do anything about it. Ottawa took advantage of Quebec's backwardness to centralize; and because of its backwardness that province was unable to participate adequately in the benefits of centralization. The vicious circle could only be broken if Quebec managed to become a modern society. But how could this be done? The very ideology which was marshalled to preserve Quebec's integrity, French-Canadian nationalism, was setting up defence mechanisms the effect of which was to turn Quebec resolutely inward and backwards. It befell the generation of French Canadians who came of age during the Second World War to break out of the dilemma; instead of bucking the rising tides of industrialization and modernization in a vain effort to preserve traditional values, they threw the flood-gates open to forces of change. And if ever proof be required that nationalism is a sterile force, let it be considered that fifteen years of systematic non-nationalism and sometimes ruthless anti-nationalism at a few key points of the society were enough to help Quebec to pass from a feudal into a modern era.

Technological factors could, practically alone, explain the sudden transformation of Quebec. But many agents from within were at work, eschewing nationalism and preparing their society to adapt itself to modern times. Typical amongst such agents were the three following. Laval's *Faculté des sciences sociales* began turning out graduates who were sufficiently well equipped to be respected members of the central representative bureaucracy. The *Confédération des travailleurs catholiques du Canada* came squarely to grips with economic reality and helped transform Quebec's working classes into active participants in the process of industrialization. The little magazine *Cité Libre* became a rallying point for progressive action and writing; moreover it understood that a modern Quebec would very soon call into question the imbalance towards which the original federal compromise had drifted, and it warned that English-Canadian nationalism was headed for a rude awakening; upholding provincial autonomy and proposing certain constitutional guarantees, it sought to re-establish the Canadian consensus on a rational basis.

The warnings went unheeded; Ottawa did not change.[19] But Quebec did: bossism collapsed, blind traditionalism crumbled, the Church was challenged, new forces were unleashed. When in Europe the dynasties and traditions had been toppled, the new societies quickly found a new cohesive agent in nationalism; and no sooner had privilege within the nation given way to internal equality than privilege *between* nations fell under attack; external equality was pursued by way of national self-determination. In Quebec today the same forces are at work: a new and modern society is being glued together by nationalism, it is discovering its potentialities as a nation, and is demanding equality with all other nations. This in turn is causing a backlash in other provinces, and Canada suddenly finds herself wondering whether she has a future. What is to be done?

If my premises are correct, nationalism cannot provide the answer. Even if massive investments in flags, dignity, protectionism, and Canadian content of television managed to hold the country together a few more years, separatism would remain a recurrent phenomenon, and very soon again new generations of Canadians and Quebeckers would be expected to pour their intellectual energies down the drain of emotionalism. If, for instance, it is going to remain *morally wrong* for Wall Street to assume control of Canada's economy, how will it become *morally right* for Bay Street to dominate Quebec's or—for that matter—Nova Scotia's?

It is possible that nationalism may still have a role to play in backward societies where the *status quo* is upheld by irrational and brutal forces; in such circumstances, *because there is no other way*, perhaps the nationalist passions will still be found useful to unleash revolutions, upset colonialism, and lay the foundations of welfare states; in such cases, the undesirable consequences will have to be accepted along with the good.

But in the advanced societies, where the interplay of social forces can be regulated by law, where the centres of political power can be made responsible to the people, where the economic victories are a function of education and automation, where cultural differentiation is submitted to ruthless competition, and where the road to progress lies in the direction of international integration, nationalism will have to be discarded as a rustic and clumsy tool.

No doubt, at the level of individual action, emotions and dreams will still play a part; even in modern man, superstition remains a powerful motivation. But magic, no less than totems and taboos, has long since ceased to play an important role in the normal governing of states. And likewise, nationalism will eventually have to be rejected as a principle of sound government. In the world of tomorrow, the expression "banana republic" will not refer to independent fruit-growing nations but to countries where formal independence has been given priority over the cybernetic revolution. In such a world, the state—if it is not to be outdistanced by its rivals—will need political instruments which are sharper, stronger, and more finely controlled than anything based on mere emotionalism: such tools will be made up of advanced technology and scientific investigation, as applied to the fields of law, economics, social psychology, international affairs, and other areas of human relations; in short, if not a pure product of reason, the political tools of the future will be designed and appraised by more rational standards than anything we are currently using in Canada today.

Let me hasten to add that I am not predicting which way Canada will turn. But because it seems obvious to me that nationalism—and of course I mean the Canadian as well as the Quebec variety—has put her on a collision course, I am suggesting that cold, unemotional rationality can still save the ship. Acton's prophecy, one hundred years ago, is now in danger of being fulfilled in Canada. "Its course," he stated of nationality, "will be marked with material as well as moral ruin, in order that a new invention may prevail over the works of God and the interests of mankind." This new invention may well be functionalism in politics; and perhaps it will prove to be inseparable from any workable concept of federalism.

NOTES

1   For a history of the use and meaning of the term, see Elie Kedourie, *Nationalism* (New York, 1960), and Hans Kohn, *The Idea of Nationalism* (New York, 1944).
2   The Abbé Gregoire had spoken of the "Archives de la nature" in 1792. See Kedourie, *Nationalism*, p. 122.
3   Reading no. 12 in Hans Kohn, *Nationalism* (New York, 1955).
4   *Cf.* A. Cobban, *Dictatorship* (New York, 1939) p. 42, and Kohn, *The Idea of Nationalism*, p. 15.
5   Eugene Forsey, "Canada: Two Nations or One?" *Canadian Journal of Economics and Political Science*, Vol. XXVIII (November 1962), p. 488. Mr. Forsey's discussion is as usual thorough and convincing.
6   *Cf.* Max Weber, *Essays in Sociology* (London, 1948), p. 176: "A nation is a community of sentiment which would adequately manifest itself in a state of its own; hence, a nation is a community which normally tends to produce a state of its own." And R. MacIver, *Society* (New York, 1937), p. 155: "There are nations then which do not rule themselves politically, but we call them nations only if they seek for political autonomy."
7   On these values see "New Treason of the Intellectuals" in P.E. Trudeau, *Federalism and the French Canadians* (Toronto: Macmillan, 1968), 151–181.

8 *Cf.* Kedourie, *Nationalism*, p. 1: "The doctrine [of nationalism] holds that ... the only legitimate type of government is national self-government."

9 Since the Government of Ireland Act, 1920, it might be more exact to think of Great Britain and Northern Ireland as forming a quasi-unitary state.

10 Ernest Renan, *Discours et conférences* (Paris, 1887), p. 307—also p. 299.

11 On the use of nationalism by the middle classes, see Cobban, *Dictatorship*, p. 140. And for a striking and original approach, see Albert Breton, "The Economics of Nationalism," *Journal of Political Economy*, August 1964.

12 Hans Kelsen, *Law and Peace* (Cambridge, 1948), pp. 1 and 7.

13 Kohn, *Nationalism*, p. 20.

14 As an example of unjustifiable centralization, J.R. Mallory mentions the federal government's policy concerning technical schools (*Montreal Star*, February 4, 1964).

15 The French language was also abolished in the territories. See F.R. Scott, *Civil Liberties and Canadian Federalism* (Toronto, 1959), p. 32.

16 The operative word here is "effective." It will be remembered that Bowell's government in Ottawa did try to remedy the situation, first by order-in-council—the dispositions of which Manitoba refused to obey—and then by a bill in the House of Commons—which was obstructed by Laurier's Liberals, who went on to win the 1896 election.

17 John Porter, "Higher Public Servants and the Bureaucratic Elite in Canada," *Canadian Journal of Economics and Political Science*, Vol XXIV (November 1958), p. 492.

18 *La Presse*, May 12, 1964. *Montreal Gazette*, May 21, 1964.

19 Who would have thought it possible, five years ago, that a prime minister of Canada, after giving into various provincial ultimata, would go on to say: "I believe that the provinces and their governments will play an increasingly important role in our national development. I for one welcome that as a healthy decentralization...."(*Montreal Star*, May 27, 1964.) Too much, too late....

FURTHER READING

Trudeau contributed many of his best essays to the radical journal *Cité Libre*; many of them are reproduced in Trudeau's edited collections *Federalism and the French Canadians* (Toronto: Macmillan, 1968) and *Against the Current: Selected Writings, 1939–96*, edited by Gérard Pelletier (Toronto: McClelland and Stewart, 1996). The best early biographies of Trudeau are Richard Gwyn, *The Northern Magus* (Toronto: McClelland and Stewart, 1980) and Walter Stewart, *Trudeau in Power* (New York: Outerbridge and Dienstfry, 1971); the best later works on Trudeau and his political legacy are by Stephen Clarkson and Christina McCall, *Trudeau and Our Times* (Toronto: McClelland and Stewart, 1990 and 1994) and *Trudeau's Shadow: The Life and Legacy of Pierre Elliott Trudeau*, edited by Andrew Cohen and J.L. Granatstein (Toronto: Random House, 1980).

12
GEORGE GRANT

INTRODUCTION

There is likely no starker contrast to Trudeau's political thought than that of George Grant (1919–1988). Deeply wary of modernity, Grant wrote passionately about the decline of spirituality and transcendence in a world overawed by technology and reason. Were it not for his powerful Christian convictions, Grant might be mistaken for an early postmodernist, as the overarching theme of his work focused consistently upon the destructive tendencies of rationalism and liberal universalism. While he refused to condemn the obvious material comforts of progress, he nonetheless despaired over the dehumanization of technology and the homogenization of mass society. Grant sought a reconciliation between faith and freedom—a philosophical understanding that could maintain both an ethic of community and a recognition of each person's spirituality. *Lament for a Nation*, his most famous work, used the argument that Canada had lost its sovereignty to the United States as a metaphor for the happy complacency in which the modern world accepted the "American" values of technological progress and materialism as satisfactory ends in themselves. *English-Speaking Justice* was a deeper philosophical analysis of some of these themes, and was originally presented as the 1974 Josiah Wood Lecture at Mount Allison University. In it, Grant traces the modern focus upon rationalism in politics from early Protestant beliefs to the rise of contractualism in contemporary liberal thought. He argues that we currently believe liberal principles to be manifestly true to rational individuals and religious ideas to be a subjective matter of faith. But, he warns, we fail to realize that these same liberal principles were themselves derived from theological tenets; and we cannot sustain them if we choose to jettison our faith.

ENGLISH-SPEAKING JUSTICE (1974)

Part I

During this century, Western civilisation has speeded its world-wide influence through the universal acceptance of its technology. The very platitudinous nature of this statement may hide the novelty which is spoken in it. The word "technology" is new, and its unique bringing together of "techne" and "logos" shows that what is common around the world is this novel interpenetration of the arts and sciences. As in all marriages, this new union of making and knowing has changed both parties, so that when we speak "technology" we are speaking a new activity which western Europeans brought into the world, and which has given them their universal-ising and homogenising influence. Kant's dictum that "the mind makes the object" were the words of blessing spoken at that wedding of knowing and production, and should be remembered when we contemplate what is common throughout the world.

The first task of thought in our era is to think what that tech-nology is: to think it in its determining power over our politics and sexuality, our music and education. Moreover we are called to think that technological civilisation in relation to the eternal fire which flames forth in the Gospels and blazes even in the presence of that determining power.

We English-speakers have a particular call to contemplate this civilisation. We have been the chief practical influence in taking technology around the world. Russians and Chinese have often communicated with each other in the language of a small island off the west coast of Europe. Bismarck said that the chief fact of nineteenth century politics was that the Americans spoke English. To assert this practical influence does not imply the absurd sugges-tion that technological civilisation is mainly a product of the English-speaking world. Names such as Heisenberg and Einstein remind us that the crowning intellectual achievement of modernity was not accomplished by English-speakers. Descartes and Rousseau, Kant and Nietzsche remind us that those who have thought most compre-hensively about modernity have often not been English-speaking. Nevertheless, in theory and practice we English-speakers have universalised technological civilisation; we have recently established its most highly explicit presence in North America. In the very fullness of this presence, we are called to think what we are.

As a small part of this multiform task, I intend in these Wood lectures to start from one fact of our situation: the close relation that there has been between the development of technology and political liberalism. By thinking about that relation, I hope to throw light on the nature of both, our liberalism and technology.

Over the last centuries, the most influential people in the English-speaking world have generally taken as their dominant form of self-definition a sustaining faith in a necessary interdependence between the developments of technological science and political liberalism. Most of our scientists have been political (and indeed moral and religious) liberals; the leading philosophic and journalistic expounders of liberalism have nearly always tied the possibility of realising a truly liberal society to the potentialities of modern mastering science. Indeed that close interdependence appears most obviously in the way that some convinced modern liberals put forth their creed as if it were a product of modern science itself; that is, speaking about it in the very language of objectivity which is appropriate to scientific discoveries, but not to an account of the political good. The expression of that close relationship has greatly varied. On the one hand, there have been those who held the identification because they believed political liberalism was the best means of guaranteeing the progress of science. (Freedom's great achievement was that it allowed modern technology to appear.) On the other hand, there have been those who emphasised that modern science was a means of actualising the good which was liberal society. (Technology's great achievement was that it allowed freedom to flourish.) Whatever these differences of emphasis, however, that close identification rested finally in a widely shared belief that the same account of reason which resulted in the discoveries of science, also expressed itself humanly in the development of political regimes ever more congruent with the principles of English-speaking liberalism. This assumed relation of modern science and modern liberalism is still our dominant form of public self-definition, whatever vagaries it has suffered in the twentieth century. Indeed, what do we English-speaking people possess of the political good, if we do not possess what is given in our particular liberalism?

It might be argued that I am incorrect to summon forth one side of that relation by the word "liberalism." It is indeed true that North

American journalists often obscure practical issues by opposing "liberalism" to "conservatism." A clearer way of speaking is to call the practical opposite of "conservatism" "progressivism." Liberalism in its generic form is surely something that all decent men accept as good—"conservatives" included. In so far as the word "liberalism" is used to describe the belief that political liberty is a central human good, it is difficult for me to consider as sane those who would deny that they are liberals. There can be sane argument concerning how far political liberty can be achieved in particular times and places, but not concerning whether it is a central human good. It may seem therefore that the use of the word "liberal" about our explicit political faith during the last centuries does nothing to specify that faith clearly, other than to state the platitude that it was part of the broad tradition of sane discourse in the Western world. Would it not be better to use for the purposes of general description the phrase "English-speaking progressivism?" Despite this argument, I will use the phrase "English-speaking liberalism," because it makes clear the two following points. First, the institutions and ideas of the English-speaking world at their best have been much more than a justification of progress in the mastery of human and non-human nature. They have affirmed that any regime to be called good, and any progress to be called good, must include political liberty and consent. It is not simply a racialist pride in our own past that allows us to make that boast. This must be reaffirmed these days, when our tradition seems often to have degenerated into an ideology the purpose of which is to justify the uninhibited progress of cybernetics, and when therefore it is very easy for decent men to attack English-speaking liberalism as a shallow ideology. Secondly, the use of the word "liberalism" rather than "progressivism" emphasises the necessary point that our English-speaking variety is not liberalism itself, but a particular species of it. This is often forgotten amongst us with the result that our account of liberalism is taken to be the only authentic account, rather than a particular expression of it. This arrogance has often made us depressingly provincial, especially in our philosophising.[1]

Two general propositions seem true about our contemporary liberalism. On the one hand, it is the only political language that can sound a convincing moral note in our public realms. On the other hand, there are signs that modern liberalism and technology, although they have been interdependent, may not necessarily be mutually sustaining, and that their identity may not be given in the nature of reason itself. These two propositions are fundamental to this writing.

The first appears to me indubitable. If argument is to appear respectable and convincing publicly, it must be spoken within the broad assumptions of modern liberalism. Arguments from outside this tradition are put out of court as irrational and probably reactionary. This response is so part of the air we breathe that we often forget its existence. For example, reactions against liberalism emerge on our continent based on local patriotisms and parochialities. These reactions are rarely able to sustain any national control of public policy, partially because the moral language in which they express themselves can easily be shown to be "irrational," in terms of liberal premises, by the dominant classes of our society and their instruments of legitimation. Or again, the language of traditional religion can sustain itself in the public realm only insofar as it responds to issues on the same side as the dominating liberalism. If it does, it is allowed to express itself about social issues. But if there is a conflict between the religious voices and the liberalism, then the religious voices are condemned as reactionary and told to confine themselves to the proper place of religion, which is the private realm. It was not surprising that an influential liberal philosopher defined religion as what we do with our solitude, and in so doing turned around the classical account of religion. Or again, people who wish to justify certain moral positions are forced to pay lip service to modern liberalism if their arguments are to be convincing. The paying of lip service is always evidence of the dominance of a particular way of thought. There was a time when lip service had to be paid to Christianity. In our present world, lip service must be paid to liberalism.

For example, the bell of liberalism sounded in the fall of Nixon. The waves of public indignation which made possible his fall were too sustained to have been produced simply because the wind machines were owned by his enemies. The fact that so many had an obvious interest in bringing about his fall must not allow one to forget that they finally depended for their success on the disinterested voices of those who truly believed in the universal principles of liberal government. Indeed, the surprise in other parts of the world that the Americans were getting rid of an effective president, simply because of a few domestic crimes, showed unawareness of the strength of political liberalism in the heartland of that empire. Those who were surprised showed that they only understood the United States as an object—that is, from outside.

The reason why modern liberalism is the only language that can seem respectable in the public realm is because the dominant people in our society still take for granted that they find in it the best expression of moral truth. This must be stated unequivocally because some of us often find ourselves on the opposite side of particular issues from that espoused by the liberal majority, and do not accept the deepest premises, which undergird liberalism, concerning what human beings are. It is disturbing to find that a belief that does not appear to one rationally convincing is nevertheless the dominating belief in the world one inhabits.

If one wants to communicate, it is constantly necessary to use language which cannot express one's own grasp of reality. The escape from this can be paranoia, which expressed itself in the U.S. as the belief that the dominance of modern liberalism was produced simply by a conspiracy of "intellectuals," "media people," "the eastern establishment" etc. Paranoia in any form is always the enemy of sanity and charity. This particular paranoia is especially dangerous because it closes the eyes to the essential fact that modern liberalism has been dominant because the dominant classes in our society have taken for granted that it expressed what is good. For a century, the majority of people have at the centre of their education received the belief that the modern liberal account of justice is the best account. To accept the implications of the fact is a "sine qua non" of any sane vision of English-speaking societies.

To turn to the second proposition: it is not difficult to point to facts which suggest that technological development does not sustain political liberalism. Abroad, the tides of American corporate technology have not washed up liberal regimes on the shores of their empire. Indeed, to put it mildly, the ferocious determination of the Americans to keep Indo-China within the orbit of their empire made clear that the rights to life, liberty and the pursuit of happiness might be politically important for members of the domestic heartland, but were not intended to be applicable to the tense outreaches of that empire. In the light of these facts, the argument is still presented by liberals that unfree regimes arise in colonial areas when they are first being modernised, but that in the long run they will develop into liberal democracies. By this argument the identity of technological advance and liberalism is preserved in thought. The strength of the argument is necessarily weakened, however, as fewer and fewer colonial regimes remain constitutional democracies. The question is then whether the argument is an appeal to progressivist hope, or to facts; or whether progressivist faith is indeed fact.[2]

However, it is in the heartlands of the English-speaking empire that the more fundamental facts appear which put in question the mutual interdependence of technological and liberal reason. The chief of these facts is that the development of technology is now increasingly directed towards the mastery of human beings. In the words of Heidegger, the sciences are now organised around cybernetics—the technology of the helmsman. To state part of what is given in that thought: technology organises a system which requires a massive apparatus of artisans concerned with the control of human beings. Such work as behaviour modification, genetic engineering, population control by abortion are extreme examples. The machinery reaches out to control more and more lives through this apparatus, and its alliance with the private and public corporations necessary to technological efficiency. The practical question is whether a society in which technology must be oriented to cybernetics can maintain the institutions of free politics and the protection by law of the rights of the individual. Behind that lies the theoretical question about modern liberalism itself. What were the modern assumptions which at one and the same time exalted human freedom and encouraged that cybernetic mastery which now threatens freedom?

Moreover, what can be the place of representative government in the immense society ruled by private and public corporations with their complex bureaucracies?[3] The great founders of our liberalism believed that the best regime required that the choices of all its members should have influence in the governing of the society. It was also hoped that free and equal individuality would be expressed in our work as a field for our choices. The free society would require the overcoming of the division of labour, so that our individuality could be expressed in an egalitarian variety of work. How are either of these possible when the dominant decisions come forth from private and public corporations? In this situation, the institutions of representative government seem increasingly to wither in their effectiveness. Lip service is paid to them; but institutions such as elections and parliaments seem to have less and less constitutive authority. The work of most human beings is intensely specialised, and proceeds from routines which have little to do with individual spontaneity. The widespread concentration of most North Americans on private life, and their acceptance that the public realm is something external to them, takes us far away from the original liberal picture of autonomous and equal human beings participating in the government and production of their society.

Indeed, the current concentration on private life, and the retreat from the public realm as something which is other, raises questions beyond the practical failures of our liberalism. It raises fundamental questions about what is being spoken about human beings in that liberalism. Its theoretical founders asserted that justice was neither a natural nor supernatural virtue, but arose from the calculations necessary to our acceptance of the social contract. In choosing the benefits of membership in organised society, we choose to obey the contractual rules of justice. But is not the present retreat into the private realm not only a recognition of the impotence of the individual, but also a desire to leave the aridity of a realm where all relations are contractual, and to seek the comfort of the private where the supracontractual is possible? For example, the contemporary insistence on sexual life as the chief palliative of our existence is clearly more than a proper acceptance of sexuality after nineteenth century repressions. It is also a hunger and thirst for ecstatic relations which transcend the contractual. After all, mutual orgasmic intercourse cannot finally be brought under the rules of contract, because it takes one beyond the realm of bargains. Therefore human beings rely on its immediacy partially as a retreat from the arid world of public contractualism. In this sense, the retirement of many from the public realm raises deeper questions about modern liberalism than its practical failure to achieve its ideals. It raises questions about the heart of liberalism: whether the omnipresence of contract in the public realm produces a world so arid that most human beings are unable to inhabit it, except for dashes into it followed by dashes out. But such a tenuous relation to the public realm is far from the intentions of the early founders of modern liberalism. This leads to asking: was the affirmation by those founders that justice is based on contract ever sufficient to support a politics of consent and justice? This questions modern liberalism at its theoretical heart.

To sum up: we are faced by two basic facts about our moral tradition. First, our liberalism is the only form of political thought which can summon forth widespread public action for the purposes of human good. Secondly, this liberalism seems presently to speak with a confused voice in the face of the technology it has encouraged and this confusion puts in question the theoretical roots of that liberalism. These lectures will, therefore, try to enucleate what is being spoken about human and non-human beings in that liberal tradition. Only in the light of such an enucleation can one turn to the more difficult question of what is the relation between technological reason and modern liberal reason....

Part III

While the theoretical foundations of our justice came increasingly to be understood as simply contractual, nevertheless decent legal justice was sustained in our regimes. This can only be comprehended in terms of the intimate and yet ambiguous co-penetration between contractual liberalism and Protestantism in the minds of generations of our people. I am not capable of enucleating the nature of that relation, and it can only be hinted at here. Indeed one can use of that co-penetration the words of one who battled with it in his own being: there is "the sense, in the whole element, of things too numerous, too deep, too obscure, too strange or even simply too beautiful, for any ease of intellectual relation."4 Perhaps more than any other European country, England's practical flesh and bones have been fed till recently by its remarkable religious traditions. They may not have been the home of much philosophy, but they were a deeply religious people. The more uncouth and less integrated Protestantism of North America has sustained certain forms of justice, at least for those of European origin. Several elementary comments about liberalism and Protestantism are necessary to the understanding of our surviving justice.

To start at the surface: it is clear why the English free church tradition feared established Christianity, or any close connection between church and state. The Calvinists had only gained political control for a very short period. They therefore saw in the secularisation of the state a means to their freedom against established religion. Beyond the political, moreover, the fearful solitariness in the Calvinists' account of the meeting between God and his creatures encouraged that individualism which was at home with a politics essentially defined in terms of individual right. It is not necessary to enter the debate between Marxist and Weberians to recognise the truth understood by both: namely that Calvinist individualism and the development of capitalism went hand in hand, and that the contractualist political regime was a useful expression for both. Indeed one can say that the extraordinary compact between God and man in Calvinism strangely prepares people for contractual human relations. As secular liberalism became increasingly progressivist, the millenarianism in extreme forms of Protestantism often seemed to be saying the same thing as the secular idea of progress. The religion which has in its heart "He has put down the mighty from their seats and has exalted them of low degree" must have some connection with equality. Less obviously, there was an intimate relation between the development of modern positive science and the positivist account of revelation in Calvinism.5 It is often forgotten by those outside theology that English Protestantism was overwhelmingly Calvinist or Anglican, not Lutheran. Such fates are consummate. Modern European history brings forth the comparison: Germany with its philosophy and music, its political immaturities and extremities; England with its poverty in music and contemplation; its political moderation and judgement. Whatever forces were operating, one of them was their differing Protestantisms. Indeed in England the long consensus about political good, which was sustained by this ambiguous union between Protestantism and secularity, had much to do with protecting that civilisation from the worst extremities of the twentieth century. Whatever else may be said about England, there has been more moderation in its domestic politics so far than in any of the other dominating Western societies. The English were indeed willing to be more extreme towards non-Europeans than they were at home; but there were some restraints even in their imperial adventures. In his fight for Indian independence, Gandhi had to deal with Lord Halifax, not with Himmler or Beria.

In the United States, the Protestantism was of a more unflinching, more immoderate and less thoughtful sort than in England.

The Puritan seekers after a new world were escaping the public demands of an Anglicanism which at its heart was not Calvinist. This rougher Protestantism was more suited to the violent situation of conquering a new continent, first emptied of its French and Spanish opposition and some easily conquered Indians. Indeed the Puritan interpretation of the Bible produced more a driving will to right-eousness than a hunger and thirst for it. As it became secularised in America, that will became the will of self-righteousness, and produced its own incarnation in Emerson. Nevertheless, even in the immoderation—indeed the ferocity—which has been so manifest in American history, that Protestantism gave a firmer and more unyielding account of justice to its country's constitutionalism than would have been forthcoming from any simply contractual account. The continuing power of American Protestantism in popular life today comes from the fact that it has been a less thoughtful species of religion than the originating Protestantism of Europe, and there-fore less vulnerable to modernity. That Protestantism is today above all pietist. This has given it the strength to continue even through all the modernising of rural and small town America. But this pietism has little intellectual bite compared to the Calvinism it replaced, so that its direct practical effect on the control of technology (the central political question) is generally minimal.

All this can be easily said by modern historians. It is more impor-tant to recognise the dependence of secular liberalism for its moral bite upon the strength of Protestantism in English-speaking soci-eties. Most of our history is written by secularists who see the signif-icant happening as the development of secular liberalism. They are therefore likely to interpret the Protestants as passing if useful allies in the realisation of our modern regimes. This allows them to patro-nise Protestant superstitions in a friendly manner, as historically helpful in the development of secularism. To put the ethical rela-tion clearly: if avoidance of violent death is our highest end (albeit negative), why should anyone make sacrifices for the common good which entail that possibility? Why should anyone choose to be a soldier or policeman, if Lockean contractualism is the truth about justice? Yet such professions are necessary if any approximation to justice and consent are to be maintained. Within a contractualist belief, why should anyone care about the reign of justice more than their life? The believing Protestants provided that necessary moral cement which could not be present for those who were consistently directed by contractualism or utilitarianism or a combination of both. This fundamental political vacuum at the heart of contractual liberalism was hidden for generations by the widespread acceptance of Protestantism. At one and the same time, believing Protestants were likely to back their constitutional regimes; yet they backed them without believing that the avoidance of violent death was the highest good, or that justice was to be chosen simply as the most convenient contract.

The word "dialectic" used about "history" has had such cruel consequences for so many people that one is loath to use it even loosely. Nevertheless the relation between Protestants and the growing explicitness of secular liberals can be expressed in the political dialectic between them. The more Protestants came to be influenced by the theoretical foundations of the liberalism which they had first accepted for practical reasons, the less were they able to sustain their prime theological belief which had allowed them to support justice in a more than contractual way; therefore they were less able to provide the moral cement which had given vigour to the liberal regimes. The more secular liberals were able to make explicit that their belief in freedom was not simply a matter of political consent, but implied that human beings were the makers of their own laws, the less could they receive from their Protestant supporters that moral force which made their regimes nobler than an individualism which calculated its contracts.

The long history of the gradual secularising of Protestant faith would require a detailed discussion of its relation to the discoveries of modern science and the formulations of modern philosophy. Protestant faith was not only undermined by the objective discoveries of the sciences, but equally by the affirmations concerning humanity in the dominant philosophies. On the scientific side, for example, it was Darwinism which gave Protestant faith its intellectual "coup de grace" among so many of our bourgeois. On the philosophic side, as "enlightened" human beings came to express their self-understanding as autonomy—that is, to believe themselves the makers of their own laws—any formulation of Christianity became unthinkable.

This co-penetration of Protestantism and liberalism must not be understood in terms of a simply passive overriding in which

Protestantism gradually lost itself. It was a veritable co-penetration in which Protestantism shaped as well as being shaped. In writing of the positive influence of Protestantism on our liberalism, one is forced to touch, however hesitantly, upon the most difficult matter which faces anybody who wishes to understand technology. This is the attempt to articulate that primal Western affirmation which stands shaping our whole civilization, before modern science and technology, before liberalism and capitalism, before our philosophies and theologies. It is present in all of us, and yet hidden to all of us; it originates somewhere and sometime which nobody seems quite to know. Nobody has been able to bring it into the full light of understanding. In all its unfathomedness, the closest I can come to it is the affirmation of human beings as "will," the content of which word has something to do with how Westerners took the Bible as a certain kind of exclusivity. The Calvinist form of Protestantism was a strong breaking forth of that primal and unfathomed affirmation, because "will" and exclusivity were so central to its theology. Calvinist theological voluntarism made it utterly a modern Western theology as distinguished from the theologies of the Platonic world. Hooker saw this with hard practical clarity when he wrote against the Calvinists at the time of their beginnings: "They err who think that of the will of God to do this or that, there is no reason beside his will."[6] In that sense Calvinists were not simply the passive victims of secularisation, but were formulators of it even in their definitions of God and humanity as "will." Calvinist secularism is as useful a substantive as secularised Calvinism. Because of their rootedness in what is thought in the word "will," these Calvinist secularists were particularly open to that definition of will as autonomy. This openness is central to the nemesis of their faith. But in that very nemesis, Calvinism remained a continuing influence in formulating our new "self-definitions." An intellectual example from Europe is the fact that thinkers such as Rousseau and Sartre, who were such formulators of human beings as freedom, were both impregnated with Calvinism in their origins. A more important and immediate example is the sheer conflict of competing wills which has characterised the history of American contractualism. "Winning isn't everything; it's all there is."

To turn back from the depths of technology's origins, it may be said simply that the nobility of English-speaking Protestants often

lay in what was given them in the word "freedom," and the consequences of this for the political realm. Nevertheless what was there
given them made them prone to take the meaning of the will to be
autonomy. But clearly once that Rubicon is crossed, no form of
Christianity can consistently stand. As the Protestants accepted the
liberalism of autonomous will, they became unable to provide their
societies with the public sustenance of uncalculated justice which
the contractual account of justice could not provide from itself.

This ambiguous relation between Protestants and secularisation
was expressed academically in the influence of Kant among generations of professors—particularly those making the first or second
steps away from the pulpit, and finding in the teaching of philosophy an acceptable substitute for preaching. Intellectuals wanted
to seem emancipated from Protestantism, even as they were strongly
held by it. They liked to see themselves as the friends of freedom
and the new technologies, while at the same time they needed to
believe that the new society would incorporate the "absolute moral
values" of Protestantism. They could not accept the account of liberalism given in its strictly worldly forms. Kant seemed to tell them
how all these needs could be met.

They could be moderns and maintain the "values" of their past.
He seemed to show them how they could believe in freedom as
autonomy and in an "absolute morality" as well. He offered them
a Protestantism purified of superstitions and open to progress. A
comparison can be drawn between the hopes of these gentle minis-
ters-cum-professors and the more tragic history of the relations
between philosophic Jews and German society. The most remarkable of the "neo-Kantians" was Hermann Cohen, and as late as this
century he seems to have been close to identifying the coming of
the Messiah with the full realisation of the German liberal state.

In the United States, contractualism was later to be buttressed
by other forms of Biblical religion which came with the later immigrants. Both Judaism and Roman Catholicism gave a firmer bite to
the political justice lived out under the American constitution than
that implied by contractualism. Nevertheless, because the primal
formation of that constitutionalism was in the meeting of
Protestantism and secular accounts of legality, it cannot be my
purpose here to describe how the later immigrant forms of Biblical
religion gave force to justice in those institutions, nor to describe

how those religions were transformed by existing within English-speaking institutions.7

To sum up: the principles of our political and legal institutions did not need to be justified in thought, because they were justified in life. They were lived out by practical people for whom they provided the obvious parameters of any decent society. Anyone who wished to act outside these parameters had rightly to feel or assume shame. They were identified with the coming to be of progressive technological society; they justified and were justified by that coming to be. Through that long period when our bourgeois societies were not only stable at home but increasingly dominant throughout the world, the liberalism could simply be lived in without contemplation. If those who considered themselves political philosophers questioned whether decent rules of justice could be expected to come forth from the foundational affirmation that political relations are simply calculated contracts, they were cushioned from clarity by a long tradition of justice otherwise sustained, and new progressivist hopes. Such intellectuals lived in societies which were enfolded in a sufficiently widespread public religion to produce believers who accepted the liberal state, and yet did not believe that justice was good simply because it was the product of calculated contract. The story has been told many times of how most intellectuals in our societies scorned the fundamental beliefs of the public religion, and yet counted on the continuance of its moral affirmations to serve as the convenient public basis of justice. Clever people generally believed that the foundational principles of justice were chosen conveniences, because of what they had learnt from modern science; nevertheless they could not turn away from a noble content to that justice, because they were enfolded more than they knew in long memories and hopes. They were so enfolded even as they ridiculed the beliefs that kept those memories alive among the less articulate. Intellectual oblivion of eternity could not quickly kill that presence of eternity given in the day to day life of justice. The strength of those very memories held many intellectuals from doubting whether justice is good, and from trying to think why it is good in the light of what we have been told about the whole in modern science. This combination of the public successes of liberalism with these memories and hopes inhibited the thought which asks if justice is more than contractually founded, and whether it can be sustained in the world if it be considered simply a chosen convenience. The very decency and confidence of English-speaking politics was related to the absence of philosophy....

Part IV

For the last centuries a civilisational contradiction has moved our Western lives. Our greatest intellectual endeavour—the new co-penetration of "logos" and "techne"—affirmed at its heart that in understanding anything we know it as ruled by necessity and chance. This affirmation entailed the elimination of the ancient notion of good from the understanding of anything. At the same time, our day-to-day organisation was in the main directed by a conception of justice formulated in relation to the ancient science, in which the notion of good was essential to the understanding of what is. This civilisational contradiction arose from the attempt of the articulate to hold together what was given them in modern science with a content of justice which had been developed out of an older account of what is.

It must be emphasised that what is at stake in this contradiction is not only the foundations of justice, but more importantly its content. Many academics in many disciplines have described the difference between the ancient and modern conceptions of justice as if it were essentially concerned with differing accounts of the human situation. The view of traditional philosophy and religion is that justice is the overriding order which we do not measure and define, but in terms of which we are measured and defined. The view of modern thought is that justice is a way which we choose in freedom, both individually and publicly, once we have taken our fate into our own hands, and know that we are responsible for what happens. This description of the difference has indeed some use for looking at the history of our race—useful both to those who welcome and those who deplore the change of view. Nevertheless, concentration on differing "world views" dims the awareness of what has been at stake concerning justice in recent Western history. This dimming takes place in the hardly conscious assumption that while there has been change as to what can be known in philosophy, and change in the prevalence of religious belief among the educated, the basic content of justice in our societies will somehow remain the same. The theoretical differences in "world views" are turned over to the domain of "objective" scholarship, and this scholarship is carried out in protected private provinces anaesthetised from any touch with what is happening to the content of justice in the heat of the world. To feel the cutting edge of what is at stake in differing foundations of justice it is necessary to touch those foundations as they are manifested in the very context of justice.

The civilisational contradiction which beset Europe did not arise from the question whether there is justice, but what justice is. Obviously any possible society must have some system of organisation to which the name "justice" can be given. The contradiction arose because human beings held onto certain aspects of justice which they had found in the ancient account of good, even after they no longer considered that that account of good helped them to understand the way things are. The content of justice was largely given them from its foundations in the Bible (and the classical philosophy which the early Christians thought necessary for understanding the Bible), while they understood the world increasingly in terms of modern technological science.

The desire to have both what was given in the new knowledge, and what was given us about justice in the religious and philosophical traditions, produced many conscious and unconscious attempts at practical and theoretical reconciliations. It is these attempts which make it not inaccurate to call the early centuries of modern liberal Europe the era of secularised Christianity. It is an often repeated platitude that thinkers such as Locke and Rousseau, Kant and Marx were secularised Christians. (Of the last name it is perhaps better to apply the not so different label—secularised Jew.) The reason why an academic such as Professor Rawls has been singled out for attention in this writing is as an example of how late that civilisational contradiction has survived in the sheltered intellectual life of the English-speaking peoples.

Indeed the appropriateness of calling modern contractualism "secularised Christianity" may be seen in the difference between modern contractualism and the conventionalism of the ancient world. Although the dominant tradition of the ancient world was that justice belonged to the order of things, there was a continuing minority report that justice was simply a man-made convention. But what so startlingly distinguishes this ancient conventionalism from our contractualism is that those who advocated it most clearly also taught that the highest life required retirement from politics. According to Lucretius, the wise man knows that the best life is one of isolation from the dynamism of public life. The dominant contractualist teachers of the modern world have advocated an intense concern with political action. We are called to the supremacy of the practical life in which we must struggle to establish the just contract of equality. When one asks what had been the chief new public intellectual influence between ancient and modern philosophy, the answer must be Western Christianity, with its insistence on the primacy of charity and its implications for equality. Modern contractualism's determined political activism relates it to its seedbed in Western Christianity. Here again one comes upon that undefined primal affirmation which has been spoken of as concerned with "will," and which is prior both to technological science and to revolution.

This public contradiction was not first brought into the light of day in the English-speaking world. It was exposed in the writings of Nietzsche. The Germans had received modern ways and thought later than the French or the English and therefore in a form more explicitly divided from the traditional thought. In their philosophy, these modern assumptions are most uncompromisingly brought into the light of day. Nietzsche's writings may be singled out as a Rubicon, because more than a hundred years ago he laid down with incomparable lucidity that which is now publicly open: what is given about the whole in technological science cannot be thought together with what is given us concerning justice and truth, reverence and beauty, from our tradition. He does not turn his ridicule primarily against what has been handed to us in Christian revelation and ancient philosophy. What was given there has simply been killed as given, and all that we need to understand is why it was once thought alive. His greatest ridicule is reserved for those who want to maintain a content to "justice" and "truth" and "goodness" out of the corpse that they helped to make a corpse. These are the intellectual democrats who adopt modern thought while picking and choosing among the ethical "norms" from a dead past. Justice as equality and fairness is that bit of Christian instinct which survives the death of God. As he puts it: "The masses blink and say: 'We are all equal—Man is but man, before God—we are all equal.' Before God! But now this God has died."

Particularly since Hume, the English moralists had pointed out that moral rules were useful conventions, but had also assumed that the core of English justice was convenient. Hume's "monkish virtues"—the parts of the tradition which did not suit the new bourgeoisie—could be shown to be inconvenient; but the heart of the tradition could be maintained and extended in the interests of property and liberty. It could be freed from its justification in terms of eternity, and its rigour could be refurbished by some under the pseudo-eternity of a timeless social contract. But Nietzsche makes clear that if the "justice" of liberty and equality is only conventional, we may find in the course of an ever-changing history that such content is not convenient. He always puts the word "justice" in quotation marks to show that he does not imply its traditional content, and that its content will vary through the flux of history. The English moralists had not discovered that realm of beings we moderns call "history," and therefore they did not understand the dominance of historicism over all other statements. Their social contract was indeed a last effort to avoid that dominance, while they increasingly accepted the ways of thought that led ineluctably to historicism. The justice of liberty and equality came forth from rationalists who did not think "historically." For whom is such justice convenient when we know that the old rationalism can no longer be thought as "true?"

However, it is Kant who is singled out by Nietzsche as the clearest expression of this secularised Christianity. Kant's thought is the consummate expression of wanting it both ways. Having understood what is told us about nature in our science, and having understood that we will and make our own history, he turned away from the consequence of those recognitions by enfolding them in the higher affirmation that morality is the one fact of reason, and we are commanded to obedience. According to Nietzsche, he limited autonomy by obedience. Because this comfortable anaesthetising from the full consequences of the modern was carried out so brilliantly in the critical system, Nietzsche calls Kant "the great delayer." Kant persuaded generations of intellectuals to the happy conclusion that they could keep both the assumptions of technological secularism and the absolutes of the old morality. He allowed them the comfort of continuing to live in the civilisational contradiction of accepting both the will to make one's own life and the old content of justice. He delayed them from knowing that there are no moral facts, but only the moral interpretation of facts, and that these interpretations can be explained as arising from the historical vicissitudes of the instincts. Moral interpretations are what we call our "values," and these are what our wills impose upon the facts. Because of the brilliance of Kant's delaying tactics, men were held from seeing that justice as equality was a secularised survival of an archaic Christianity, and the absolute commands were simply the man-made "values" of an era we have transcended.

Nietzsche was the first to make clear the argument that there is no reason to continue to live in that civilisational contradiction. Societies will always need legal systems—call them systems of "justice" if you like the word. Once we have recognised what we can now will to create through our technology, why should we limit such creation by basing our systems of "justice" on presuppositions which have been shown to be archaic by the very coming to be of technology? As we move into a society where we will be able to shape not only non-human nature but humanity itself, why should we limit that shaping by doctrines of equal rights which come out of a world view that "history" has swept away. Does not the production of quality of life require a legal system which gives new range to the rights of the creative and the dynamic? Why should that range be limited by the rights of the weak, the uncreative and the immature? Why should the liberation of women to quality of life be limited by restraints on abortion, particularly when we know that the foetuses are only the product of necessity and chance? Once we have recognised "history" as the imposing of our wills on an accidental world, does not "justice" take on a new content?[8]

Against this attack on our "values," our liberalism so belongs to the flesh and bones of our institutions that it cannot be threatened by something as remote as ontological questioning. The explicit statements of the American constitution guard their system of justice; the British constitution guards the same shape of rights in a less explicit but in a more deeply rooted way. These living forces of allegiance protect the common sense of practical men against the follies of ideologues. Anyway, did not the English-speaking peoples win the wars against the Germans, and win them in the name of liberalism, against the very "philosophy" that is said to assail that liberalism?

It is also argued that the very greatness of American pluralism, founded upon the contract, is that out of it have come forth continuous religious revivals which produce that moral sustenance necessary to the justice of their society. Is it not a reason for confidence that in the election of 1976 the two candidates competed in allegiance to the traditions of religion, and that there is a renewed interest in religion among the young in the contractual society? Where is the atheism of the right in the United States? Does not the greatness of the American constitution lie in the fact that the general outlines of social cooperation are laid down and maintained by a secular contract, while within those general rules the resources of religious faith can flourish, as long as such faiths do not transgress that general outline? The greatness of the system is that the tolerance of pluralism is combined with the strength of religion. God has not died, as European intellectuals believed; it is just that our differing apprehensions of deity require that the rules of the game are not defined in terms of any of them. The rules of the game are defined in terms of the calculation of worldly self-interest; beyond that, citizens may seek the eternal as they see fit.

Indeed, any sane individual must be glad that we face the unique event of technology within a long legal and political tradition founded on the conception of justice as requiring liberty and equality. When we compare what is happening to multitudes in Asia who live the event of technology from out of ancient and great traditions, but without a comparable sense of individual right, we may count ourselves fortunate to live within our tradition. Asian people often have great advantages over us in the continuing strength of rite; our advantage is in the continuing strength of right. Also our liberalism came from the meeting of Christian tradition with an early form of modern thought, so that our very unthinking confidence in that liberalism has often saved us from modern political plagues which have been devastating in other western societies. At the practical level, it is imprudent indeed to speak against the principles, if not the details, of those legal institutions which guard our justice.9

Nevertheless, it must be stated that our justice now moves to a lowered content of equal liberty. The chief cause of this is that our justice is being played out within a destiny more comprehensive than itself. A quick name for this is "technology." I mean by that word the endeavour which summons forth everything (both human and non-human) to give its reasons, and through the summoning forth of those reasons turns the world into potential raw material, at the disposal of our "creative" wills.[10] The definition is circular in the sense that what is "creatively" willed is further expansion of that union of knowing and making given in the linguistic union of "techne," and "logos." Similar but cruder: it has been said that communism and contractual capitalism are predicates of the subject technology. They are ways in which our more comprehensive destiny is lived out. But clearly that technological destiny has its own dynamic conveniences, which easily sweep away our tradition of justice, if the latter gets in the way. The "creative" in their corporations have been told for many generations that justice is only a convenience. In carrying out the dynamic convenience of technology, why should they not seek a "justice" which is congruent with those conveniences, and gradually sacrifice the principles of liberty and equality when they conflict with the greater conveniences? What is it about other human beings that should stand in the way of such convenience? The tendency of the majority to get together to insist on a contract guaranteeing justice to them against the "creative" strong continues indeed to have some limiting power. Its power is, however, itself limited by the fact that the majority of that majority see in the very technological endeavour the hope for their realisation of "the primary goods," and therefore will often not stand up for the traditional justice when it is inconvenient to that technological endeavour. The majority of the acquiescent think they need the organisers to provide "the primary goods" more than they need justice.

In such a situation, equality in "primary goods" for a majority in the heartlands of the empire is likely; but it will be an equality which excludes liberal justice for those who are inconvenient to the "creative." It will exclude liberal justice from those who are too weak to enforce contracts—the imprisoned, the mentally unstable, the unborn, the aged, the defeated, and sometimes even the morally unconforming. The price for large-scale equality under the direction of the "creative" will be injustice for the very weak. It will be a kind of massive "equality" in "primary goods," outside a concern for justice. As Huey Long put it: "When fascism comes to America, it will come in the name of democracy." We move to such a friendly and smooth faced organisation that it will not be recognised for what it is. This lack of recognition is seen clearly when the President of France says he is working for "an advanced liberal society," just as he is pushing forward laws for the mass destruction of the unborn. What he must mean by liberal is the society organised for the human conveniences which fit the conveniences of technology.

As justice is conceived as the external convenience of contract, it obviously has less and less to do with the good ordering of the inward life. Among the majority in North America, inward life then comes to be ordered around the pursuit of "primary goods," and/or is taken in terms of a loose popular Freudianism, mediated to the masses by the vast array of social technicians.[11] But it is dangerous to mock socially the fact of contradiction. The modern account of "the self" is at one with the Nietzschean account. This unity was explicitly avowed by Freud. With its affirmation of the instrumentality of reason, how can it result in a conception of "justice" similar to that of our tradition? In such a situation, the majorities in the heartlands of the empires may be able to insist on certain external equalities. But as justice is conceived as founded upon contract, and as having nothing to do with the harmony of the inward life, will it be able to sustain the inconveniences of public liberty?

In the Western tradition it was believed that the acting out of justice in human relationships was the essential way in which human beings are opened to eternity. Inward and outward justice were considered to be mutually interdependent, in the sense that the inward openness to eternity depended on just practice, and just practice depended on that inward openness to eternity. When public justice is conceived as conventional and contractual, the division between inward and outward is so widened as to prevent any such mutual interdependence. Both openness to eternity and practical justice are weakened in that separation. A.N. Whitehead's shallow dictum that religion is what we do with our solitude aptly expresses that modern separation. It is a destructive half-truth because it makes our solitude narcissistic, and blunts our cutting edge in public justice.

Above all, we do not correctly envisage what is happening when we take our situation simply as new practical difficulties for liberalism, arising from the need to control new technologies, themselves external to that liberalism. Such an understanding of our situation prevents us from becoming aware that our contractual liberalism is not independent of the assumptions of technology in any way that allows it to be the means of transcending those technologies. Our situation is rather that the assumptions underlying contractual liberalism and underlying technology both come from the same matrix of modern thought, from which can arise no reason why the justice of liberty is due to all human beings, irrespective of convenience. In so far as the contemporary systems of liberal practice hold onto the content of free and equal justice, it is because they still rely on older sources which are more and more made unthinkable in the very realisation of technology. When contractual liberals hold within their thought remnants of secularised Christianity or Judaism, these remnants, if made conscious, must be known as unthinkable in terms of what is given in the modern. How, in modern thought, can we find positive answers to the questions: (i) what is it about human beings that makes liberty and equality their due? (ii) why is justice what we are fitted for, when it is not convenient? Why is it our good? The inability of contractual liberals (or indeed Marxists) to answer these questions is the terrifying darkness which has fallen upon modern justice.

Therefore, to those of us who for varying reasons cannot but trust the lineaments of liberal justice, and who somehow have been told that some such justice is due to all human beings and that its living out is, above all, what we are fitted for—to those of such trust comes the call from that darkness to understand how justice can be thought together with what has been discovered of truth in the coming to be of technology. The great theoretical achievements of the modern era have been quantum physics, the biology of evolutionism, and the modern logic. (All other modern theoretical claims, particularly those in the human sciences, remain as no more than provisional, or even can be known as simply expressions of that oblivion of eternity which has characterised the coming to be of technology.) These are the undoubtable core of truth which has come out of technology, and they cry out to be thought in harmony with the conception of justice as what we are fitted for.

The danger of this darkness is easily belittled by our impoverished use of the word "thought." This word is generally used as if it meant an activity necessary to scientists when they come up against a difficulty in their research, or some vague unease beyond calculation when we worry about our existence. Thought is steadfast attention to the whole. The darkness is fearful, because what is at stake is whether anything is good. In the pretechnological era, the central Western account of justice clarified the claim that justice is what we are fitted for. It clarified why justice is to render each human being their due, and why what was due to all human beings was "beyond all bargains and without an alternative." That account of justice was written down most carefully and most beautifully in *The Republic* of Plato. For those of us who are Christians, the substance of our belief is that the perfect living out of that justice is unfolded in the Gospels. Why the darkness which enshrouds justice is so dense—even for those who think that what is given in *The Republic* concerning good stands forth as true—is because that truth cannot be thought in unity with what is given in modern science concerning necessity and chance. The darkness is not simply the obscurity of living by that account of justice in the practical tumult of the technological society. Nor is it the impossibility of that account coming to terms with much of the folly of modernity, e.g., the belief that there is a division between "facts" and "values"; nor the difficulty of thinking its truth in the presence of historicism. Rather, it is that this account has not been thought in unity with the greatest theoretical enterprises of the modern world. This is a great darkness, because it appears certain that rational beings cannot get out of the darkness by accepting either truth and rejecting the other. It is folly simply to return to the ancient account of justice as if the discoveries of the modern science of nature had not been made. It is folly to take the ancient account of justice as simply of antiquarian interest, because without any knowledge of justice as what we are fitted for, we will move into the future with a "justice" which is terrifying in its potentialities for mad inhumanity of action. The purpose of this writing has been to show the truth of the second of these propositions. In the darkness one should not return as if the discoveries of modern science had not taken place; nor should one give up the question of what it means to say that justice is what we are fitted for; and yet who has been able to think the two together? For those of us who are lucky enough to know that we have been told that justice is what we are fitted for, this is not a practical darkness, but simply a theoretical one. For those who do not believe that they have been so told it is both a practical and theoretical darkness which leads to an ever greater oblivion of eternity.

In the task of lightening the darkness which surrounds justice in our era, we of the English-speaking world have one advantage and one great disadvantage. The advantage is practical: the old and settled legal institutions which still bring forth loyalty from many of the best practical people. The disadvantage is that we have been so long disinterested or even contemptuous of that very thought about the whole which is now required. No other great Western tradition has shown such lack of interest in thought, and in the institutions necessary to its possibility. We now pay the price for our long tradition of taking the goods of practical confidence and competence as self-sufficiently the highest goods. In what is left of those secular institutions which should serve the purpose of sustaining such thought—that is, our current institutions of higher learning—there is little encouragement to what might transcend the technically competent, and what is called "philosophy" is generally little more than analytical competence. Analytical logistics plus historicist scholarship plus even rigorous science do not when added up equal philosophy. When added together they are not capable of producing that thought which is required if justice is to be taken out of the darkness which surrounds it in the technological era. This lack of tradition of thought is one reason why it is improbable that the transcendence of justice over technology will be lived among English-speaking people.

NOTES

¹ This second point, which would appear to be obvious, has been greatly obscured by recent propagandists for English-speaking liberalism, who in their desire to defend that tradition have denied that other traditions of liberalism have any right to be called "liberal" at all. At its silliest, this kind of writing is to be found in Professor K. Popper's *The Open Society and Its Enemies*, particularly in its polemics against Plato and Hegel. It is obviously the proper work of political philosophy to argue, as Montesquieu does so brilliantly in *The Spirit of the Laws*, that the modern English polity is a higher regime than the Athenian polis, and that modern philosophers understand the good of liberty in a fuller way than the ancients. Whether Plato understood the good of liberty as well as Locke is a question for serious and difficult argument. But to argue, as Popper does, that Plato and Hegel denied that political liberty was a central human good, and were indeed progenitors of modern totalitarianism, must have required such a casual reading of these two writers that his book can only be considered trivial propaganda. How is it possible to read through *The Apology* or *The Philosophy of Right* and believe that the writers of either did not believe that political liberty was a central human good? Rather similar arguments have been advanced by English-speaking liberals against the tradition of European liberalism which originates with Rousseau. See for example Bertrand Russell's account of Rousseau in his *A History of Western Philosophy* or J.L. Talmon's *The Origins of Totalitarian Democracy*. The danger of such writings is that they have encouraged in our universities a provincial approach

towards the history of political thought, just at a time when our situation required the opposite. For the continuing health of the liberal tradition, what we least needed was a defensive exclusion of the classical and European traditions from the canon of liberalism. At a time when massive technological advance has presented the race with unusual difficulties concerning political liberty, what was needed from our academics was an attempt to think through all that was valuable from the great western traditions which could help us in dealing with these difficulties. Instead, what we got from men such as Russell and Popper was a procrustean affirmation of the self-sufficiency of English liberalism. To put the matter crudely: in a time of great intellectual confusion, our crimes at home and abroad should not prevent us from trying to see what good is present in English-speaking liberalism, any more than the crimes of the Soviet Union should prevent us from trying to see what good is present in the tradition that proceeds from Rousseau, or indeed any more than ancient slavery and imperialism should prevent us looking clearly at classical political philosophy.

2 It is of course true that the dilemma arising within liberalism, because of its imperial as well as its domestic role, existed as much in the European empires of the nineteenth century as in the American. Indeed, Plato's sustained attacks on Athenian imperialism, and its close relation to democracy, deals with a comparable situation, except for the presence of technology in our day. In England, modern liberalism was above all the creed of the new bourgeois, in that the insistence on political liberties was related to the liberation of dynamic commercial technology, and thus with the expansion of that dynamism around the world. The claim to legal and political freedoms at home was not a claim that could be universally applied abroad to alien races who had to be made the subjects of that commercial technology. This was an even more pressing difficulty for the French, because after the revolution their ideology more explicitly universalised the rights of man. Western principles of right in claiming universality became at one and the same time the basis for anti-imperialism both at home and abroad, yet also a justification for western expansion as the bringing of enlightenment into "backward" parts of the world. Liberalism as a justification for imperialism can be seen very clearly in the work of Macauley. His account of English history is a panegyric to modern liberalism, with the world-historical good of England's greatness. In India he was the chief instrument in westernising education, and above all for substituting English for Sanskrit in that education. He once said that "All the lore of India is not equal to Aesop's fables." In the intense competition for the world's crassest remark, this one has a high claim. On the other hand, as imperialism developed, the western critique of it came forth largely in the name of liberalism. The antiprogressivist critics of imperialism, such as Cunningham Graham, spoke after all in voices which were not easily understood in modern Europe. Indeed the dilemma became increasingly obvious; in so far as modern liberals put their trust in the development of commerce and technology, they were inevitably identifying themselves with the spread of imperialism; in so far as liberalism became explicitly a universal doctrine of human rights, the liberals had to become critics of their imperialism. A similar dilemma was present from the beginnings of American imperialism, and erupted into immediate political significance over the Vietnam war. The part of F.D. Roosevelt at one and the same time was domestically the liberal part, and abroad established the highest tide of American imperialism. Yet the dominant force in the American protest against that war came from people who protested in the name of liberalism. However ashamed we English-speaking people should be of that war, it should not be forgotten that the strongest anti-imperialist protest in western history occurred in the U.S.A. It may be that the majority of protesters accepted the high consumption due to their imperialism, nevertheless that protest says something about the authenticity of American liberalism.

3 The word "hierarchy" is still often used as the political opposite to "equality." This is bad usage because the subordinations and superordinations of our bureaucracies are

not intended to be "sacred orders" given in the nature of things. There seems to be no current positive word which expresses clearly the opposite of equality. Is this because our liberal language has become increasingly egalitarian, and the lip service we pay to this principle makes it impossible to find accurate words to express what is happening in our institutions?

4 Henry James's preface to *The Aspern Papers*. That relation has been illumined by the massive historical scholarship about it in the last generation; but such a relation clearly cannot be fathomed by scholarship. Even Weber or Troeltsch, as they move beyond scholarship towards philosophy, are still unable to catch that self-definition of our wills which arose from the co-penetration. For my comments see *Technology and Empire: Perspectives on North America*, Toronto, 1969.

5 In the fine writing on this matter recently, e.g., the books of Trevor-Roper, Webster, Yates, etc., it is still necessary to single out the early articles of M.B. Foster as most theoretically illuminating. See *Mind* 1934: 35–36.

6 *The Laws of Ecclesiastical Polity*, Book I, chap. 2.

7 It is often pointed out that Jewish people remain the most fervent and articulate advocates of our contractualism. Therefore a word must be appended about the relation between Judaism and modern English-speaking regimes. It is obvious why the Jewish community has always welcomed and supported modern liberalism. In western and eastern Europe, Jews had lived for centuries under regimes in which some form of Christianity was the official religion, and under which their survival required both fortitude and patience. As the regimes became secularised, they presented Jews with the possibility of living openly in the civil society. Beyond this obvious fact, it is necessary to understand the deeper question of why Jews have exerted such a formative influence on American society, far beyond their percentage of the population. Perhaps it is that in Judaism worship of God is closely bound together with the existence of a particular historical nation, and that this sense of being a people has given Jews sources of strength when they move out into the impersonal and individualistic public realm consequent on contractualism. Its members have been able to live forcefully in the unblinking public light, because they could retire into the shade of a community not only based on the universality of religion, but on the particularity of nationhood, and these two bound together in a quite unique way. In a society in which contractual relations define more and more human encounters, the Jews have maintained a public force from that given union of worship and nationality, which could only exist sporadically among Christians because of the very nature of Christ's message.

8 To put the matter politically: the early public atheism of Europe generally came from "the left." Its adherents attacked the traditional religion while taking for granted almost unconsciously that "the right" would continue to live within its religious allegiances. "The left" could attack religion partially because it relied on "the right" having some restraint because of its religion. Philosophers cannot be subsumed under their political effects, but with Nietzsche the atheism of "the right" enters the western scene. One definition of national socialism is a strange union of the atheisms of "the right" and of "the left."

9 It is well to remember that the greatest contemporary philosopher, Heidegger, published in 1953 *An Introduction to Metaphysics* in which he wrote of National Socialism: "The inner truth and greatness of this movement (namely the encounter between global technology and modern man)." One theoretical part of that encounter was the development of a new jurisprudence, which explicitly distinguished itself from our jurisprudence of rights, because the latter belonged to an era of plutocratic democracy which needed to be transcended in that encounter. Such arguments must make one extremely careful of the ontological questioning of our jurisprudence, even in its barest contractual form.

10 See M. Heidegger *Der Satz Vom Grund*, Pfullingen, 1957.

[11] We are fortunate these days when the social technicians are controlled by something as human as popular Freudianism. Whatever its defects, popular Freudianism is surely superior to the "new brutalism" of behaviour modification carried out by behaviourist techniques.

FURTHER READING

Except for *Lament for a Nation* (Ottawa: Carleton University Press, 1982) and *English-Speaking Justice* (Toronto: Anansi, 1985), George Grant mainly published collections of essays, including *Philosophy in the Mass Age* (1959), *Technology and Empire* (1969), and *Technology and Justice* (1986). Grant's works are now available in omnibus form, published as *The Collected Works of George Grant*, edited by Arthur Davis and Peter Emberley (Toronto: University of Toronto Press, 2000). Commentaries include Larry Schmidt, *George Grant in Progress* (Toronto: Anansi, 1978), Joan O'Donovan, *George Grant and the Twilight of Justice* (Toronto: University of Toronto Press, 1984), and Arthur Davis, ed. *George Grant and the Subversion of Modernity* (Toronto: University of Toronto Press, 1990); but the best work on George Grant remains William Christian's marvellous biography, *George Grant* (Toronto: University of Toronto Press, 1993).

13 GAD HOROWITZ

INTRODUCTION

Why is the political culture of Canada so different from that of the United States? Gad Horowitz (b. 1936) argues that the fundamental reason for this distinction is due to the historical significance of the "tory touch" in Canada. He begins with Louis Hartz's "fragment theory," which states that political culture is irretrievably shaped by the particular cultural fragment that establishes itself in a new territory. Horowitz objects to Hartz's assertion that no substantial difference exists between the United States and Canada, and he argues that Hartz underestimates the significance of the small tory fragment that established itself in Canada along with the liberal one. Canadian socialism, states Horowitz, developed as a natural reaction to this small but consequential tory influence. Thus, while socialism never became accepted by the American mainstream due to its "German, Marxist, and other-worldly" nature, the ideas of the left are more readily accepted in Canada because they were seen as more "British, non-Marxist, and worldly." While left-wing politics are still a small component of Canadian politics overall, he concludes, the "antagonistic symbiosis" between the left and the Liberal party has left an indelible mark upon Canadian political culture.

CONSERVATISM, LIBERALISM, AND SOCIALISM IN CANADA: AN INTERPRETATION (1966)

1. Introduction: The Hartzian Approach

In the United States, organized socialism is dead; in Canada socialism, though far from national power, is a significant political force. Why this striking difference in the fortunes of socialism in two very similar societies?

Any attempt to account for the difference must be grounded in a general comparative study of the English-Canadian and American societies. It will be shown that the relative strength of socialism in Canada is related to the relative strength of toryism, and to the different position and character of liberalism in the two countries.

In North America, Canada is unique. Yet there is a tendency in Canadian historical and political studies to explain Canadian phenomena not by contrasting them with American phenomena but by identifying them as variations on a basic North American theme. I grant that Canada and the United States are similar, and that the similarities should be pointed out. But the pan-North American approach, since it searches out and concentrates on similarities, cannot help us to understand Canadian uniqueness. When this approach is applied to the study of English-Canadian socialism, it discovers, first, that like the American variety it is weak, and second, that it is weak for much the same reasons. These discoveries perhaps explain why Canadian socialism is weak in comparison to European socialism; they do not explain why Canadian socialism is so much stronger than American socialism.

The explanatory technique used in this study is that developed by Louis Hartz in *The Liberal Tradition in America*[1] and *The Founding of New Societies*.[2] It is applied to Canada in a mildly pan-North American way by Kenneth McRae in "The Structure of Canadian History," a contribution to the latter book.

The Hartzian approach is to study the new societies founded by Europeans (the United States, English Canada, French Canada, Latin America, Dutch South Africa, Australia) as "fragments" thrown off from Europe. The key to the understanding of ideological development in a new society is its "point of departure" from Europe: the ideologies borne by the founders of the new society are not representative of the historic ideological spectrum of the mother country. The settlers represent only a fragment of that spectrum. The complete ideological spectrum ranges—in chronological order, and from right to left—from feudal or tory through liberal whig to liberal democrat to socialist. French Canada and Latin America are "feudal fragments." They were founded by bearers of the feudal or tory values of the organic, corporate, hierarchical community; their point of departure from Europe is before the liberal revolution. The United States, English Canada, and Dutch South Africa are "bourgeois fragments," founded by bearers of liberal individualism who have left the tory end of the spectrum behind them. Australia is the one "radical fragment," founded by bearers of the working class ideologies of mid-nineteenth-century Britain.

The significance of the fragmentation process is that the new society, having been thrown off from Europe, "loses the stimulus to change that the whole provides."3 The full ideological spectrum of Europe develops only out of the continued confrontation and interaction of its four elements; they are related to one another, not only as enemies, but as parents and children. A new society which leaves part of the past behind it cannot develop the future ideologies which need the continued presence of the past in order to come into being. In escaping the past, the fragment escapes the future, for "the very seeds of the later ideas are contained in the parts of the old world that have been left behind."4 The ideology of the founders is thus frozen, congealed at the point of origin.

Socialism is an ideology which combines the corporate-organic-collectivist ideas of toryism with the rationalist-egalitarian ideas of liberalism. Both the feudal and the bourgeois fragments escape socialism, but in different ways. A feudal fragment such as French Canada develops no whig (undemocratic) liberalism; therefore it does not develop the democratic liberalism which arises out of and as a reaction against whiggery; therefore it does not develop the socialism which arises out of and as a reaction against liberal democracy. The corporate-organic-collectivist component of socialism is present in the feudal fragment—it is part of the feudal ethos—but the radical rationalist-egalitarian component of socialism is missing. It can be provided only by whiggery and liberal democracy, and these have not come into being.

In the bourgeois fragment, the situation is the reverse: the radical rationalist-egalitarian component of socialism is present, but the corporate-organic-collectivist component is missing, because toryism has been left behind. In the bourgeois fragments "Marx dies because there is no sense of class, no yearning for the corporate past."5 The absence of socialism is related to the absence of toryism.

It is *because* socialists have a conception of society as more than an agglomeration of competing interests—a conception close to the tory view of society as an organic community—that they find the liberal idea of equality (equality of opportunity) inadequate.

Socialists disagree with liberals about the essential meaning of equality because socialists have a tory conception of society.

In a liberal bourgeois society which has never known toryism the demand for equality will express itself as left-wing or democratic liberalism as opposed to whiggery. The left will point out that all are not equal in the competitive pursuit of individual happiness. The government will be required to assure greater equality of opportunity—in the nineteenth century, by destroying monopolistic privileges; in the twentieth century by providing a welfare "floor" so that no one will fall out of the race for success, and by regulating the economy so that the race can continue without periodic crises.

In a society which thinks of itself as a community of classes rather than an aggregation of individuals, the demand for equality will take a socialist form: for equality of condition rather than mere equality of opportunity; for co-operation rather than competition; for a community that does more than provide a context within which individuals can pursue happiness in a purely self-regarding way. At its most "extreme," socialism is a demand for the *abolition* of classes so that the good of the community can truly be realized. This is a demand which cannot be made by people who can hardly see class and community: the individual fills their eyes.

2. The Application to Canada

It is a simple matter to apply the Hartzian approach to English Canada in a Pan-North American way. English Canada can be viewed as a fragment of the American liberal society, lacking a feudal or tory heritage and therefore lacking the socialist ideology which grows out of it. Canadian domestic struggles, from this point of view, are a northern version of the American struggle between big-propertied liberals on the right and *petit bourgeois* and working-class liberals on the left; the struggle goes on within a broad liberal consensus, and the voice of the tory or the socialist is not heard in the land. This pan–North American approach, with important qualifications, is adopted by Hartz and McRae in *The Founding of New Societies*. English Canada, like the United States, is a bourgeois fragment. No toryism in the past; therefore no socialism in the present.

But Hartz notes that the liberal society of English Canada has a "tory touch," that it is "etched with a tory streak coming out of the

American revolution."[6] The general process of bourgeois fragmentation is at work in both English Canada and the United States,
but there are differences between the two fragments which Hartz
describes as "delicate contrasts,"[7] McRae as "subtle" and "minor."[8]
Put in the most general way, the difference is that while the United
States is the perfect bourgeois fragment, the "archetype" of monolithic liberalism unsullied by tory or socialist deviations, English
Canada is a bourgeois fragment marred by non-liberal "imperfections"—a tory "touch," and therefore a socialist "touch." The way
Hartz and McRae would put it is that English Canada and the United
States are "essentially" alike; differences are to be found but they
are not "basic." Surely, however, whether one describes the differences as delicate, subtle, and minor or as basic, significant, and
important depends on one's perspective, on what one is looking for,
on what one wishes to stress. Hartz himself points out that "each of
the fragment cultures ... is 'unique'; a special blend of European
national tradition, historical timing,"[9] and so on. He is "concerned
with both general processes and the individuality of the settings in
which they evolve."[10] Nevertheless, his main focus is on the unifor-
mities, the parallel lines of development discovered in the comparative study of the United States and English Canada. This follows
quite naturally from his world historical perspective, his emphasis
on the three-way contrast of feudal, liberal, and radical fragments.
From this perspective, the differences between English Canada and
the United States are indeed "subtle" and "minor." But they are not
absolutely minor: they are minor only in relation to the much larger
differences among feudal, bourgeois, and radical fragments. If one
shifts one's perspective, and considers English Canada from within
the world of bourgeois fragments, the differences suddenly expand.
If one's concern is to understand English-Canadian society in its
uniqueness, that is, in contrast to American society, the differences
become not "delicate" but of absolutely crucial importance.

Hartz's pan–North Americanism is a matter of perspective: he
recognizes the un-American characteristics of English Canada, but
considers them minor in relation to the much larger differences
between bourgeois and other fragments. McRae's pan–North
Americanism, however, is not merely a matter of perspective, for he
seems to consider English Canada's un-American characteristics to
be absolutely "minor." For McRae, they are minor not only from the

world perspective, but from the narrower perspective which considers the bourgeois fragments alone.

Take as an example the central concern of this study—the differing weights of Canadian and American socialism. From the world perspective, the difference is perhaps "insignificant." As Hartz says, "there may be a Tory touch in English Canada, but the fragment, despite the C.C.F. of recent times, has not yielded a major socialist movement."[11] From the narrower perspective, however, the presence of a socialist movement in English Canada is remarkable. The danger of a pan–North American approach is that it tends either to ignore the relative strength of Canadian socialism or to dismiss it as a freak. It explains away, rather than explains, the strength of Canadian socialism. This is the approach adopted by McRae. Hartz is content to point out that English Canada does not have a *major* socialist movement. McRae's stress on English-Canadian–American similarity is so strong, however, that it is no longer a question of perspective but of error, for he attempts to boil a minor socialist movement away into *nothing*, and thence to conclude that there is no "basic" difference between the two bourgeois fragments.

The first step in his argument is to point out that socialism was "successful" only among Saskatchewan farmers, that it "failed" in the industrial areas. The CCF was therefore "basically" a movement of agrarian protest similar to American farmers' protests; its failure in urban Canada, parallel with the failure of socialism as a working class movement in the United States.[12] But words like "success" and "failure" are dangerous because they hide degrees of success and failure. The CCF failed to become a major party in urban Canada, but it succeeded in becoming a significant minor party—a success denied to the American socialists. This is a difference, not a similarity. Furthermore, McRae ignores the fact that in one urban Canadian province—British Columbia—the CCF *did* succeed in becoming a major party. And he ignores the ties between the Canadian labour movement and the CCF-NDP (surely a phenomenon worthy of explanation) by identifying the Canadian labour movement "in broad terms" with the American, as one "not significantly attracted to socialism."[13]

In the second step of the argument, the success of the CCF in Saskatchewan is explained away by dismissing Saskatchewan socialism as just another American agrarian protest. This is also an error, because unlike the American movements the Saskatchewan CCF was *socialist.* Confronting this hard fact, McRae attempts to explain it by noting that the Canadian prairies were generously sprinkled with British immigrants already familiar with Fabian socialism.[14] But is it not *significant* that immigrants who brought socialist ideas to the American liberal society had to abandon them in the process of Americanization, while those who brought these ideas to Canada built a major (provincial) party with them?

McRae's *coup de grace* to Canadian socialism is the observation that "with the formation of the NDP ... the last half realized elements of socialism ... seem to have been absorbed into the liberal tradition."[15] The error here is to ascribe the moderation or liberalization of "doctrinaire" socialism in Canada to a special *Canadian* circumstance—the (overestimated) power of liberalism when it is in fact a part of a general process of liberalization of socialism which is going on in every country of the West. The doctrine of the NDP is no more liberal than that of many other Western socialist parties.

The most important un-American characteristics of English Canada, all related to the presence of toryism, are: (a) the presence of tory ideology in the founding of English Canada by the Loyalists, and its continuing influence on English-Canadian political culture; (b) the persistent power of whiggery or right-wing liberalism in Canada (the Family Compacts) as contrasted with the rapid and easy victory of liberal democracy (Jefferson, Jackson) in the United States; (c) the ambivalent centrist character of left-wing liberalism in Canada as contrasted with the unambiguously leftist position of left-wing liberalism in the United States; (d) the presence of an influential and legitimate socialist movement in English Canada as contrasted with the illegitimacy and early death of American socialism; (e) the failure of English-Canadian liberalism to develop into the one true myth, the nationalist cult, and the parallel failure to exclude toryism and socialism as "un-Canadian"; in other words, the legitimacy of ideological diversity in English Canada.

From a world perspective, these imperfections in English Canada's bourgeois character may appear insignificant. From the point of view of one who is interested in understanding English Canada not merely as a bourgeois fragment, but as a unique bourgeois fragment, the imperfections are significant.

3. The Presence of Toryism and its Consequences

Many students have noted that English-Canadian society has been powerfully shaped by tory values that are "alien" to the American mind. The latest of these is Seymour Martin Lipset, who stresses the relative strength in Canada of the tory values of "ascription" and "elitism" (the tendency to defer to authority), and the relative weakness of the liberal values of "achievement" and "egalitarianism."[16] He points to such well-known features of Canadian history as the absence of a lawless, individualistic-egalitarian American frontier, the preference for Britain rather than the United States as a social model, and generally, the weaker emphasis on social equality, the greater acceptance by individuals of the facts of economic inequality, social stratification, and hierarchy. One tory touch in English Canada which is not noted by Lipset, but has been noted by many others (including McRae), is the far greater willingness of English-Canadian political and business elites to use the power of the state for the purpose of developing and controlling the economy.

Lipset accepts the notion, common among Canadian historians, that the Loyalist émigrés from the American revolution were a genuine tory element; that their expulsion from the United States to Canada accounts for the development of the United States in a liberal direction and of English Canada in a conservative direction. English Canada's "point of departure," in this view, is not liberal but conservative. The idea is that English Canada was founded by British tories whose purpose was to build a society which would be not liberal like the American but conservative like the British.

McRae correctly finds this notion to be an exaggeration of the difference between the Loyalists and the revolutionaries, between English Canada and the United States.[17] The picture of English Canada as a feudal fragment rather than a bourgeois fragment (which is what is implied by the Loyalist myth) is indeed a false one. McRae argues correctly that the Loyalists and the Family Compacts did not represent British toryism, but pre-revolutionary American whiggery with a "tory touch." But he errs in underestimating the significance of the "touch." He notes several factors differentiating the Loyalists, and subsequently English Canadians in general, from the revolutionary Americans: belief in monarchy and empire unity, greater stress on "law and order," revulsion against American populistic excesses, different frontier experiences, and so on. But he notes them only to dismiss them. "Basically," the Loyalist, and therefore the English Canadian, *is* the American liberal.[18] He is not "exactly" like the American,[19] McRae adds, but nevertheless he is the American. This is going too far. It is legitimate to point out that Canada is not a feudal (tory) fragment but a bourgeois (liberal) fragment touched with toryism. It is not legitimate to boil the tory touch away to nothing. If the tory touch was strong enough to produce all the un-American characteristics we are considering, it becomes misleading to identify the English Canadian with the American liberal.

Possibly McRae is pushed into his pan–North Americanism by his assumption that a *significant* tory presence in English Canada can be derived only from the discovery of a similar presence in pre-revolutionary America, and thus from an interpretation of the American revolution as a genuine social revolution directed against a significant tory presence in the United States[20]—which would indeed be a false interpretation. But no such interpretation is necessary. Let us put it this way: pre-revolutionary America was a liberal fragment with insignificant traces of toryism, extremely weak feudal survivals. But they were insignificant in the *American* setting; they were far overshadowed by the liberalism of that setting. The Revolution did not have to struggle against them, it swept them away easily and painlessly, leaving no trace of them in the American memory. But these traces of toryism were expelled into a *new* setting, and in this setting they were no longer insignificant. In this new setting, where there was no pre-established overpowering liberalism to force them into insignificance, they played a large part in shaping a new political culture, significantly different from the American. As Nelson wrote in *The American Tory*, "the Tories' organic conservatism represented a current of thought that failed to reappear in America after the revolution. A substantial part of the whole spectrum of European ... philosophy seemed to slip outside the American perspective."[21] But it *reappeared* in Canada. Here the sway of liberalism has proved to be not total, but considerably mitigated by a tory presence initially and a socialist presence subsequently. There is no need, in order to support this view, to return to the discredited interpretation of the American revolution as a social revolution.

One Canadian-American difference strikes both Hartz and McRae with particular force: the persistent power of Family Compact whiggery in Canada as contrasted with the rapid and easy victories of Jeffersonian and Jacksonian democracy in the United States. In the United States the Federalist-Whigs are easily defeated, and the democratization of political life occurs swiftly and thoroughly. Later the Whigs give up their antipathy to the people, adopt the rhetoric of democracy and egalitarianism, and return to power as Republicans through adroit appeals to the Horatio Alger dream, the "capitalist lust" of the American little man. By contrast, in Canada, the Family Compacts were able to maintain ascendancy and delay the coming of democracy because of the tory touch "inherited in part from American Loyalism, which restrained egalitarian feeling in Canada."[22] McRae notes that even with the coming of responsible government, "there was no complete repudiation of the Compacts and what they stood for.... Something of the old order" was preserved even after its disappearance.[23]

Despite the importance which Hartz and McRae ascribe to the persistence of whiggery as one of the factors which differentiate English Canada from the United States, the most significant aspect of the phenomenon from their point of view is that it ultimately disappeared.[24] The American and English-Canadian bourgeois fragments, though separated at the beginning by the power of the Canadian whigs, ultimately move together, close to the point of almost exact similarity. From my point of view, however, the early power of whiggery serves to emphasize the importance of the tory touch in English Canada. After all, whiggery "ultimately" fell not only in the United States and Canada, but everywhere. The significant contrast is not between situations in which it falls and those in which it does not fall, but between situations in which it falls quickly and those in which it persists.

In the United States, the masses could not be swayed by the Federalist-Whig appeals to anti-egalitarian sentiments. In Canada the masses *were* swayed by these appeals; the role of the Compacts was to save "the colonial masses from the spectre of republicanism and democracy."[25] What accounts for this is the tory presence in English-Canadian political culture—the "greater acceptance of limitation, of hierarchical patterns."[26] As McRae admits, this outlook did not disappear with the defeat of the Compacts, and the character of Canadian right-wing liberalism continued to be distinctive after the coming of democracy. The American Whigs returned to power as Republicans by encouraging the dream of the little man to be equal with the big man; the notions of capitalism and democracy had to be thoroughly merged. In Canada there was "greater acceptance of hierarchical patterns"; the Alger dream was much weaker in the masses, so there was no need to harness it in order to keep the right wing in the saddle.

The next step in tracing the development of the English-Canadian political culture must be to take account of the tremendous waves of British immigration which soon engulfed the original American Loyalist fragment. Here McRae's concern is to argue that the liberal ideology of the Loyalist fragment had already "frozen, congealed at the point of origin"; that the national ethos had already been fully formed (an American liberalism not "exactly" like American liberalism); that the later waves of immigration played no part in the formation of English-Canadian political culture; that they found an established culture, and were impelled to acclimatize to it.[27] It is important for McRae to prove this point, for while there is room for the argument that the Loyalists were American whigs with a tory touch, the later British immigrants had undoubtedly been heavily infected with non-liberal ideas, and these ideas were undoubtedly in their heads as they settled in Canada. The political culture of a new nation is not necessarily fixed at the point of origin or departure; the founding of a new nation can go on for generations. If the later waves of immigration arrived before the point *of congealment* of the political culture, they must have participated actively in the process of culture formation. If this be so, the picture of English Canada as an almost exactly American liberal society becomes very difficult to defend. For *even if* it be granted that the Loyalists were (almost exactly) American liberals, it is clear that later participants in the formation of the culture were not.

Between 1815 and 1850 almost one million Britons emigrated to Canada. The population of English Canada doubled in twenty years and quadrupled in forty. The population of Ontario increased tenfold in the same period—from about 95,000 in 1814 to about 950,000 in 1851.[28] McRae himself admits that "it would be inaccurate to say that this wave of migration was absorbed into the original fragment: an influx of these proportions does not permit of simple assimilation."[29]

Nevertheless, he concludes that "despite the flood tide of immigration ... the original liberal inheritance of English Canada survived and dominated."[30] According to McRae, the universal urge to own property and the classlessness of North American society had such a powerful impact on the immigrants that they simply "forgot their old notions of social hierarchy" and became American liberals.[31] Surely this argument is an instance of stretching the facts in order to fit a theory! Do people simply "forget" their old notions so quickly and so completely? Is it not possible that the immigrants, while they were no doubt considerably liberalized by their new environment, also brought to it non-liberal ideas which entered into the political culture mix, and which perhaps even reinforced the non-liberal elements present in the original fragment? If the million immigrants had come from the United States rather than Britain, would English Canada not be "significantly" different today?

The difficulty in applying the Hartzian approach to English Canada is that although the point of departure is reasonably clear, it is difficult to put one's finger on the point of congealment. Perhaps it was the Loyalist period; perhaps it was close to the mid-century mark; there are grounds for arguing that it was in the more recent past. But the important point is this: no matter where the point of congealment is located in time, the tory streak is present before the solidification of the political culture, and it is strong *enough* to produce significant "imperfections," or non-liberal, un-American attributes of English-Canadian society.

My own opinion is that the point of congealment came later than the Loyalists. The United States broke from Britain early, and the break was complete. Adam Smith and Tom Paine were among the last Britons who were spiritual founding fathers of the United States. Anything British, if it is of later than eighteenth century vintage, is un-American. The American mind long ago cut its ties with Britain and began to develop on its own. When did Canada break from Britain? When did the Canadian mind begin to develop on its own? Not very long ago most Canadians described themselves as followers of the "British way of life," and many railed against egalitarian ideas from south of the border as "alien." Nineteenth-century British ideologists are among the spiritual founding fathers of Canada. In the United States they are alien, though we may make an exception for Herbert Spencer.

The indeterminate location of the point of congealment makes it difficult to account in any *precise* way for the presence of socialism in the English-Canadian political culture mix, though the presence itself is indisputable. If the point of congealment came *before* the arrival of the first radical or socialist-minded immigrants, the presence of socialism must be ascribed primarily to the earlier presence of toryism. Since toryism is a significant part of the political culture, at least part of the leftist reaction against it will sooner or later be expressed in its own terms, that is, in terms of *class* interests and the good of the community as a corporate entity (socialism) rather than in terms of the individual and his vicissitudes in the competitive pursuit of happiness (liberalism). If the point of congealment is very early, socialism appears at a later point not primarily because it is imported by British immigrants, but because it is contained as a potential in the original political culture. The immigrants then find that they do not have to give it up—that it is not un-Canadian—because it "fits" to a certain extent with the tory ideas already present. If the point of congealment is very late, the presence of socialism must be explained as a result of *both* the presence of toryism and the introduction of socialism into the cultural mix before congealment. The immigrant retains his socialism not only because it "fits" but also because nothing really *has* to fit. He finds that his socialism is not un-Canadian partly because "Canadian" has not yet been defined.

Canadian liberals cannot be expected to wax enthusiastic about the non-liberal traits of their country. They are likely to condemn the tory touch as anachronistic, stifling, undemocratic, out of tune with the essentially American ("free," "classless") spirit of English Canada. They dismiss the socialist touch as an "old-fashioned" protest, no longer necessary (if it ever was) in this best (liberal) of all possible worlds in which the "end of ideology" has been achieved. The secret dream of the Canadian liberal is the removal of English Canada's "imperfections"—in other words, the total assimilation of English Canada into the larger North American culture. But there is a flaw in this dream which might give pause even to the liberal. Hartz places special emphasis on one very unappetizing characteristic of the new societies—intolerance—which is strikingly absent in English Canada. Because the new societies other than Canada are unfamiliar with legitimate ideological diversity, they are unable to accept it and deal with it in a rational manner, either internally or on the level of international relations.

The European nation has an "identity which transcends any ideologist and a mechanism in which each plays only a part."[32] Neither the tory, nor the liberal, nor the socialist, has a monopoly of the expression of the "spirit" of the nation. But the new societies, the fragments, contain only one of the ideologies of Europe; they are one-myth cultures. In the new setting, freed from its historic enemies past and future, ideology transforms itself into nationalism. It claims to be a moral absolute, "the great spirit of a nation."[33] In the United States, liberalism becomes "Americanism"; a political philosophy becomes a civil religion, a nationalist cult. The American attachment to Locke is "absolutist and irrational."[34] Democratic capitalism is the American way of life; to oppose it is to be un-American.

To be an American is to be a bourgeois liberal. To be a French Canadian is to be a pre-Enlightenment Catholic; to be an Australian is to be a prisoner of the radical myth of "mateship"; to be a Boer is to be a pre-Enlightenment bourgeois Calvinist. The fragments escape the need for philosophy, for thought about values, for "where perspectives shrink to a single value, and that value becomes the universe, how can value itself be considered?"[35] The fragment demands solidarity. Ideologies which diverge from the national myth make no impact; they are not understood, and their proponents are not granted legitimacy. They are denounced as aliens, and treated as aliens, because they *are* aliens. The fragments cannot understand or deal with the fact that *all* men are *not* bourgeois Americans, or radical Australians, or Catholic French Canadians, or Calvinist South Africans. They cannot make peace with the loss of ideological certainty.

The specific weakness of the United States is its "inability to understand the appeal of socialism" to the third world.[36] Because the United States has "buried" the memory of the organic medieval community "beneath new liberal absolutisms and nationalisms"[37] it cannot understand that the appeal of socialism to nations with a predominantly non-liberal past (including French Canada) consists precisely in the promise of "continuing the corporate ethos in the very process" of modernization.[38] The American reacts with isolationism, messianism, and hysteria.

English Canada, because it is the most "imperfect" of the fragments, is not a one-myth culture. In English Canada ideological diversity has not been buried beneath an absolutist liberal nationalism. Here Locke is not the one true god; he must tolerate lesser tory and socialist deities at his side. The result is that English Canada does not direct an uncomprehending intolerance at heterodoxy, either within its borders or beyond them. (What a "backlash" Parti-Pris or PSQ-type separatists would be getting if Quebec were in the United States!) In English Canada it has been possible to consider values without arousing the all-silencing cry of treason. Hartz observes that "if history had chosen English Canada for the American role" of directing the Western response to the world revolution, "the international scene would probably have witnessed less McCarthyite hysteria, less Wilsonian messianism."[39]

Americanizing liberals might consider that the Pearsonian rationality and calmness which Canada displays on the world stage—the "mediating" and "peace-keeping" role of which Canadians are so proud—is related to the un-American (tory and socialist) characteristics which they consider to be unnecessary imperfections in English-Canadian wholeness. The tolerance of English-Canadian domestic politics is also linked with the presence of these imperfections. If the price of Americanization is the surrender of legitimate ideological diversity, even the liberal might think twice before paying it.

McRae comes close to qualifying his pan–North Americanism out of existence by admitting at one point that "it would be a mistake to underrate the emotional attachment that many Canadians ... still feel for British institutions.... English Canadians ... cap the foundations of their North American liberal social ethos with a superstructure embodying elements of the wider British political heritage."[40] But the pan-North Americanism wins in the end; the *foundations* of English Canada are American liberal, only the *superstructure* is British. My argument is essentially that non-liberal British elements have entered into English-Canadian society *together* with American liberal elements at the foundations. The fact is that Canada has been greatly influenced by both the United States and Britain. This is not to *deny* that liberalism is the dominant element in the English-Canadian political culture; it is to stress that it is not the sole element, that it is accompanied by vital and legitimate streams of toryism and socialism which have as close a relation to English Canada's "essence" or "foundations" as does liberalism. English Canada's "essence" is both liberal and non-liberal. Neither the British nor the American elements can be explained away as "superstructural" excrescences.

4. Un-American Aspects of Canadian Conservatism

So far, I have been discussing the presence of toryism in Canada without referring to the Conservative party. This party can be seen as a party of right-wing or business liberalism, but such an interpretation would be far from the whole truth; the Canadian Conservative party, like the British Conservative party and unlike the Republican party, is not monolithically liberal. If there is a touch of toryism in English Canada, its primary carrier has been the Conservative party. It would not be correct to say that toryism is *the* ideology of the party, or even that some Conservatives are tories. These statements would not be true even of the British Conservative party. The primary component of the ideology of business-oriented parties is liberalism; but there are powerful traces of the old pre-liberal outlook in the British Conservative party,[41] and less powerful but still perceptible traces of it in the Canadian party. A Republican is always a liberal. A Conservative may be at one moment a liberal, at the next moment a tory, and is usually something of both.

If it is true that the Canadian Conservatives can be seen from some angles as right-wing liberals, it is also true that figures such as R.B. Bennett, Arthur Meighen, and George Drew cannot be understood simply as Canadian versions of William McKinley, Herbert Hoover, and Robert Taft. Canadian Conservatives have something British about them that American Republicans do not. It is not simply their emphasis on loyalty to the crown and to the British connection, but a touch of the authentic tory aura—traditionalism, elitism, the strong state, and so on. The Canadian Conservatives lack the American aura of rugged individualism. Theirs is not the characteristically American conservatism which conserves only *liberal* values.[42]

It is possible to perceive in Canadian conservatism not only the elements of business liberalism and orthodox toryism, but also an element of "tory democracy"—the paternalistic concern for the "condition of the people," and the emphasis on the tory party as their champion—which, in Britain, was expressed by such figures as Disraeli and Lord Randolph Churchill. John A. Macdonald's approach to the emergent Canadian working class was in some respects similar to that of Disraeli. Later Conservatives acquired the image of arch reactionaries and arch enemies of the workers, but let us not forget that "Iron Heel" Bennett was also the Bennett of the Canadian New Deal.

The question arises: why is it that in Canada the *Conservative* leader proposes a New Deal? Why is it that the Canadian counterpart of Hoover apes *Roosevelt*? This phenomenon is usually interpreted as sheer historical accident, a product of Bennett's desperation and opportunism. But the answer may be that Bennett was not Hoover. Even in his "orthodox" days Bennett's views on the state's role in the economy were far from similar to Hoover's; Bennett's attitude was that of Canadian, not American, conservatism. Once this is recognized, it is possible to entertain the suggestion that Bennett's sudden radicalism, his sudden concern for the people, may not have been mere opportunism. It may have been a manifestation, a sudden activation under pressure, of a latent tory-democratic streak. Let it be noted also that the depression produced two Conservative splinter parties, both with "radical" welfare state programmes, and both led by former subordinates of Bennett: H.H. Stevens' Reconstruction party and W.D. Herridge's New Democracy.

The Bennett New Deal is only the most extreme instance of what is usually considered to be an accident or an aberration—the occasional manifestation of "radicalism" or "leftism" by otherwise orthodox Conservative leaders in the face of opposition from their "followers" in the business community. Meighen, for example, was constantly embroiled with the "Montreal interests" who objected to his railway policies. On one occasion he received a note of congratulation from William Irvine: "The man who dares to offend the Montreal interests is the sort of man that the people are going to vote for."[43] This same Meighen expressed on certain occasions, particularly after his retirement, an antagonism to big government and creeping socialism that would have warmed the heart of Robert Taft; but he combined his business liberalism with gloomy musings about the evil of universal suffrage[44]—musings which Taft would have rejected as un-American. Meighen is far easier to understand from a British than from an American perspective, for he combined, in different proportions at different times, attitudes deriving from all three Conservative ideological streams: right-wing liberalism, orthodox toryism, and tory democracy.

The Western or agrarian Conservatives of the contemporary period, John Diefenbaker and Alvin Hamilton, who are usually dismissed as "prairie radicals" of the American type, might represent not only anti-Bay Street agrarianism but *also* the same type of tory democracy which was expressed before their time by orthodox business-sponsored Conservatives like Meighen and Bennett. The populism (anti-elitism) of Diefenbaker and Hamilton is a genuinely foreign element in Canadian conservatism, but their stress on the Tory party as champion of the people and their advocacy of welfare state policies are in the tory democratic tradition. Their attitudes to the monarchy, the British connection, and the danger of American domination are entirely orthodox Conservative attitudes. Diefenbaker Conservatism is therefore to be understood not simply as a Western populist phenomenon, but as an odd *combination* of traditional Conservative views with attitudes absorbed from the Western Progressive tradition.

Another aberration which may be worthy of investigation is the Canadian phenomenon of the red tory. At the simplest level, he is a Conservative who prefers the CCF-NDP to the Liberals, or a socialist who prefers the Conservatives to the Liberals, without really knowing why. At a higher level, he is a conscious ideological Conservative with some "odd" socialist notions (W.L. Morton) or a conscious ideological socialist with some "odd" tory notions (Eugene Forsey). The very suggestion that such affinities might exist between Republicans and Socialists in the United States is ludicrous enough to make some kind of a point.

Red toryism is, of course, one of the results of the relationship between toryism and socialism which has already been elucidated. The tory and socialist minds have some crucial assumptions, orientations, and values in common, so that from certain angles they may appear not as enemies, but as two different expressions of the same basic ideological outlook. Thus, at the very highest level, the red tory is a philosopher who combines elements of socialism and toryism so thoroughly in a single integrated *Weltanschauung* that it is impossible to say that he is a proponent of either one as *against* the other. Such a red tory is George Grant, who has associations with both the conservative party and the NDP, and who has recently published a book which defends Diefenbaker, laments the death of "true" British conservatism in Canada, attacks the Liberals as individualists and Americanizers, and defines socialism as a variant of conservatism (each "protects the public good against private freedom").45

5. The Character of Canadian Socialism

Canadian socialism is un-American in two distinct ways. It is un-American in the sense that it is a significant and legitimate political force in Canada, insignificant and alien in the United States. But Canadian socialism is also un-American in the sense that it does not speak the same language as American socialism. In Canada, socialism is British, non-Marxist, and worldly; in the United States it is German, Marxist, and other-worldly.

I have argued that the socialist ideas of British immigrants to Canada were not sloughed off because they "fit" with a political culture which already contained non-liberal components, and probably also because they were introduced into the political culture mix before the point of congealment. Thus socialism was not alien here. But it was not alien in yet another way; it was not borne by foreigners. The personnel and the ideology of the Canadian Labour and socialist movements have been primarily British. Many of those who built these movements were British immigrants with past experience in the British labour movement; many others were Canadian-born children of such immigrants. And in British North America, Britons could not be treated as foreigners.

When socialism was brought to the United States, it found itself in an ideological environment in which it could not survive because Lockean individualism had long since achieved the status of a national religion; the political culture had already congealed, and socialism did not fit. American socialism was alien not only in this ideological sense, but in the ethnic sense as well; it was borne by foreigners from Germany and other continental European countries. These foreigners sloughed off their socialist ideas not simply because such ideas did not "fit" ideologically, but because as foreigners they were going through a general process of Americanization; socialism was only one of many ethnically alien characteristics which had to be abandoned. The immigrant's ideological change was only one incident among many others in the general process of changing his entire way of life. According to David Saposs, "the factor that contributed most tellingly to the decline of the socialist movement was that its chief following, the immigrant workers, ... had become Americanized."[46]

A British socialist immigrant to Canada had a far different experience. The British immigrant was not an "alien" in British North America. The English-Canadian culture not only granted legitimacy to his political ideas and absorbed them into its wholeness; it absorbed him as a person into the English-Canadian community, with relatively little strain, without demanding that he change his entire way of life before being granted full citizenship. He was acceptable to begin with, by virtue of being British. It is impossible to understand the differences between American and Canadian socialism without taking into account this immense difference between the ethnic contexts of socialism in the two countries.

The ethnic handicap of American socialism consisted not only in the fact that its personnel was heavily European. Equally important was the fact that it was a *brand* of socialism—Marxism—which found survival difficult not only in the United States but in all English-speaking countries. Marx has not found the going easy in the United States; but neither has he found the going easy in Britain, Canada, Australia, or New Zealand. The socialism of the United States, the socialism of De Leon, Berger, Hillquit, and Debs, is predominantly Marxist and doctrinaire, because it is European. The socialism of English Canada, the socialism of Simpson, Woodsworth, and Coldwell, is predominantly Protestant, labourist, and Fabian, because it is British.

The prevalence of doctrinaire Marxism helps to explain the sectarianism of the American Socialist party. The distinctive quality of a sect is its "other-worldliness." It rejects the existing scheme of things entirely; its energies are directed not to devising stratagems with which to lure the electorate, but to elaborating its utopian theory. Daniel Bell describes the American Socialist party as one "whose main preoccupation has been the refinement of 'theory' at the cost, even, of interminable factional divisions."[47] "It has never, even for a single year, been without some issue which threatened to split the party."[48] For Bell, the failure of American socialism is its failure to make the transition from sect to party, to concern itself with popular issues rather than theoretical disputes. The unfortunate decisions made by the party—especially the decisions to oppose the two world wars—were a result of this sectarianism, this refusal to compromise with the world.

The CCF has not been without its otherworldly tendencies; there have been doctrinal disagreements, and the party has always had a left wing interested more in "socialist education" than in practical political work. But this left wing has been a constantly declining minority. The party has expelled individuals and small groups—mostly Communists and Trotskyites—but it has never split. Its life has never been threatened by disagreement over doctrinal matters. It is no more preoccupied with theory than the British Labour party. It sees itself, and is seen by the public, not as a coterie of ideologists but as a party like the others, second to none in its avidity for office. If it has been attacked from the right for socialist "utopianism" and "impracticality," it has also been attacked from the right for abandoning the "true" socialist faith in an unprincipled drive for power.

The contrast between American Marxist socialism and Canadian non-Marxist socialism, and the weakness of Marxism not only in America but in all other English speaking countries, at first led me to think that Hartz's "single factor" explanation of the illegitimacy of American socialism might be overdone. This question arose: was it socialism *per se* that could not live in the United States, or only Marxist socialism? What if American socialism had looked to Britain rather than Germany, if it had been "empirical" rather than doctrinaire Marxist? The answer that suggested itself was that if American socialism had not been handicapped by its Marxian character—if it had been handicapped only by the fact that America had not known toryism and therefore would not listen to socialism—it might have been able to live a little longer and might not have died such a horrible death.

What this line of reasoning ignored was the fact that there *was* an impact in America of British socialist thought which was, however, even weaker than the Marxist impact. Why, in America, an English-speaking country, should the British influence on socialism have been so much weaker than the German? Precisely because the "single factor" explanation is not overdone. Socialism could not attain any degree of strength in America, for the Hartzian reason, except for a short while as a socialism *in* America but not *of* America, that is to say, except among unassimilated foreign groups. There *was* an unassimilated continental European group;

there was never an unassimilated British group. The British influence was therefore much weaker than the Marxist.

At first I thought that since Marxism fails not only in the United States but in all English-speaking countries, *peculiarly American* characteristics cannot be the explanation of its failure in the United States. This is true; the peculiarly American characteristics account for the failure of *all* socialisms, *even* English-speaking socialism, in the United States. The failure of Marxian socialism is less complete and less rapid than the failure of the others precisely because of the peculiar American cultural characteristics which mean doom for all socialisms *except* those sustained by immigrants prior to their Americanization. The strength of Marx relative to other socialisms in America is a confirmation of the Hartzian hypothesis.

6. Canadian Liberalism: The Triumphant Centre

Canadian Conservatives are not American Republicans; Canadian socialists are not American socialists; Canadian Liberals are not American liberal Democrats.

The un-American elements in English Canada's political culture are most evident in Canadian conservatism and socialism. But Canadian liberalism has British colour too. The liberalism of Canada's Liberal party should not be identified with the liberalism of the American Democratic party. In many respects they stand in sharp contrast to one another.

The three components of the English-Canadian political culture have not developed in isolation from one another; each has developed in interaction with the others. Our toryism and our socialism have been moderated by liberalism. But by the same token, our liberalism has been rendered "impure," in American terms, through its contacts with toryism and socialism. If English-Canadian liberalism is less individualistic, less ardently populistic-democratic, more inclined to state intervention in the economy, and more tolerant of "feudal survivals" such as monarchy, this is due to the uninterrupted influence of toryism upon liberalism, an influence wielded in and through the conflict between the two. If English-Canadian liberalism has tended since the depression to merge at its leftist edge with the democratic socialism of the CCF-NDP, this is due to the influence which socialism has exerted upon liberalism, in and through the conflict between them. The key to understanding the Liberal party in Canada is to see it as a *centre* party, with *influential* enemies on both right and left.

Hartz's comparison of the Liberal Reform movements of the United States and Europe casts light on the differences between American and English-Canadian liberalism. Hartz defines Liberal Reform as the movement "which emerged toward the end of the nineteenth century to adapt classical liberalism to the purposes of small propertied interests and the labouring class and at the same time which rejected socialism."49 The fact that European Liberal Reform was confronted with a significant socialist challenge meant (a) that liberals, influenced by socialist theory, tried to "transcend the earlier individualism" and recognized "the need for collective action to solve the class problem,"50 and (b) that liberals, faced with powerful enemies on both the left and the right, presented an ambivalent conservative-radical image; they attacked the tories and the *status quo*, but they also defended the *status quo* from its socialist enemies.

American liberals, impervious to the socialist challenge and therefore unaffected by socialist ideas, remained "enslaved" to individualism. "Even in its midnight dreams" American Liberal Reform "ruled out the concepts of socialism."51 Its goal was not to reform modern capitalism by abandoning Lockean individualism and moving in the direction of socialism, but, by smashing or controlling trusts and bosses, to restore the old individualistic way of life. It struggled to retain individualism and yet to recognize the new problems of a modern industrial society: "An agonized reluctance ... characterized the outlook of Progressivism toward the positive legislation advanced everywhere by Western Liberal Reform."52 Yet American Liberal Reform had an unambiguous radical image; its only enemies were the big-propertied liberals of the right. American Liberal Reformers were thus "saved from a defensive appearance, were able to emerge as pure crusaders."53 If they had had to answer socialist attacks, they would have appeared much less radical.

The relevance of this analysis for the English-Canadian situation is apparent. In English Canada Liberal Reform, represented by King's Liberal party, has had to face the socialist challenge. Under socialist influence, it abandoned its early devotion to "the lofty principles of Gladstone, the sound economics of Adam Smith, and the glories of laissez faire."54 King's *Industry and Humanity* and the Liberal platform of 1919 mark the transition of English-Canadian federalism from the old individualism to the new Liberal Reform.55

King's Liberal Reform, since it had to answer attacks from the left as well as from the right, projected a notoriously ambivalent conservative-radical image:

> Truly he will be remembered
> Wherever men honor ingenuity
> Ambiguity, inactivity, and political longevity.

When he faced Bennett and Meighen, King was the radical warrior, the champion of the little people against the interests. When he turned to face Woodsworth and Coldwell, he was the cautious conservative, the protector of the *status quo*. He

> ... never let his on the one hand
> Know what his on the other hand was doing.56

Roosevelt's New Deal involved "departures from the liberal faith of a very substantive kind."57 Unlike the earlier Progressivism it did not shun state action. But neither did it consciously abandon Locke. Since Roosevelt did not have to face the socialist challenge, he did not have to "spell out his liberal premises. He did not have to spell out any real philosophy at all. His 'radicalism' could consist of what he called 'bold and persistent experimentation' which of course meant nothing in terms of large social faiths and was indeed perfectly compatible with Americanism."58 The Republican opposition tried to alert the American people to the fact that Roosevelt's experiments were indeed socialistic and un-American, but the American people did not listen. They were convinced by Roosevelt's plea that his legislative schemes were "mere technical gadgetry,"59 that questions of political philosophy were not relevant. Roosevelt and the American people, by closing their eyes to the philosophical implications of the New Deal, had their cake and ate it too; they subverted Lockean individualism in fact, but they held on to their Americanism, their Lockean individualist faith.

Hartz points out that this "pragmatism" of the New Deal enabled it to go farther, to get more things done, than European Liberal

Reform. "The free-wheeling inventiveness typified by the TVA, the NRA, the WPA, the SEC"[60] was nowhere to be found in Europe. Defending itself against socialism, European Liberal Reform could not submerge questions of theory; it had to justify innovations on the basis of a revised liberal ideology; it had to stop short of socialism openly. The New Deal, since it was not threatened by socialism, could ignore theory; it "did not need to stop short of Marx openly"; hence it could accomplish more than European Liberal Reform.

King had to face the socialist challenge. He did so in the manner of European Liberal Reform. No need to worry about abandoning individualism; Locke was not Canada's national god; like European liberalism, Canadian liberalism had been revised. The similarity of socialism and Liberal Reform could be acknowledged; indeed it could be emphasized and used to attract the socialist vote. At the same time, King had to answer the arguments of socialism, and in doing so he had to spell out his liberalism. He had to stop short of socialism openly.[61] Social reform, yes; extension of public ownership, yes; the welfare state, yes; increased state control of the economy, yes; but not too much. Not socialism. The result was that King, like the European liberals, could not go as far as Roosevelt.

"What makes the New Deal 'radical'," says Hartz, "is the smothering by the American Lockian faith of the socialist challenge to it." Roosevelt did not need to reply to Norman Thomas as the European liberals had to reply to their socialists. Roosevelt therefore did not have to "spell out his liberal premises and hence create the atmosphere of indecision which this necessarily involved."[62] Atmosphere of indecision: Is this not the characteristic atmosphere of King Liberalism?

Hartz asks: "What would Roosevelt have said had he ... been compelled to take Thomas ... seriously?"[63] and shows that Roosevelt would have been forced to defend private property against nationalization, to attack "bureaucracy" and the all-powerful state, to criticize "utopianism" and "impracticability" in politics. He would have had to qualify his radicalism by an attack on the larger radicalism which faced him to the left.

In other words, instead of being "radical," he would be half radical and half conservative, which is precisely the position that the Liberal Reformers of Europe were compelled to occupy. Instead of enlisting the vigorous passions of youth, he might easily be described as a tired man who could not make up his mind; a liberal who tried to break with Adam Smith but could not really do so.[64]

What Roosevelt *would* have said if he had answered Norman Thomas is what King *did* say in answering Woodsworth and Coldwell. Like the Europeans, and unlike Roosevelt, he had to defend private property, he had to attack excessive reliance on the state, he had to criticize socialism as "impracticality" and "utopianism." Half radical and half conservative—a tired man who could not make up his mind—is this not the living image of Mackenzie King?

"In America, instead of being a champion of property, Roosevelt became the big antagonist of it; his liberalism was blocked by his radicalism."[65] In Canada, since King had to worry not only about Bennett and Meighen and Drew, but also about Woodsworth and Coldwell and Douglas, King had to embark upon a defence of private property. *He* was no traitor to his class. Instead of becoming the antagonist of property, he became its champion; his radicalism was blocked by his liberalism.

An emphasis on the solidarity of the nation as against divisive "class parties" of right and left was "of the very essence of the Reformist Liberal position in Europe." "Who," asks Hartz, "would think of Roosevelt as a philosopher of class solidarity?"[66] Yet that is precisely what Roosevelt would have been if he had had to respond to a socialist presence in the American political culture. And that is precisely what King was in fact in Canada. His party was "the party of national unity." One of the most repeated charges against the CCF was that it was a divisive "class party"; the purpose of the Liberal party, on the other hand, was to preserve the solidarity of the Canadian people—the solidarity of its classes as well as the solidarity of French and English.

Hartz sums up Roosevelt in these words: "What emerges then ... is a liberal self that is lost from sight: a faith in property, a belief in class unity, a suspicion of too much state power, a hostility to the utopian mood, all of which were blacked out by the weakness of the socialist challenge."[67] King's liberal self was not lost from sight, for the socialist challenge was stronger in Canada than in the United States.

The Liberal party has continued to speak the language of King: ambiguous and ambivalent, presenting first its radical face and then its conservative face, urging reform and warning against hasty, ill-considered change, calling for increased state responsibility but stopping short of socialism openly, speaking for the common people but preaching the solidarity of classes.[68]

In the United States, the liberal Democrats are on the left. There is no doubt about that. In Canada, the Liberals are a party of the centre, appearing at times leftist and at times rightist. As such, they are much closer to European, especially British, Liberal Reform than to the American New Deal type of liberalism.

In the United States, the liberal Democrats are the party of organized labour. The new men of power, the labour leaders, have arrived politically; their vehicle is the Democratic party. In English Canada, if the labour leaders have arrived politically, they have done so in the CCF-NDP. They are nowhere to be found in the Liberal party. The rank and file, in the United States, are predominantly Democrats; in Canada at least a quarter are New Democrats, and the remainder show only a relatively slight, and by no means consistent, preference for the Liberals as against the Conservatives.

In the United States, left-wing "liberalism," as opposed to right wing "liberalism," has always meant opposition to the domination of American life by big business, and has expressed itself in and through the Democratic party; the party of business is the Republican party. In Canada, business is close to both the Conservatives and the Liberals. The business community donates to the campaign funds of both and is represented in the leadership circles of both.

A comparison of two election broadsides, one by an American liberal Democrat and one by a Canadian Liberal, is most instructive. *Kennedy or Nixon*, by Arthur Schlesinger Jr., is suffused with the spirit of the New Deal. Liberalism is defined as "opposition to control of the government by the most powerful group in the community."[69] The Democratic party is described as the party which unites all other groups, including individual "nonconformist businessmen" who have transcended their class interests, for the struggle against the forces of business orthodoxy, against the *status quo*. The Republican party is labelled as the party of the orthodox business "establishment."[70] The book closes with an attack on bankers, owners of television stations, Wall Street brokers, General Motors, Du Pont, and the American Medical Association.

The Liberal Party, by J.W. Pickersgill, is suffused with the ambivalent, centrist, radical-conservative spirit of Mackenzie King. The Liberal party is for judicious reform, against unreasoning attachment to the *status quo,* but of course it is also opposed to headstrong and irreverent socialism. Schlesinger does not hesitate to relate liberalism to the conflicting interests of specific social forces. Pickersgill defines liberalism in vague, inoffensive generalities: "The first principle of Liberalism is that the state ... exist[s] to serve man, and not man to serve the state. The second principle of Liberalism is that the family is the foundation of human society and that it is the duty of all governments to promote the welfare of the family and the sanctity of the home."[71]

The Liberal party in Canada does not represent the opposition of society to domination by organized business. It claims to be based on no particular groups, but on *all.* It is not against any particular group; it is for *all.* The idea that there is any real conflict between groups is dismissed, and the very terms "right" and "left" are rejected: "The terms 'right' and 'left' belong to those who regard politics as a class struggle.... The Liberal view is that true political progress is marked by ... the reconciliation of classes, and the promotion of the general interest above all particular interests."...[72]

NOTES

1 New York: Harcourt, Brace (Toronto: Longmans), 1955; hereafter cited as *Liberal Tradition.*

2 New York: Harcourt, Brace and World (Toronto: Longmans, 1964); hereafter cited as *New Societies.*

3 Hartz, *New Societies,* 3.

4 *Ibid.,* 25.

5 *Ibid.,* 7.

6 *Ibid.,* 34.

7 *Ibid.,* 71.

8 Kenneth McRae, "The Structure of Canadian History," in *ibid.,* 239.

9 *Ibid.,* 72.

10 *Ibid.,* 34.

11 *Ibid.*

12 *Ibid.,* 269–70.

13 *Ibid.,* 269.

14 *Ibid.*

15 *Ibid.,* 273.

16 In *The First New Nation* (New York, 1963), esp. chap. 7.

17 *New Societies,* 235–40.

18 *Ibid.,* 234.

19 *Ibid.,* 238.

20 *Ibid.*, 235.

21 William Nelson, *The American Tory* (New York, 1961), 189–90.

22 Hartz, *New Societies*, 91.

23 *Ibid.*, 244.

24 *Ibid.*, 37.

25 *Ibid.*, 243.

26 Lipset, *The New First Nation*, 251.

27 *New Societies*, 244–7.

28 *Ibid.*, 245.

29 *Ibid.*, 246.

30 *Ibid.*, 247.

31 *Ibid.*, 246.

32 *Ibid.*, 15.

33 *Ibid.*, 10.

34 Hartz, *Liberal Tradition*, 11.

35 Hartz, *New Societies*, 23.

36 *Ibid.*, 119.

37 *Ibid.*, 35.

38 *Ibid.*, 119.

39 *Ibid.*, 120.

40 *Ibid.*, 267.

41 See Samuel Beer, *British Politics in the Collectivist Age* (New York, 1965), esp. chaps. 3 and 9–13.

42 Historic toryism finds expression today in the writings of Conservatives like W.L. Morton, who describes America as a liberal society integrated from below, by a *covenant* of brothers, and Canada as a monarchial society held together at the top, integrated by loyalty to the Crown. (*The Canadian Identity* [Toronto, 1961], 99–114.) In another of his writings Morton stresses the tory belief in personal leadership, in loyalty to leaders and readiness to let them govern. ("Canadian Conservatism Now," in Paul Fox, ed., *Politics: Canada* [Toronto, 1962], 287.) He takes an organic view of society, stresses the values of authority and tradition, rejects the liberal values of individualism and egalitarianism. He calls for the rejection of the "dangerous and improper idea of the electoral mandate" (*ibid.*, 289). He calls for the "creation of a Canadian system of honours" (*ibid.*, 290). And he exhorts Canadian Conservatives frankly and loyally to accept the welfare state, since "laissez faire and rugged individualism" are foreign to "conservative principles" (*ibid.*, 289). Canadian and British tories are able to rationalize their parties' grudging acceptance of the welfare state by recalling their precapitalist collectivist traditions. Can one conceive of a respected spokesman of traditional Republicanism denouncing "rugged individualism" as un-Republican?

43 Roger Graham, *Arthur Meighen*, vol. II (Toronto, 1963), 269.

44 *Ibid.*, vol. III (Toronto, 1965), 71–4.

45 George Grant, *Lament for a Nation* (Toronto, 1965), 71. See Gad Horowitz, "Tories, Socialists and the Demise of Canada," *Canadian Dimension*, May-June 1965, 12–15.

46 *Communism in American Unions* (New York, 1959), 7.

47 "The Background and Development of Marxian Socialism in the United States," in D. Igbert and S. Persons, eds., *Socialism in American Life* (Princeton, 1952), 401.

48 *Ibid.*, 221.

49 *Liberal Tradition*, p. 228.

50 *Ibid.*, 231.

51 *Ibid.*, 234.

52 *Ibid.*, 243.

53 *Ibid.*, 229.

54 Bruce Hutchison, *The Incredible Canadian* (Toronto, 1952), 6. Hutchison writes (p.

39) of *Industry and Humanity.* "In almost every respect this book repudiates the historic Liberalism of Canada, denounces the economic system which Liberal politics have nurtured, proposes a society of an entirely different sort, edges uncomfortably close to the theories of the Socialist CCF." See also F.A. McGregor, *The Fall and Rise of Mackenzie King: 1911–1919* (Toronto, 1962), 230–47.

55 Before the thirties there was no strong socialist party in Canada. I would therefore be on safer ground if I were to locate the socialist challenge and liberal response in the thirties rather than at the time of the First World War. Nevertheless, the King of *Industry and Humanity* and the platform of 1919 does manifest the kind of transition from individualism to a socialized Liberal Reform that occurred in Europe. The socialist challenge *was* there, not in the form of a menace at the polls, but "in the air," in the political culture as a *legitimate* ideology which evoked response—rejection and incorporation—from other ideologies, even though it was not yet a power at the polls. And from 1921—the time of Woodsworth's election to the Commons—the *direct* political influence of Woodsworth on King comes into the picture, even though Woodsworth in the twenties did not present a significant electoral danger. American liberalism did not have to answer socialist attacks not primarily because of the weakness of socialism at the polls but because of its weakness in the political *culture*—its alien, illegitimate, un-American character. I might also mention that British liberalism began to revise itself in response to the socialist challenge long before socialism became a significant electoral menace.

56 P.R. Scott, "W.L.M.K.," *The Blasted Pine*, ed. F.R. Scott and A.J.M. Smith (Toronto, 1962), 28.

57 Hartz, *Liberal Tradition*, p. 263.

58 *Ibid.*

59 *Ibid.*, 260.

60 *Ibid.*, 271.

61 Speaking in the Commons on February 27, 1933, King assured the socialists that their objectives were not alien to the spirit of Liberalism. His objection was to their "implied method of reform through dictatorship." Norman McL. Rogers, *Mackenzie King* (Toronto, 1935), 188.

62 Hartz, *Liberal Tradition*, p. 261.

63 *Ibid.*, 262.

64 *Ibid.*

65 *Ibid.*, 267.

66 *Ibid.*

67 *Ibid.*, 270.

68 "The Canadian voter is in favour of progress *and* against social experimentation" (my emphasis). (National Liberal Federation, *The Liberal Party of Canada* [Ottawa: National Liberal Federation, 1957], 15.) "Liberalism accepts social security but rejects socialism; it accepts free enterprise but rejects economic anarchy; it accepts humanitarianism but rejects paternalism." (Lester Pearson, Introduction to J.W. Pickersgill, *The Liberal Party* [Toronto, 1962], x.) "Liberalism insists that the government must not stand by helpless in the face of ... human suffering.... Liberals, however, do not believe in socialism, with its veneration of the powerful state; with its emphasis on bureaucracy; with its class consciousness." (Pickersgill, *The Liberal Party*, p. 115.)

69 (New York, 1960), 43.

70 *Ibid.*, 50.

71 Pickersgill, *The Liberal Party*, 64.

72 *Ibid..*, 68. David Marquand notes that the British Liberal party's "proudest boast is that they are not tied to the great power blocs of modern society, that they are a party of individuals and not of interests.... Their ideology ... is characterized by a pervasive disdain for the unpleasant realities of social and political conflict and a refusal to admit that society is made up of opposing groups." ("Has Lib-Lab a Future?" *Encounter*, April 1962, 64.)

FURTHER READING

This succinct account of Horowitz's argument is presented in more detail in *Canadian Labour in Politics* (Toronto: University of Toronto Press, 1968), a book developed from Horowitz's Harvard PhD thesis. Influenced by Herbert Marcuse's fusing of Marxism and psychoanalysis, Horowitz went on to publish *Repression: Basic and Surplus Repression in Psychoanalytic Theory—Freud, Reich, and Marcuse* (Toronto: University of Toronto Press, 1977). His current work is strongly influenced by the poststructuralist movement, yet maintains its focus upon understanding the nature of political repression in modern society.

For a better understanding of the "Hartz-Horowitz" account, read Hartz's original works outlining the fragment theory, *The Liberal Tradition in America* (New York: HBJ, 1955) and *The Founding of New Societies* (New York: HBJ, 1964). H.D. Forbes writes an excellent critique of the "Hartz-Horowitz" thesis in "Hartz-Horowitz at twenty: nationalism, toryism, and socialism in Canada and the United States," *Canadian Journal of Political Science* 20.2 (June 1987): 287–315; and Forbes and Nelson Wiseman debate the applicability of this theory to Quebec in Wiseman, "A note on 'Hartz-Horowitz at twenty': the case of French Canada," *Canadian Journal of Political Science* 21.4 (December 1988): 795–806 and in Forbes, "Rejoinder," *Canadian Journal of Political Science* 21.4 (December 1988): 807–11. An interesting anthology focusing on the nature of Canada's ideological roots is *Canada's Origins: Liberal, Tory, or Republican?*, edited by Janet Ajzenstadt and Peter J. Smith (Ottawa: Carleton University Press, 1995).

14 RENÉ LÉVESQUE

INTRODUCTION

More political manifesto than theoretical discourse, *An Option for Quebec* is nonetheless the distillation and result of several generations of political thought in Quebec. In this document, René Lévesque (1922–87) crisply sets forth the justification for political independence for Quebec. Originally a journalist, Lévesque became a Liberal member of Quebec's Legislative Assembly in 1960 and was a key figure in Quebec's Quiet Revolution. In 1967, when the Liberals refused to consider Quebec sovereignty as a serious policy alternative, Lévesque and several others left the Liberal Party to establish the Parti Québécois in 1968. Two unsuccessful elections later, the Parti Québécois gained power in 1976, but sovereignty-association was rejected in referenda both in 1980 and 1995 even as the Parti Québécois and the federal Bloc Québécois became part of the established political landscape of Canada.

AN OPTION FOR QUEBEC (1968)

1. "Belonging"

We are *Québécois*.

What that means first and foremost—and if need be, all that it means—is that we are attached to this one corner of the earth where we can be completely ourselves: this Quebec, the only place where we have the unmistakable feeling that "here we can be really at home."

Being ourselves is essentially a matter of keeping and developing a personality that has survived for three and a half centuries.

At the core of this personality is the fact that we speak French. Everything else depends on this one essential element and follows from it or leads us infallibly back to it.

In our history, America began with a French look, briefly but gloriously given it by Champlain, Joliet, La Salle, La-Verendrye.... We learn our first lessons in progress and perseverance from Maisonneuve, Jeanne Mance, Jean Talon; and in daring or heroism from Lambert Closse, Brébeuf, Frontenac, d'Iberville....

Then came the conquest. We were a conquered people, our hearts set on surviving in some small way on a continent that had become Anglo-Saxon.

Somehow or other, through countless changes and a variety of regimes, despite difficulties without number (our lack of awareness and even our ignorance serving all too often as our best protection), we succeeded.

Here again, when we recall the major historical landmarks, we come upon a profusion of names: Etienne Parent and Lafontaine and the Patriots of '37; Louis Riel and Honoré Mercier, Bourassa, Philippe Hamel; Garneau and [É]douard Montpetit and Asselin and Lionel Groulx.... For each of them, the main driving force behind every action was the will to continue, and the tenacious hope that they could make it worth while.

Until recently in this difficult process of survival we enjoyed the protection of a certain degree of isolation. We lived a relatively sheltered life in a rural society in which a great measure of unanimity reigned, and in which poverty set its limits on change and aspiration alike.

We are children of that society, in which the *habitant,* our father or grandfather, was still the key citizen. We also are heirs to that fantastic adventure—that early America that was almost entirely French. We are, even more intimately, heirs to the group obstinacy which has kept alive that portion of French America we call *Québec.*

All these things lie at the core of this personality of ours. Anyone who does not feel it, at least occasionally, is not—is no longer— one of us.

But *we* know and feel that these are the things that make us what we are. They enable us to recognize each other wherever we may be. This is our own special wave-length on which, despite all interference, we can tune each other in loud and clear, with no one else listening.

This is how we differ from other men and especially from other North Americans, with whom in all other areas we have so much in common. This basic "difference" we cannot surrender. That became impossible a long time ago.

More is involved here than simple intellectual certainty. This is a physical fact. To be unable to live as ourselves, as we should live, in our own language and according to our own ways, would be like living without an arm or a leg—or perhaps a heart.

Unless, of course, we agreed to give in little by little, in a decline which, as in cases of pernicious anaemia, would cause life to slip slowly away from the patient.

Again, in order not to perceive this, one has to be among the *déracinés*, the uprooted and cut-off.

2. The Acceleration of History

On the other hand, one would have to be blind not to see that the conditions under which this personality must assert itself have changed in our lifetime, at an extremely rapid and still accelerating rate.

Our traditional society, which gave our parents the security of an environment so ingrown as to be reassuring and in which many of us grew up in a way that we thought could, with care, be preserved indefinitely; that "quaint old" society has gone.

Today, most of us are city dwellers, wage-earners, tenants. The standards of parish, village, and farm have been splintered. The automobile and the airplane take us "outside" in a way we never could have imagined thirty years ago, or even less. Radio and films, and now television, have opened for us a window onto everything that goes on throughout the world: the events—and the ideas too— of all humanity invade our homes day after day.

The age of automatic unanimity thus has come to an end. The old protective barriers are less and less able to mark safe pathways for our lives. The patience and resignation that were preached to us in the old days with such efficiency now produce no other reactions than scepticism or indifference, or even rebellion.

At our own level[,] we are going through a universal experience. In this sudden acceleration of history, whose main features are the unprecedented development of science, technology, and economic activity, there are potential promises and dangers immeasurably greater than any the world ever has known.

The promises—if man so desires—are those of abundance, of

liberty, of fraternity; in short, of a civilization that could attain heights undreamed of by the most unrestrained Utopians.

The dangers—unless man can hold them in check—are those of insecurity and servitude, of inhuman governments, of conflicts among nations that could lead to extermination.

In this little corner of ours, we already are having a small taste of the dangers as well as the promises of this age.

A Balance Sheet of Vulnerability

The dangers are striking enough.

In a world where, in so many fields, the only stable law seems to have become that of perpetual change, where our old certainties are crumbling one after the other, we find ourselves swept along helplessly by irresistible currents. We are not at all sure that we can stay afloat, for the swift, confusing pace of events forces us to realize as never before our own weaknesses, our backwardness, our terrible collective vulnerability.

Endlessly, with a persistence almost masochistic, we draw up list after list of our inadequacies. For too long we despised education. We lack scientists, administrators, qualified technical people. Economically, we are colonials whose three meals a day depend far too much on the initiative and goodwill of foreign bosses. And we must admit as well that we are far from being the most advanced along the path of social progress, the yard-stick by which the quality of a human community can best be measured. For a very long time we have allowed our public administration to stagnate in negligence and corruption, and left our political life in the hands of fast talkers and our own equivalent of those African kings who grew rich by selling their own tribesmen.

We must admit that our society has grave, dangerous, and deep-rooted illnesses which it is absolutely essential to cure if we want to survive.

Now, a human society that feels itself to be sick and inferior, and is unable to do anything about it, sooner or later reaches the point of being unacceptable even to itself.

For a small people such as we are, our minority position on an Anglo-Saxon continent creates from the very beginning a permanent temptation to such a self-rejection, which has all the attraction of a gentle downward slope ending in a comfortable submersion in the Great Whole.

There are enough sad cases, enough among us who have given up, to show us that this danger does exist.

It is, incidentally, the only danger that really can have a fatal effect upon us, because it exists within ourselves.

And if ever we should be so unfortunate as to abandon this individuality that makes us what we are, it is not "the others" we would have to blame, but only our own impotence and resulting discouragement.

The only way to overcome the danger is to face up to this trying and thoughtless age and make it accept us as we are, succeeding somehow in making a proper and appropriate place in it for ourselves, in our own language, so that we can feel we are equals and not inferiors. This means that in our homeland we must be able to earn our living and pursue our careers in French. It also means that we must build a society which, while it preserves an image that is our own, will be as progressive, as efficient, and as "civilized" as any in the world. (In fact, there are other small peoples who are showing us the way, demonstrating that maximum size is in no way synonymous with maximum progress among human societies.)

To speak plainly, we must give ourselves sufficient reason to be not only sure of ourselves but also, perhaps, a little proud.

3. The Quiet Revolution

Now, in the last few years we have indeed made some progress along this difficult road of "catching up," the road which leads to the greater promise of our age.

At least enough progress to know that what comes next depends only on ourselves and on the choices that only we can make.

The enticements toward progress were phrases like "from now on," or "it's got to change," or "masters in our own house," etc.

The results can be seen on every side. Education, for us as for any people desirous of maintaining its place in the world, has finally become the top priority. With hospital insurance, family and school allowances, pension schemes, and the beginnings of medicare, our social welfare has made more progress in a few years than in the whole preceding century; and for the first time we find ourselves, in many of the most important areas, ahead of the rest of the country. In the economic field, by nationalizing electric power, by created the S.G.F., *Soquem,* and the *Caisse de Dépôts*[1] we have taken the first steps toward the kind of collective control of certain essential services without which no human community can feel secure. We also, at last, have begun to clean up our electoral practices, to modernize and strengthen our administrative structures, to give our land the roads that are indispensable to its future, and to study seriously the complex problems of our outmoded municipalities and under-developed regions.

To be sure, none of this has been brought to completion. What has been done is only a beginning, carried out in many cases without the co-ordination that should have been applied—and far too often in circumstances dictated by urgency or opportunity. All along the way there have been hesitations and, God knows, these still exist. In all these accomplishments mistakes have been made and gaps have been left—and whatever happens, even if we do a hundred times as much, this always will be so.

No One Will Do It For You

But in the process we have learned certain things, things which are both simple and revolutionary.

The first is that we have the capacity to do the job ourselves, and the more we take charge and accept our responsibilities, the more efficient we find we are; capable, all things considered, of succeeding just as well as anyone else.

Another is that there is no valid *excuse*, that it is up to us to find and apply to our problems the solutions that are right for us; for no one else can, much less wants to, solve them for us.

Yet another thing we have learned—and perhaps the most important: "The appetite comes with the eating." This is a phenomenon we can see everywhere as soon as a human group decides to move forward. It is called the "revolution of rising expectations."

This is the main driving force at our disposal for continued progress. We must calculate its use as precisely as possible, to avoid costly diversions; but even more we must take care not to stifle it, for without this we shall experience the collective catastrophe of an immobilized society, at a time when those who fail to advance automatically retreat, and to a point which can easily become one of no return.

In other words, above all we must guard against loss of impetus, against the periodic desire to slow down, against the belief that we are moving too quickly when in reality—despite a few wanderings—we are just beginning to reach the speed our age demands. In this, a nation is like an individual: those who succeed are those who are unafraid of life.

The fact is that we are condemned to progress *ad infinitum.*

Not only are we just beginning, but we shall always be just beginning, as far as we can see ahead. On the horizon are further changes and adaptations; on the horizon is the hope that we will be wise enough to make the right choices, with the courage and vitality called for by the ceaseless pursuit of progress and the acceptance of every challenge on the way.

4. The Basic Minimums

On this road where there can be no more stopping are a number of necessary tasks which must be attended to without delay. Neglecting them would endanger the impetus we have acquired, perhaps would slow it down irreparably.

And here we encounter a basic difficulty which has become more and more acute in recent years. It is created by the political regime under which we have lived for over a century.

We are a nation within a country where there are two nations. For all the things we mentioned earlier, using words like "individuality," "history," "society," and "people," are also the things one includes under the word "nation." It means nothing more than the collective will to live that belongs to any national entity likely to survive.

Two nations in a single country: this means, as well, that in fact there are *two majorities,* two "complete societies" quite distinct from each other trying to get along within a common framework. That this number puts us in a minority position makes no difference: just as a civilized society will never condemn a little man to feel inferior beside a bigger man, civilized relations among nations demand that they treat each other as equals in law and in fact.

Now we believe it to be evident that the hundred-year-old framework of Canada can hardly have any effect other than to create increasing difficulties between the two parties insofar as their mutual respect and understanding are concerned, as well as impeding the changes and progress so essential to both.

It is useless to go back over the balance sheet of the century just past, listing the advantages it undoubtedly has brought us and the obstacles and injustices it even more unquestionably has set in our way.

The important thing for today and for tomorrow is that both sides realize that this regime has had its day, and that it is a matter of urgency either to modify it profoundly or to build a new one.

As we are the ones who have put up with its main disadvantages, it is natural that we also should be in the greatest hurry to be rid of it; the more so because it is we who are menaced most dangerously by its current paralysis.

Primo Vivere

Almost all the essential tasks facing us risk being jeopardized, blocked, or quietly undone by the sclerosis of Canadian institutions and the open or camouflaged resistance of the men who manipulate them.

First, we must secure once and for all, in accordance with the complex and urgent necessities of our time, the safety of our collective "personality." This is the distinctive feature of the nation, of this majority that we constitute in Quebec—the only true fatherland left us by events, by our own possibilities, and by the incomprehension and frequent hostility of others.

The prerequisite to this is, among other things, the power for unfettered action (which does not exclude co-operation) in fields as varied as those of citizenship, immigration, and employment; the great instruments of "mass culture"—films, radio, and television; and the kind of international relations that alone permit a people to breathe the air of a changing and stimulating world, and to learn to see beyond itself. Such relations are especially imperative for a group whose cultural connections in the world are as evident and important as ours.

Our collective security requires also that we settle a host of questions made so thorny by the present regime that each is more impossible than the next. Let us only mention as examples the integrity of Quebec's territory, off-shore rights, the evident inacceptibility of an institution like the Supreme Court, and Quebec's need to be able to shape freely what we might term its internal constitution.

That collective personality which constitutes a nation also cannot tolerate that social security and welfare—which affect it daily in the most intimate ways—should be conceived and directed from outside. This relates to the oft-repeated demand for the repatriation of old-age pensions, family allowances, and, when it comes into being, medicare.

By the same token, and even more so, it relates to the most obvious needs of efficiency and administrative responsibility. In this whole vast area there are overlapping laws, regulations, and organizations whose main effect is to perpetuate confusion and, behind this screen, to paralyze change and progress.

The Madhouse

Mutatis mutandis, we find similar situations with equally disastrous results in a multitude of other areas: the administration of justice, jurisdiction in fields such as insurance, corporations, bankruptcies, financial institutions, and, in a general way, all economic activities which have become the most constant pre-occupations of all men today and also the aspect of society in which modern states have seen their sphere of action grow most dramatically in the last couple of generations.

On this point, here is how the C.S.N., the F.T.Q., and the U.C.C.[2] describe the situation in their joint memorandum to the Quebec Legislature's Constitutional Committee:

The fact that certain economic tools belong to the federal government, while other powers whose exercise also influences economic life belong to the provinces, creates a difficult problem in the rational planning of economic activity in general. Thinking in terms of a more advanced socialization than that which we know today, this situation, along with opportunity given one government to thwart the actions of [the] other, may lead to conflict, and is in any case of such a nature that it could, at these two levels of government, result in impotence in attacking the economic problems of the country with any kind of resolution or efficiency. Any duplication of institutions should be avoided, moreover, if it leads to a duplication of costs. This situation should demand our attention all the more urgently because of the fact that already (for example, in agriculture) laws and regulations at the two levels of government, and especially their application, because of their overlapping, their duplication, their superimposition of their lack of co-ordination, cause many grave difficulties and are often most prejudicial to the citizens involved,

especially those of Quebec in view of our lagging behind in a number
of areas.

Here again let us limit ourselves to citing the minimums established
by the most complete studies of recent years. And so, back to those
three organizations and the way in which they define these minimums in the cautious conclusion of their memorandum:

> The Quebec government should exercise its powers by giving direc-
> tion to the economy, rationalizing its marginal industries, developing
> secondary industry, etc. The government of Quebec should promote
> an economic policy frankly favourable to its own population and more
> demanding vis-a-vis the capitalist interests, for it is not enough only to
> appear to govern in favour of the people in this sector. In particular,
> the Quebec government must obtain the greatest advantages and royal-
> ties it can possibly extract from the exploitation of natural resources,
> taking account of the reasonable limits of this kind of policy. Activity
> just as intense and equally devoted to the interests of the people must
> spread through all departments responsible for economic matters,
> notably agriculture, industry, and commerce, and so forth.

This outline, which is necessarily incomplete ("and so forth"), hints
at a program immediately acceptable to everyone, but it poses at
once the question of means.

A Strong State

How can it be carried out? Let us mention only what is clearly obvious. Order must be re-established in the chaos of a governmental
structure created at a time when it was impossible to foresee the
scientific and technical revolution in which we now are caught up,
the endless changes it demands, the infinite variety of things
produced, the concentration of enterprises, the crushing weight
that the greatest of these impose on individual and collective life,
the absolute necessity of having a state able to direct, co-ordinate,
and above all humanize this infernal rhythm.

In this up-dating of political structures that are completely over-
taxed by an economic role they cannot refuse to play, the action
demanded of the Quebec government, to be specific, would require
at the very least new jurisdictions over industrial and commercial

corporations, fiduciary and savings institutions, and all the internal agencies of development and industrialization, as well as the power to exercise a reasonable control over the movement and investment of our own capital.

So as not to belabour the obvious, we shall mention only for the record the massive transfer of fiscal resources that would be needed for all the tasks this State of Quebec should undertake in our name—not counting the tasks it already has, tasks that daily grow more out of proportion to its inadequate means: i.e., the insatiable needs of education, urban problems without number, and the meagreness or tragic non-existence of the tools of scientific and industrial research.

Very sketchily, this would seem to be the basic minimum of change that Quebec should force the present Canadian regime to accept in order to reach both the collective security and the opportunity for progress which its best minds consider indispensable.

We could certainly add to the list. But nothing could be struck from it easily.

For us, this is, in fact, a true minimum.

5. The Blind Alley

But we would be dreaming if we believed that for the rest of the country our minimum can be anything but a frightening maximum, completely unacceptable even in the form of bare modifications or, for that matter, under the guise of the constitutional reform with which certain people say they are willing to proceed.

Not only the present attitude of the federal government, but also the painful efforts at understanding made by the opposition parties and reactions in the most influential circles in English Canada all give us reason to expect that our confrontation will grow more and more unpleasant.

From a purely revisionist point of view, our demands would seem to surpass both the best intentions displayed by the "other majority" and the very capacity of the regime to make concessions without an explosion.

If we are talking only of revision, they will tell us, our demands would lead to excessive weakening of that centralized state which English Canada needs for its own security and progress as much as we need our own State of Quebec. And they would be right.

And further, they could ask us—with understandable insistence—what in the world our political representatives would be doing in Ottawa taking part in debates and administrative acts whose authority and effectiveness we intend so largely to eliminate within Quebec.

If Quebec were to begin negotiations to revise the present frame of reference, and persisted in this course, it would not be out of the woods in the next hundred years. But by that time it is most likely that there would be nothing left worth talking about of the nation that is now trying to build a homeland in Quebec.

During the long wait we would soon fall back on the old defensive struggle, the enfeebling skirmishes that make one forget where the real battle is, the half-victories that are celebrated between two defeats, the relapse into divisive federal-provincial electoral folly, the sorry consolations of verbal nationalism and, above all, ABOVE ALL ELSE—this must be said, and repeated, and shouted if need be—above all the incredible "split-level" squandering of energy, which certainly is for us the most disastrous aspect of the present regime.

And as for this waste of energy, English Canada suffers from it, too. And there, too, the best minds have begun to realize this fact, let there be no doubt of that.

Two Paralyzed Majorities

For the present regime also prevents the English-speaking majority from simplifying, rationalizing, and centralizing as it would like to do certain institutions which it, too, realizes are obsolete. This is an ordeal which English Canada is finding more and more exhausting, and for which it blames to the exaggerated anxieties and the incorrigible intransigence of Quebec.

It is clear, we believe, that this frustration may easily become intolerable. And it is precisely among the most progressive and "nationalist" groups in English Canada, among those who are concerned about the economic, cultural, and political invasion from the United States, among those who are seeking the means to prevent the country from surrendering completely, that there is the greatest risk of a growing and explosive resentment toward Quebec for the reasons mentioned above.

And these are the very men among whom we should be able to find the best partners for our dialogue over the new order that must emerge.

We are seeking at last to carve out for ourselves a worthy and acceptable place in this Quebec which has never belonged to us as it should have. Facing us, however, a growing number of our fellow-citizens of the other majority are afraid of losing the homeland that Canada was for them in the good old days of the Empire, when they at least had the impression that they were helping to rule, and that it was all within the family. Today the centres of decision-making are shifting south of the border at a terrifying rate.

In this parallel search for two national securities, as long as the search is pursued within the present system or anything remotely resembling it, we can end up only with double paralysis. The two majorities, basically desiring the same thing—a chance to live their own lives, in their own way, according to their own needs and aspirations—will inevitably collide with one another repeatedly and with greater and greater force, causing hurts that finally would be irreparable.

As long as we persist so desperately in maintaining—with spit and chewing gum or whatever—the ancient hobble of a federalism suited to the last century, the two nations will go on creating an ever-growing jungle of compromises while disagreeing more and more strongly on essentials.

This would mean a perpetual atmosphere of instability, of wrangling over everything and over nothing. It would mean the sterilization of two collective "personalities" which, having squandered the most precious part of their potential, would weaken each other so completely that they would have no other choice but to drown themselves in the ample bosom of "America."

6. The Way of the Future

We think it is possible for both parties to avoid this blind alley. We must have the calm courage to see that the problem can't be solved either by maintaining or somehow adapting the *status quo*. One is always somewhat scared at the thought of leaving a home in which one has lived for a long time. It becomes almost "consecrated," and all the more so in this case, because what we call "Confederation" is one of the last remnants of those age-old safeguards of which modern times have robbed us. It is therefore quite normal that some people cling to it with a kind of desperation that arises far more from fear than from reasoned attachment.

But there are moments—and this is one of them—when courage and calm daring become the only proper form of prudence that a people can exercise in a crucial period of its existence. If it fails at these times to accept the calculated risk of the great leap, it may miss its vocation forever, just as does a man who is afraid of life.

What should we conclude from a cool look at the crucial crossroads that we now have reached? Clearly that we must rid ourselves completely of a completely obsolete federal regime.

And begin anew.

Begin how?

The answer, it seems to us, is as clearly written as the question, in the two great trends of our age: that of the freedom of peoples, and that of the formation by common consent of economic and political groupings.

A Sovereign Quebec

For our own good, we must dare to seize for ourselves complete liberty in Quebec, the right to all the essential components of independence, i.e., the complete mastery of every last area of basic collective decision-making.

This means that Quebec must become sovereign as soon as possible.

Thus we finally would have within our grasp the security of our collective "being" which is so vital to us, a security which otherwise must remain uncertain and incomplete.

Then it will be up to us, and us alone, to establish calmly, without recrimination or discrimination, the priority for which we are now struggling feverishly but blindly: that of our language and our culture.

Only then will we have the opportunity—and the obligation—to use our talents to the maximum in order to resolve without further excuses or evasions all the great problems that confront us, whether it be a negotiated protective system for our farmers, or decent treatment for our employees and workers in industry, or the form and evolution of the political structures we must create for ourselves.

In short, this is not for us simply the only solution to the present Canadian impasse; it also is the one and only common goal inspiring enough to bring us together with the kind of strength and unity we shall need to confront all possible futures—the supreme challenge of continuous progress within a society that has taken control of its own destiny.

As for the other Canadian majority, it will also find our solution to its advantage, for it will be set free at once from the constraints imposed on it by our presence; it will be at liberty in its own way to rebuild to its heart's desire the political institutions of English Canada and to prove to itself, whether or not it really wants to maintain and develop on this continent, an English-speaking society distinct from the United States.

—and a New Canadian Union

And if this is the case, there is no reason why we, as future neighbours, should not voluntarily remain associates and partners in a common enterprise; which would conform to the second great trend of our times: the new economic groups, customs unions, common markets, etc.

Here we are talking about something which already exists, for it is composed of the bonds, the complementary activities, the many forms of economic co-operation within which we have learned to live. Nothing says that we must throw these things away; on the contrary, there is every reason to maintain the framework. If we destroyed it, interdependent as we are, we would only be obliged sooner or later to build it up again, and then with doubtful success.

Now, it is precisely in the field of economics that we feel the pinch most painfully. In our outmoded constitutional texts and governmental structures, we flounder hopelessly over how to divide between our two states the powers, the agencies, and the means for action.

On this subject any expert with the slightest pretension to objectivity must certainly endorse the following statement by Otto Thur, Head of the Department of Economics at the University of Montreal (in a special edition of *Le Devoir*, June 30, 1967): "It is not the wording of a constitution that will solve problems [in the field of economics], but rather enlightened and consistent action, which brings about a progressive betterment of existing reality."

It seems to us, given a minimum of wisdom and, of course, self-interest—which should not be beyond the reach of our two majorities—that in the kind of association we are proposing we would have the greatest chance of pursuing jointly such a course of "enlightened and consistent action" worth more in economic affairs than all the pseudo-sacred documents with their ever-ambiguous inflexibility.

Such an association seems to us, in fact, made to measure for the purpose of allowing us, unfettered by obsolete constitutional forms, to pool our stakes with whatever permanent consultation and flexible adjustments would best serve our common economic interests: monetary union, common tariffs, postal union, administration of the national debt, co-ordination of policies, etc.

And nothing would prevent us from adding certain matters which under the present system have never had the advantage of frank discussion between equals: the question of minorities, for one; and also the questions of equal participation in a defence policy in proportion to our means, and a foreign policy that might, if conceived jointly, regain some of the dignity and dynamism that it has lost almost completely.[3]

We are not sailing off into uncharted seas. Leaving out the gigantic model furnished by the evolution of the Common Market, we can take our inspiration from countries comparable in size to our own—Benelux or Scandinavia—among whom co-operation is highly advanced, and where it has promoted unprecedented progress in the member states without preventing any of them from continuing to live according to their own tradition and preferences.

Making History Instead of Submitting To It

To sum up, we propose a system that would allow our two majorities to extricate themselves from an archaic federal frame-work in which our two very distinct "personalities" paralyze each other by dint of pretending to have a third personality common to both.

This new relationship of two nations, one with its home-land in Quebec and another free to rearrange the rest of the country at will, would be freely associated in a new adaptation of the current "common-market" formula, making up an entity which could perhaps—and if so very precisely—be called a Canadian Union.

The future of a people is never born without effort. It requires that a rather large number of "midwives" knowingly make the grave decision to work at it. For apart from other blind forces, and apart from all the imponderables, we must believe that basically it is still men who make man's history.

What we are suggesting to those who want to listen is that we devote our efforts, together, to shape the history of Quebec in the only fitting direction; and we are certain that at the same time we shall also be helping the rest of the country to find a better future of its own.

NOTES

1 S.G.F. is *la Societé Générale de Financement* (General Investment Corporation), an investment, holding, and management company designed to promote business and industry in the province, and financed by both public and private sectors. *Soquem* is *la Société Québecoise d'Exploration Minière* (Quebec Mining Exploration Co.), government-owned and the largest in the province. The *Caisse de Dépôts* is the investment arm of the Quebec Pension Plan.

2 C.S.N. is the *Confédération des Syndicats Nationaux* (Confederation of National Trade Unions) and F.T.Q. is the *Fédération des Travailleurs du Québec* (Quebec Labour Federation). These are the two largest central labour bodies in the province. The U.C.C. is the *Union Catholique des Cultivateurs,* a major farm organization sometimes known in English as the Catholic Farmers' Union or the Farmers' Catholic Union.

3 In this paragraph some people have felt obliged—and others have hastened—to find a far-too-strict limitation imposed on Quebec's sovereignty. This would indeed be true if we proposed really to include Defence and External Affairs in the areas of actual association. These two are among the most important means through which a people can express its personality. But such is not our proposal. The highly conditional form in which it is couched, and the suggestion of preliminary studies, seem to us to indicate clearly enough that we were referring to the possibility of agreements which *might* be reached, agreements that would be strictly limited in nature (e.g., joint general staffs? Certain common agencies abroad, such as commercial representatives?), which should not *a priori* be excluded in the free development of countries which are neighbours and partners. This is the sort of thing we had in mind below when we speak of these two distinct societies which "have a crying need now to give each other some breathing space, and to rediscover themselves, freely and without prejudice, creating little by little new points of contact as the need arises."

FURTHER READING

Lévesque's own writings include *La passion du Québec* (Montréal: Éditions Québec/Amérique, 1978), *Oui* (Montréal: Éditions de l'homme, 1980), *Attendez que je me rappelle* (Montréal: Éditions Québec/Amérique, 1986), and Michel Lévesque and Rachel Casaubon, eds., *René Lévesque: textes et entrevues, 1960–1987* (Sillery: Presses de l'université du Québec, 1991). A number of political and social analyses discussing Quebec are available; the best include Henry Milner, *Politics in the New Quebec* (Toronto: McClelland and Stewart, 1978); Graham Fraser, *PQ: René Lévesque and the Parti Québecois in Power*

(Toronto: Macmillan, 1984); Kenneth McRoberts, *Quebec: Social Change and Political Crisis* (Toronto: McClelland and Stewart, latest edition); Garth Stevenson, *Community Besieged: The Anglophone Minority and the Politics of Quebec* (Montreal: McGill-Queen's University Press, 1999); and Pierre Godin, *René Lévesque: l'espoir et le chagrin, 1976–1980* (Montréal: Éditions du Boréal, 2001). An excellent introductory text on Quebec politics is Alain-G Gagnon, ed. *Québec: State and Society*, 3rd ed. (Peterborough: Broadview Press, 2004).

PART
3

THE THIRD WAVE
(1980s TO THE PRESENT)

15 CHARLES TAYLOR

INTRODUCTION

Growing up in Montreal in an anglo-francophone household, Charles Taylor (b. 1931) was deeply influenced not only by the politics of nationality, but by the increasing confrontation between liberal modernity and conservative Catholicism in Quebec. These influences perhaps explain his pervasive fascination with the ideas of Hegel, although Taylor's intellectual contributions have had an impressively broad focus. He has written extensively, for example, in religious and moral theory, as well as in the philosophy of language and epistemology. In the area of political philosophy, his overarching concern has been an attempt to reconcile and integrate the inviolability of individualism with the vitality of common life. While we cannot ignore the fundamental status for individual rights that liberalism has bequeathed to us, these rights become hollow institutions when divorced from the richness and meaningfulness of community.

THE MALAISE OF MODERNITY (1991)

1. Three Malaises

I want to write here about some of the malaises of modernity. I mean by this features of our contemporary culture and society that people experience as a loss or a decline, even as our civilization "develops." Sometimes people feel that some important decline has occurred during the last years or decades—since the Second World War, or the 1950s, for instance. And sometimes the loss is felt over a much longer historical period: the whole modern era from the seventeenth century is frequently seen as the time frame of decline. Yet although the time scale can vary greatly, there is certain convergence on the themes of decline. They are often variations around a few central melodies. I want to pick out two such central themes here, and then throw in a third that largely derives from these two. These three by no means exhaust the topic, but they do get at a great deal of what troubles and perplexes us about modern society.

The worries I will be talking about are very familiar. No one needs to be reminded of them; they are discussed, bemoaned, challenged, and argued against all the time in all sorts of media. That sounds like a reason not to talk about them further. But I believe that this great familiarity hides bewilderment, that we don't really understand these changes that worry us, that the usual run of debate about them in fact misrepresents them—and thus makes us misconceive what we can do about them. The changes defining modernity are both well-known and very perplexing, and that is why it's worth talking still more about them.

(1) The first source of worry is individualism. Of course, individualism also names what many people consider the finest achievement of modern civilization. We live in a world where people have a right to choose for themselves their own pattern of life, to decide in conscience what convictions to espouse, to determine the shape of their lives in a whole host of ways that their ancestors couldn't control. And these rights are generally defended by our legal systems. In principle, people are no longer sacrificed to the demands of supposedly sacred orders that transcend them.

Very few people want to go back on this achievement. Indeed, many think that it is still incomplete, that economic arrangements, or patterns of family life, or traditional notions of hierarchy still restrict too much our freedom to be ourselves. But many of us are also ambivalent. Modern freedom was won by our breaking loose from older moral horizons. People used to see themselves as part of a larger order. In some cases, this was a cosmic order, a "great chain of Being," in which humans figured in their proper place along with angels, heavenly bodies, and our fellow earthly creatures. This hierarchical order in the universe was reflected in the hierarchies of human society. People were often locked into a given place, a role and station that was properly theirs and from which it was almost unthinkable to deviate. Modern freedom came about through the discrediting of such orders.

But at the same time as they restricted us, these orders gave meaning to the world and to the activities of social life. The things that surround us were not just potential raw materials or instruments for our projects, but they had the significance given them by their place in the chain of being. The eagle was not just another bird, but the king of a whole domain of animal life. By the same token, the rituals and norms of society had more than merely instrumental significance. The discrediting of these orders has been called the "disenchantment" of the world. With it, things lost some of their magic.

A vigorous debate has been going on for a couple of centuries as to whether this was an unambiguously good thing. But this is not what I want to focus on here. I want to look rather at what some have seen to be the consequences for human life and meaning.

The worry has been repeatedly expressed that the individual lost something important along with the larger social and cosmic horizons of action. Some have written of this as the loss of a heroic dimension to life. People no longer have a sense of a higher purpose, of something worth dying for. Alexis de Tocqueville sometimes talked like this in the last century, referring to the "petits et vulgaires plaisirs" that people tend to seek in the democratic age.[1] In another articulation, we suffer from a lack of passion. Kierkegaard saw "the present age" in these terms. And Nietzsche's "last men" are at the final nadir of this decline; they have no aspiration left in life but to a "pitiable comfort."[2]

This loss of purpose was linked to a narrowing. People lost the broader vision because they focussed on their individual lives. Democratic equality, says Tocqueville, draws the individual towards himself, "et menace de le renfermer enfin tout entier dans la solitude de son propre coeur."[3] In other words, the dark side of individualism is a centring on the self, which both flattens and narrows our lives, makes them poorer in meaning, and less concerned with others or society.

This worry has recently surfaced again in concern at the fruits of a "permissive society," the doings of the "me generation," or the prevalence of "narcissism," to take just three of the best-known contemporary formulations. The sense that lives have been flattened and narrowed, and that this is connected to an abnormal and regrettable self-absorption, has returned in forms specific to contemporary culture. This defines the first theme I want to deal with.

(2) The disenchantment of the world is connected to another massively important phenomenon of the modern age, which also greatly troubles many people. We might call this the primacy of instrumental reason. By "instrumental reason" I mean the kind of rationality we draw on when we calculate the most economical application of means to a given end. Maximum efficiency, the best cost-output ratio, is its measure of success.

No doubt sweeping away the old orders has immensely widened the scope of instrumental reason. Once society no longer has a sacred structure, once social arrangements and modes of action are no longer grounded in the order of things or the will of God, they are in a sense up for grabs. They can be redesigned with their consequences for the happiness and well-being of individuals as our goal. The yardstick that henceforth applies is that of instrumental reason. Similarly, once the creatures that surround us lose the significance that accrued to their place in the chain of being, they are open to being treated as raw materials or instruments for our projects.

In one way this change has been liberating. But there is also a widespread unease that instrumental reason not only has enlarged its scope but also threatens to take over our lives. The fear is that things that ought to be determined by other criteria will be decided in terms of efficiency or "cost-benefit" analysis, that the independent ends that ought to be guiding our lives will be eclipsed by the demand to maximize output. There are lots of things one can point to that give substance to this worry: for instance, the ways the demands of economic growth are used to justify very unequal distributions of wealth and income, or the way these same demands make us insensitive to the needs of the environment, even to the point of potential disaster. Or else, we can think of the way much of our social planning, in crucial areas like risk assessment, is dominated by forms of cost-benefit analysis that involve grotesque calculations, putting dollar assessments on human lives.4

The primacy of instrumental reason is also evident in the prestige and aura that surround technology, and makes us believe that we should seek technological solutions even when something very different is called for. We see this often enough in the realm of politics, as Bellah and his colleagues forcefully argue in their new book.5 But it also invades other domains, such as medicine. Patricia Benner has argued in a number of important works that the technological approach in medicine has often side-lined the kind of care that involves treating the patient as a whole person with a life story, and not as the locus of a technical problem. Society and the medical establishment frequently undervalue the contribution of nurses, who more often than not provide this humanly sensitive caring, as against that of specialists with high-tech knowledge.[6]

The dominant place of technology is also thought to have contributed to the narrowing and flattening of our lives that I have just been discussing in connection with the first theme. People have spoken of a loss of resonance, depth, or richness in our human surroundings. Almost 150 years ago, Marx, in the *Communist Manifesto*, remarked that one of the results of capitalist development was that "all that is solid melts in air." The claim is that the solid, lasting, often expressive objects that served us in the past are being set aside for the quick, shoddy, replaceable commodities with which we now surround ourselves. Albert Borgman speaks of the "device paradigm," whereby we withdraw more and more from "manifold engagement" with our environment and instead request and get products designed to deliver some circumscribed benefit. He contrasts what is involved in heating our homes, with the contemporary central heating furnace, with what this same function entailed in pioneer times, when the whole family had to be involved in cutting and stacking the wood and feeding the stove or fireplace.[7] Hannah Arendt focussed on the more and more ephemeral quality of modern objects of use and argued that "the reality and reliability of the human world rest primarily on the fact that we are surrounded by things more permanent than the activity by which they are produced."[8] This permanence comes under threat in a world of modern commodities.

This sense of threat is increased by the knowledge that this primacy is not just a matter of a perhaps unconscious orientation, which we are prodded and tempted into by the modern age. As such it would be hard enough to combat, but at least it might yield to persuasion. But it is also clear that powerful mechanisms of social life press us in this direction. A manager in spite of her own orientation may be forced by the conditions of the market to adopt a maximizing strategy she feels is destructive. A bureaucrat, in spite of his personal insight, may be forced by the rules under which he operates to make a decision he knows to be against humanity and good sense.

Marx and Weber and other great theorists have explored these impersonal mechanisms, which Weber has designated by the evocative term of "the iron cage." And some people have wanted to draw from these analyses the conclusion that we are utterly helpless in the face of such forces, or at least helpless unless we totally dismantle the institutional structures under which we have been operating for the last centuries—that is, the market and the state. This aspiration seems so unrealizable today that it amounts to declaring us helpless.

I want to return to this below, but I believe that these strong theories of fatality are abstract and wrong. Our degrees of freedom are not zero. There is a point to deliberating what ought to be our ends, and whether instrumental reason ought to have a lesser role in our lives than it does. But the truth in these analyses is that it is not just a matter of changing the outlook of individuals, it is not just a battle of "hearts and minds," important as this is. Change in this domain will have to be institutional as well, even though it cannot be as sweeping and total as the great theorists of revolution proposed.

(3) This brings us to the political level, and to the feared consequences for political life of individualism and instrumental reason. One I have already introduced. It is that the institutions and structures of industrial-technological society severely restrict our choices, that they force societies as well as individuals to give a weight to instrumental reason that in serious moral deliberation we would never do, and which may even be highly destructive. A case in point is our great difficulties in tackling even vital threats to our lives from environmental disasters, like the thinning ozone layer. The society structured around instrumental reason can be seen as imposing a great loss of freedom, on both individuals and the group—because it is not just our social decisions that are shaped by these forces. An individual life-style is also hard to sustain against the grain. For instance, the whole design of some modern cities makes it hard to function without a car, particularly where public transport has been eroded in favour of the private automobile.

But there is another kind of loss of freedom, which has also been widely discussed, most memorably by Alexis de Tocqueville. A society in which people end up as the kind of individuals who are "enclosed in their own hearts" is one where few will want to participate actively in self-government. They will prefer to stay at home and enjoy the satisfactions of private life, as long as the government of the day produces the means to these satisfactions and distributes them widely.

This opens the danger of a new, specifically modern form of despotism, which Tocqueville calls "soft" despotism. It will not be a tyranny of terror and oppression as in the old days. The government will be mild and paternalistic. It may even keep democratic forms, with periodic elections. But in fact, everything will be run by an "immense tutelary power,"9 over which people will have little control. The only defence against this, Tocqueville thinks, is a vigorous political culture in which participation is valued, at several levels of government and in voluntary associations as well. But the atomism of the self-absorbed individual militates against this. Once participation declines, once the lateral associations that were its vehicles wither away, the individual citizen is left alone in the face of the vast bureaucratic state and feels, correctly, powerless. This demotivates the citizen even further, and the vicious cycle of soft despotism is joined.

Perhaps something like this alienation from the public sphere and consequent loss of political control is happening in our highly centralized and bureaucratic political world. Many contemporary thinkers have seen Tocqueville's work as prophetic.10 If this is so, what we are in danger of losing is political control over our destiny, something we could exercise in common as citizens. This is what Tocqueville called "political liberty." What is threatened here is our dignity as citizens. The impersonal mechanisms mentioned above may reduce our degrees of freedom as a society, but the loss of political liberty would mean that even the choices left would no longer be made by ourselves as citizens, but by irresponsible tutelary power.

These, then, are the three malaises about modernity that I want to deal with.... The first fear is about what we might call a loss of meaning, the fading of moral horizons. The second concerns the eclipse of ends, in face of rampant instrumental reason. And the third is about a loss of freedom.

Of course, these are not uncontroversial. I have spoken about worries that are widespread and mentioned influential authors, but nothing here is agreed. Even those who share some form of these worries dispute vigorously how they should be formulated. And there are lots of people who want to dismiss them out of hand. Those who are deeply into what the critics call the "culture of narcissism" think of the objectors as hankering for an earlier, more oppressive age. Adepts of modern technological reason think the critics of the primacy of the instrumental are reactionary and obscurantist, scheming to deny the world the benefits of science. And there are proponents of mere negative freedom who believe that the value of political liberty is overblown, and that a society in which scientific management combines with maximum independence for each individual is what we ought to aim at. Modernity has its boosters as well as its knockers.

Nothing is agreed here, and the debate continues. But in the course of this debate, the essential nature of the developments, which are here being decried, there being praised, is often misunderstood. And as a result, the real nature of the moral choices to be made is obscured. In particular, I will claim that the right path to take is neither that recommended by straight boosters nor that favoured by outright knockers. Nor will a simple trade-off between the advantages and costs of, say, individualism, technology, and bureaucratic management provide the answer. The nature of modern culture is more subtle and complex than this. I want to claim that both boosters and knockers are right, but in a way that can't be done justice to by a simple trade-off between advantages and costs. There is in fact both much that is admirable and much that is debased and frightening in all the developments I have been describing, but to understand the relation between the two is to see that the issue is not how much of a price in bad consequences you have to pay for the positive fruits, but rather how to steer these developments towards their greatest promise and avoid the slide into the debased forms.

Now I have nothing like the space I would need to treat all three of these themes as they deserve, so I propose a short-cut. I will launch into a discussion of the first theme, concerning the dangers of individualism and the loss of meaning....

2. The Inarticulate Debate

We can pick it up through a very influential recent book in the United States, Allan Bloom's *The Closing of the American Mind.* The book itself was a rather remarkable phenomenon: a work by an academic political theorist about the climate of opinion among today's students, it held a place on the *New York Times* best-seller list for several months, greatly to the surprise of the author. It touched a chord.

The stance it took was severely critical of today's educated youth. The main feature it noted in their outlook on life was their acceptance of a rather facile relativism. Everybody has his or her own "values," and about these it is impossible to argue. But as Bloom noted, this was not just an epistemological position, a view about the limits of what reason can establish; it was also held as a moral position: one ought not to challenge another's values. That is their concern, their life choice, and it ought to be respected. The relativism was partly grounded in a principle of mutual respect.

In other words, the relativism was itself an off-shoot of a form of individualism, whose principle is something like this: everyone has a right to develop their own form of life, grounded on their own sense of what is really important or of value. People are called upon to be true to themselves and to seek their own self-fulfilment. What this consists of, each must, in the last instance, determine for him- or herself. No one else can or should try to dictate its content.

This is a familiar enough position today. It reflects what we could call the individualism of self-fulfilment, which is widespread in our times and has grown particularly strong in Western societies since the 1960s. It has been picked up on and discussed in other influential books: Daniel Bell's *The Cultural Contradictions of Capitalism*, Christopher Lasch's *The Culture of Narcissism* and *The Minimal Self*, and Gilles Lipovetsky's *L'ère du vide*.

The tone of concern is audible in all these, although perhaps less marked in Lipovetsky. It runs roughly along the lines I outlined above under theme 1. This individualism involves a centring on the self and a concomitant shutting out, or even unawareness, of the greater issues or concerns that transcend the self, be they religious, political, historical. As a consequence, life is narrowed or flattened.[11] And the worry characteristically spills over into the third area I described: these authors are concerned about the possibly dire political consequences of this shift in the culture.

Now there is much that I agree with in the strictures these writers make of contemporary culture. As I shall explain in a minute, I think the relativism widely espoused today is a profound mistake, even in some respects self-stultifying. It seems true that the culture of self-fulfilment has led many people to lose sight of concerns that transcend them. And it seems obvious that it has taken trivialized and self-indulgent forms. This can even result in a sort of absurdity, as new modes of conformity arise among people who are striving to be themselves, and beyond this, new forms of dependence, as people insecure in their identities turn to all sorts of self-appointed experts and guides, shrouded with the prestige of science or some exotic spirituality.

But there is something I nevertheless want to resist in the thrust of the arguments that these authors present. It emerges clearest in Bloom, perhaps most strongly in his tone of contempt for the culture he is describing. He doesn't seem to recognize that there is a powerful moral ideal at work here, however debased and travestied its expression might be. The moral ideal behind self-fulfilment is that of being true to oneself, in a specifically modern understanding of that term. A couple of decades ago, this was brilliantly defined by Lionel Trilling in an influential book, in which he encapsulated that modern form and distinguished it from earlier ones. The distinction is expressed in the title of the book, *Sincerity and Authenticity*, and following him I am going to use the term "authenticity" for the contemporary ideal.

What do I mean by a moral ideal? I mean a picture of what a better or higher mode of life would be, where "better" and "higher" are defined not in terms of what we happen to desire or need, but offer a standard of what we ought to desire.

The force of terms like "narcissism" (Lasch's word), or "hedonism" (Bell's description), is to imply that there is no moral ideal at work here; or if there is, on the surface, that it should rather be seen as a screen for self-indulgence. As Bloom puts it, "The great majority of students, although they as much as anyone want to think well of themselves, are aware that they are busy with their own careers and their relationships. There is a certain rhetoric of self-fulfilment that gives a patina of glamor to this life, but they can see that there is nothing particularly noble about it. Survivalism has taken the place of heroism as the admired quality."[12] I have no doubt that this describes some, perhaps lots, of people, but it is a big mistake to think that it allows us insight into the change in our culture, into the power of this moral ideal—which we need to understand if we are to explain even why it is used as a hypocritical "patina" by the self-indulgent.

What we need to understand here is the moral force behind notions like self-fulfilment. Once we try to explain this simply as a kind of egoism, or a species of moral laxism, a self-indulgence with regard to a tougher, more exigent earlier age, we are already off the track. Talk of "permissiveness" misses this point. Moral laxity there is, and our age is not alone in this. What we need to explain is what is peculiar to our time. It's not just that people sacrifice their love relationships, and the care of their children, to pursue their careers. Something like this has perhaps always existed. The point is that today many people feel *called* to do this, feel they ought to do this, feel their lives would be somehow wasted or unfulfilled if they didn't do it.

Thus what gets lost in this critique is the moral force of the ideal of authenticity. It is somehow being implicitly discredited, along with its contemporary forms. That would not be so bad if we could turn to the opposition for a defence. But here we will be disappointed. That the espousal of authenticity takes the form of a kind of soft relativism means that the vigorous defence of any moral ideal is somehow off limits. For the implications, as I have just described them above, are that some forms of life are indeed *higher* than others, and the culture of tolerance for individual self-fulfilment shies away from these claims. This means, as has often been pointed out, that there is something contradictory and self-defeating in their position, since the relativism itself is powered (at least partly) by a moral ideal. But consistently or not, this is the position usually adopted. The ideal sinks to the level of an axiom, something one doesn't challenge but also never expounds.

In adopting the ideal, people in the culture of authenticity, as I want to call it, give support to a certain kind of liberalism, which has been espoused by many others as well. This is the liberalism of neutrality. One of its basic tenets is that a liberal society must be neutral on questions of what constitutes a good life. The good life is what each individual seeks, in his or her own way, and government would be lacking in impartiality, and thus in equal respect for all citizens, if it took sides on this question.[13] Although many of the writers in this school are passionate opponents of soft relativism (Dworkin and Kymlicka among them), the result of their theory is to banish discussions about the good life to the margins of political debate.

The result is an extraordinary inarticulacy about one of the constitutive ideals of modern culture.[14] Its opponents slight it, and its friends can't speak of it. The whole debate conspires to put it in the shade, to render it invisible. This has detrimental consequences. But before going on to these, I want to mention two other factors that conspire to intensify this silence.

One of them is the hold of moral subjectivism in our culture. By this I mean the view that moral positions are not in any way grounded in reason or the nature of things but are ultimately just adopted by each of us because we find ourselves drawn to them. On this view, reason can't adjudicate moral disputes. Of course, you can point out to someone certain consequences of his position he may not have thought about. So the critics of authenticity can point to the possible social and political results of each person seeking self-fulfilment. But if your interlocutor still feels like holding to his original position, nothing further can be said to gainsay him.

The grounds for this view are complex and go far beyond the moral reasons for soft relativism, although subjectivism clearly provides an important backing for this relativism. Obviously, lots of people into the contemporary culture of authenticity are happy to espouse this understanding of the role (or non-role) of reason. What is perhaps more surprising, so are a great many of their opponents, who therefore are led to despair all the more of reforming contemporary culture. If the youth really don't care for causes that transcend the self, then what can you say to them?

Of course, there are critics who hold that there are standards in reason.[15] They think that there is such a thing as human nature, and that an understanding of this will show certain ways of life to be right and others wrong, certain ways to be higher and better than others. The philosophical roots of this position are in Aristotle. By contrast, modern subjectivists tend to be very critical of Aristotle, and complain that his "metaphysical biology" is out of date and thoroughly unbelievable today.

But philosophers who think like this have generally been opponents of the ideal of authenticity; they have seen it as part of a mistaken departure from the standards rooted in human nature. They had no reason to articulate what it is about; while those who upheld it have been frequently discouraged from doing so by their subjectivist views.

A third factor that has obscured the importance of authenticity as a moral ideal has been the normal fashion of social science explanation. This has generally shied away from invoking moral ideals and has tended to have recourse to supposedly harder and more down to earth factors in its explanation. And so the features of modernity I have been focussing on here, individualism and the expansion of instrumental reason, have often been accounted for as by-products of social change: for instance, as spin-offs from industrialization, or greater mobility, or urbanization. There are certainly important causal relations to be traced here, but the accounts that invoke them frequently skirt altogether the issue whether these changes in culture and outlook owe anything to their own inherent power as moral ideals. The implicit answer is often negative.[16]

Of course, the social changes that are supposed to spawn the new outlook must themselves be explained, and this will involve some recourse to human motivations, unless we suppose that industrialization or the growth of cities occurred entirely in a fit of absence of mind. We need some notion of what moved people to push steadily in one direction, for example towards the greater application of technology to production, or towards greater concentrations of population. But what are often invoked are motivations that are non-moral. By that I mean motivations that can actuate people quite without connection to any moral ideal, as I defined this earlier. So we very often find these social changes explained in terms of the desire for greater wealth, or power, or the means of survival or control over others. Though all these things can be woven into moral ideals, they need not be, and so explanation in terms of them is considered sufficiently "hard" and "scientific."

Even where individual freedom and the enlargement of instrumental reason are seen as ideas whose intrinsic attractions can help explain their rise, this attraction is frequently understood in non-moral terms. That is, the power of these ideas is often understood not in terms of their moral force but just because of the advantages they seem to bestow on people regardless of their moral outlook, or even whether they have a moral outlook. Freedom allows you to do what you want, and the greater application of instrumental reason gets you more of what you want, whatever that is.[17]

The result of all this has been to thicken the darkness around the moral ideal of authenticity. Critics of contemporary culture tend to disparage it as an ideal, even to confound it with a non-moral desire to do what one wants without interference. The defenders of this culture are pushed into inarticulacy about it by their own outlook. The general force of subjectivism in our philosophical world and the power of neutral liberalism intensify the sense that these issues can't and shouldn't be talked about. And then on top of it all, social science seems to be telling us that to understand such phenomena as the contemporary culture of authenticity, we shouldn't have recourse in our explanations to such things as moral ideals but should see it all in terms of, say, recent changes in the mode of production,[18] or new patterns of youth consumption, or the security of affluence.

Does this matter? I think so, very much. Many of the things critics of contemporary culture attack are debased and deviant forms of this ideal. That is, they flow from it, and their practitioners invoke it, but in fact they don't represent an authentic (!) fulfilment of it. Soft relativism is a case in point. Bloom sees that it has a moral basis: "The relativity of truth is not a theoretical insight but a moral postulate, the condition of a free society, or so [the students] see it."[19] But in fact, I would like to claim, it travesties and eventually betrays this moral insight. So far from being a reason to reject the moral ideal of authenticity, it should itself be rejected in its name. Or so I would like to argue.

A similar point can be made for those appeals to authenticity that justify ignoring whatever transcends the self: for rejecting our past as irrelevant, or denying the demands of citizenship, or the duties of solidarity, or the needs of the natural environment. Similarly, justifying in the name of authenticity a concept of relationships as instrumental to individual self-fulfilment should also be seen as a self-stultifying travesty. The affirmation of the power of choice as itself a good to be maximized is a deviant product of the ideal.

Now if something like this is true, then it matters to be able to say it. For then one *has* something to say, in all reason, to the people who invest their lives in these deviant forms. And this may make a difference to their lives. Some of these things may be heard. Articulacy here has a moral point, not just in correcting what may be wrong views but also in making the force of an ideal that people are already living by more palpable, more vivid for them; and by making it more vivid, empowering them to live up to it in a fuller and more integral fashion.

What I am suggesting is a position distinct from both boosters and knockers of contemporary culture. Unlike the boosters, I do not believe that everything is as it should be in this culture. Here I tend to agree with the knockers. But unlike them, I think that authenticity should be taken seriously as a moral ideal. I differ also from the various middle positions, which hold that there are some good things in this culture (like greater freedom for the individual), but that these come at the expense of certain dangers (like a weakening of the sense of citizenship), so that one's best policy is to find the ideal point of trade-off between advantages and costs.

The picture I am offering is rather that of an ideal that has degraded but that is very worthwhile in itself, and indeed, I would like to say, unrepudiable by moderns. So what we need is neither root-and-branch condemnation nor uncritical praise; and not a carefully balanced trade-off. What we need is a work of retrieval, through which this ideal can help us restore our practice....

NOTES

[1] Alexis de Tocqueville, *De la Démocratie en Amérique* vol. 2 (Paris: Garnier-Flammarion, 1981), p. 385.

[2] "Erbärmliches Behagen"; *Also Sprach Zarathustra*, Zarathustra's Preface, sect. 3.

[3] Tocqueville, *De la Démocratie*, p. 127.

[4] For the absurdities of these calculations, see R. Bellah et al., *The Good Society* (Berkeley: University of California Press, 1991), pp. 114–19.

[5] Bellah et al., *The Good Society*, chapter 4.

[6] See especially Patricia Benner and Judith Wrubel, *The Primacy of Caring: Stress and Coping in Health and Illness* (Menlo Park, CA: Addison-Wesley, 1989).

[7] Albert Borgman, *Technology and the Character of Contemporary Life* (Chicago: University of Chicago Press, 1984), pp. 41–42. Borgman even seems to echo Nietzsche's picture of the "last men" when he argues that the original liberating promise of technology can degenerate into "the procurement of frivolous comfort" (p. 39).

[8] Hannah Arendt, *The Human Condition* (Garden City, NJ: Doubleday, Anchor Edition, 1959), p. 83.

[9] Tocqueville, *De la Démocratie*, p. 385.

[10] See for instance R. Bellah et al., *Habits of the Heart* (Berkeley: University of California Press, 1985).

[11] This image occurs in Bloom, *The Closing of the American Mind* (New York: Simon and Schuster, 1987): "The loss of the books has made them narrower and flatter. Narrower because they lack what is most necessary, a real basis for discontent with the present and awareness that there are alternatives to it. They are both more contented with what is and despairing of ever escaping from it.... Flatter, because without interpretations of things, without the poetry or the imagination's activity, their souls are like mirrors, not of nature, but of what is around" (p. 61).

12 Bloom, *The Closing of the American Mind*, p. 84.

13 See John Rawls, *A Theory of Justice* (Cambridge: Harvard University Press, 1971), and "The idea of an overlapping consensus," in *Philosophy and Public Affairs* 17 (1988); Ronald Dworkin, *Taking Rights Seriously* (London: Duckworth, 1977) and *A Matter of Principle* (Cambridge: Harvard University Press, 1985); also Will Kymlicka, *Liberalism, Community and Culture* (Oxford: The Clarendon Press, 1989).

14 I have written about this at greater length in *Sources of the Self* (Cambridge: Harvard University Press, 1989), chapter 3.

15 See especially Alasdair MacIntyre, *After Virtue* (Notre Dame: University of Notre Dame Press, 1981) and *Whose Justice? Which Rationality?* (Notre Dame: University of Notre Dame Press, 1988).

16 Of course, for a certain vulgar Marxism, the negative answer is quite explicit. Ideas are the product of economic changes. But much non-Marxist social science operates implicitly on similar premises. And this in spite of the orientation of some of the great founders of social science, like Weber, who recognized the crucial role of moral and religious ideas in history.

17 Individualism has in fact been used in two quite different senses. In one it is a moral ideal, one facet of which I have been discussing. In another, it is an amoral phenomenon, something like what we mean by egoism. The rise of individualism in this sense is usually a phenomenon of breakdown, where the loss of a traditional horizon leaves mere anomie in its wake, and everybody fends for themselves—e.g., in some demoralized, crime-ridden slums formed by newly urbanized peasants in the Third World (or in nineteenth-century Manchester). It is, of course, catastrophic to confuse these two kinds of individualism, which have utterly different causes and consequences. Which is why Tocqueville carefully distinguishes "individualism" from "egoism."

18 See David Harvey, *The Condition of Post-modernity* (Oxford: Blackwell, 1989).

18 Bloom, *The Closing of the American Mind*, p. 25.

FURTHER READING

Next to *The Malaise of Modernity*, the most accessible of Taylor's political philosophy is his extended essay *Multiculturalism and the "Politics of Recognition,"* in a volume with commentaries, edited by Amy Gutman (Princeton: Princeton University Press, 1992). The most extensive examination of Taylor's thought is by Ruth Abbey in *Charles Taylor* (Princeton University Press, 2000); but another good compilation is *Philosophy in an Age of Pluralism: The Philosophy of Charles Taylor in Question,* edited by James Tully (Cambridge: Cambridge University Press, 1994). A collection of Taylor's more political writings is *Reconciling the Solitudes: Essays on Canadian Federalism and Nationalism,* edited by Guy LaForest (Montreal: McGill-Queen's University Press, 1993). More confident readers may wish to try Taylor's *Hegel* (Cambridge and New York: Cambridge University Press, 1975), *Sources of the Self: The Making of Modern Identity* (Cambridge, MA: Harvard University Press, 1989), or *Modern Social Imaginaries* (Durham, NC: Duke University Press, 2004).

16

JAMES TULLY

INTRODUCTION

The political thought of James Tully (b. 1946), like that of Charles Taylor, is rooted in a deep understanding of the development of western political ideas. Understanding the historical context within which contemporary ideas have evolved, in Tully's view, allows us to challenge the accepted political assumptions that underpin institutions such as private property, constitutionalism, or civic freedom. An acclaimed Locke scholar, Tully is as comfortable discussing the political debates of the seventeenth and eighteenth centuries as he is with contemporary debates over globalization or environmentalism: indeed, we cannot fully grasp the complexities of the latter without a clear comprehension of the former.

STRANGE MULTIPLICITY (1995)

A Summary of Contemporary Constitutionalism

The survey of the composite language of contemporary constitutionalism suggests that the constitutions of contemporary societies are considerably different from the picture given by the modern theories and the three authoritative schools. Where the machinery of modern constitutionalism has not clear-cut the living cultural diversity, because the sovereign people have said enough and refused to submit, the resulting common ground is a multiplicity. These constitutions are based on the sovereignty of culturally diverse citizens here and now, not on abstract forgeries of culturally homogeneous individuals, communities or nations. The aspectival character of the constitutions is not grasped by a comprehensive representation, but by participation in a practical dialogue where limited and complementary stories are exchanged. Constitutional negotiations are not monologues in an imperial voice, but inter-cultural dialogues where the post-imperial majesty of *audi alteram partem* always has her final say.

These constitutions are not causal stages high above the ancient ones of early modern Europeans or Aboriginal peoples, but contin-uous with them. They preserve legal, political and cultural plural-ity rather than impose uniformity and regularity. There is not one national narrative that gives the partnership its unity, but a diver-sity of criss-crossing and contested narratives through which citi-zens participate in and identify with their association. Constitutions are not fixed and unchangeable agreements reached at some foun-dational moment, but chains of continual intercultural negotia-tions and agreements in accord with, and violation of the conventions of mutual recognition, continuity and consent. In sum, as the people remove modern constitutionalism from its imperial throne and put it in its proper place, what remains to be seen looks to me like the outlines of the black canoe in dawn's early light....

Contemporary constitutionalism is just because it rests on the three venerable conventions of justice that survived our critical survey. It is also worthy of our hearing, and perhaps allegiance, because it furthers the liberty of self rule. Since there is no greater value in Western civil-isation, and perhaps in any civilisation, this is no small recommen-dation for the vision presented here for your consideration.

Moreover, the path from modern to contemporary constitu-tionalism was not taken lightly or without due consideration of the other side. To recall, Hobbes founded the comprehensive and exclu-sive authority of modern constitutionalism on its scientific status. Hale replied that the model of science is inapplicable to the tangled domain of constitutionalism. It cannot provide knowledge of how constitutional actors ought to be governed because they are not, and cannot be coerced to be, governed by comprehensive rules as the model presupposes. The hermeneutical sciences sought to restore comprehensive theory to office on the basis of rules implicit in practice. Nationalism, communitarianism and practice-based liberalism rested their comprehensive claims on this version of the model. Wittgenstein demurred, pointing out that this revised model is equally inappropriate to the aspectual domain of human action. The hundreds of voices heard in the survey support Hale and Wittgenstein in dethroning modern constitutionalism. The final irony of modern constitutionalism's long reign is that the model of science on which its authority rested is even a false representation of the natural sciences. As Clifford Geertz demonstrates, natural scientists too study individual cases, advance limited and competing sketches, draw analogies with other cases and discuss these with as many colleagues as possible.[1]

Instead of grand theory, constitutional knowledge appears to be a humble and practical dialogue in which interlocutors from near and far exchange limited descriptions of actual cases, learning as they go along. Accordingly, the language and institutions of modern constitutionalism should now take their democratic place among the multiplicity of constitutional languages and institutions of the world and submit their limited claims to authority to the three conventions, just like all the others.

Hence, in this post-imperial view of constitutionalism the value of progress is also preserved and transformed. Progress is not the ascent out of the ancient cultural assemblage until one reaches the imaginary uniform modern republic, from which one ranks and judges the less developed others on the rungs far below. Rather, it consists in learning to recognise, converse with and be mutually accommodating to the culturally diverse neighbours in the city we inhabit here and now. This is the reversal of worldview called for, as Jamake Highwater warns, citing the Mexican essayist Octavio Paz, if the family of humankind is to survive:[2]

> What sets worlds in motion is the interplay of differences, their attractions and repulsions. Life is plurality, death is uniformity. By suppressing differences and peculiarities, by eliminating different civilizations and cultures, progress weakens life and favors death. The ideal of a single civilization for everyone, implicit in the cult of progress of technique, impoverishes and mutilates us. Every view of the world that becomes extinct, every culture that disappears, diminishes a possibility.

This quotation turns on a connection suggested by the term "culture" itself. The value of continuing the overlapping, interacting and contested forms of life we call human cultures is analogous to the value of preserving the equally interdependent plant and animal cultures. Since both Aboriginal and non-Aboriginal ecologists concur that all forms of life are suspended in this delicately balanced labyrinth of biodiversity, the value is life itself. And, on the other side, there is a connection, as William Cronon, Carolyn Merchant, David Maybury-Lewis, Alfred Crosby and Julian Burger have shown beyond reasonable doubt, between the global spread of modern constitutionalism, with its policies of discontinuity and assimilation, and the ecological imperialism and destruction that continues to accompany it. The kinship between the recognition of human and ecological cultures is effortlessly expressed by Bill Reid in his meditation on the meaning of "Haida":[3]

> As for what constitutes a Haida—well, Haida only means human being, and as far as I'm concerned, a human being is anyone who respects the needs of his fellow man, and the earth which nurtures and shelters us all. I think we could find room in South Moresby [one of the islands of *Haida Gwai*] for quite a few Haida no matter what their ethnic background.

Notwithstanding these arguments in support of contemporary constitutionalism, I have not responded directly to four objections voiced by the guardians of modern constitutionalism in the course of our survey. Contemporary constitutionalism conflicts with national integrity in nationalism, violates individual freedom and autonomy in liberalism, protects enclaves of anti-democratic rule and leads to disunity in practice. I address these legitimate concerns in the next section. A consideration of the two public goods of contemporary constitutionalism follows in the third section....

Replies to Four Objections to Contemporary Constitutionalism

The post-imperial constitutionalism of this book is incompatible with the "integrity" of the nation in nationalism in one sense of this term. If the integrity of the nation is a code word for an ethnic nation, then ... it is empirically false. Nations are, in William McNeill's phrase, polyethnic. This has not stopped the ideologists of the ethnic nation state from making their false claims.... Anthony Smith explains that ethnicity has been a feature of the modern concept of a nation from the seventeenth century to the racial versions of the nineteenth and twentieth centuries. It is lodged in place by the broader assumption that cultures and nations constitute a world system of separate, closed and homogeneous units at various stages of development.

The integrity of the ethnic nation is more often a claim that the nation should be purified, rather than a claim that it is pure, although the two are often connected. The policies of "forging" a nation ... and the justifications of Lord Durham and John Stuart Mill ... are classic examples of how modern nation states have attempted to construct dominant ethnic identities. These attempts to assimilate the ethnic citizens who fail to fit the mould have been, and continue to be, disastrous and abhorrent failures.

The abandonment of the set of assumptions that held ethnic nationalism in place and the adoption of the more accurate picture of cultural diversity is certainly incompatible with ethnic nationalism and any other form of exclusive nationalism. However, it is not incompatible with the sense of belonging to a people or a nation who govern themselves by their own laws and ways. This aspiration to belong to a self-governing nation is and has been central to the politics of recognition, in spite of the attempts of Lord Durham and others to reduce it to an ethnic struggle. The type of nationalism which survives is conceived in awareness of the cultural diversity of any nation....

Let us now view contemporary constitutionalism from the perspective of modern liberals and their objection. A constitution ought to provide the foundation for the individual freedom and dignity of all citizens in both the public and private spheres. It should enable them to participate freely and with equal dignity in the governing of their society and to live their private lives in accord with their own choice and responsibility. In recent years, liberal philosophers have asked how these values of civic and private, freedom and responsibility can be preserved in the culturally diverse societies of today. They argue that the social condition of being able to exercise individual freedom in both the civic and private spheres is that citizens are members of viable cultures. The reason for this is that a viable culture is a necessary and partly constitutive context for individual freedom and autonomy. Consequently, although liberals place no value on cultures in their own right, they are now classified as a primary good of a liberal society because they provide the support for liberal values.

The older imperial liberals agreed with this, but they presumed that modern European cultures were the superior cultural bases for individual freedom. Within their stages vision of history, they believed that these superior cultures developed as a causal result of the processes of modernisation, supplemented where necessary by policies of reform and socialisation. Accordingly, liberal governments could look on the destruction of the diversity of primitive cultures and the inculcation of European culture with moral approval.

In hindsight, some liberals now see the error of their ways. The imperial liberals from Locke to Mill were not only mistaken in their presumption that modernisation causes cultural convergence. As Daniel Weinstock, a liberal, explains in a dialogue on cultural diversity with a communitarian and a nationalist, they also overlooked the social preconditions of one of liberalism's primary goods: individual self respect. Citizens can take part in popular sovereignty, by having a say in constitutional negotiations, and exercise their civic and private freedom only if they have a threshold of self respect. Self respect is a sense of one's own value and the relatively secure conviction that what one has to say and do in politics and life is worthwhile. The social basis of this threshold sense of self respect is that others recognise the value of one's activities and goals; that there is an association in which individuals can acquire a level of confidence in the worth of what they say and do. Since what a person says and does and the plans he or she formulates and revises are partly characterised by his or her cultural identity, the condition of self respect is met only in a society in which the cultures of all the members are recognised and affirmed by others, both by those who do and those who do not share those cultures. A complementary argument, also starting from Rawls' concept of self respect, is advanced by Susan James from a liberal feminist perspective.

Consequently, a constitutional association whose members view the disappearance of the cultures of other members with moral approval or moral indifference, and who treat other cultures with condescension and contempt, destroys the self respect of those members. In so doing, the ability of those citizens to exercise their individual freedom and autonomy in constitutional negotiations, civic participation and private life is undermined. This is scarcely a new discovery. In *A vindication of the rights of woman*, Mary Wollstonecraft catalogued the debilitating effects on women of the degrading stereotypes and education upheld by men. The disastrous effects of policies of cultural destruction and assimilation on the self respect and self esteem of Aboriginal peoples proves this obvious but overlooked point beyond reasonable doubt.

If a liberal constitution is to provide the basis for its most important values of freedom and autonomy, it thus must protect the cultures of its members and engender the public attitude of mutual respect for cultural diversity that individual self respect requires. To put this differently, the primary good of self respect requires that popular sovereignty is conceived as an intercultural dialogue. The various cultures of the society need to be recognised in public institutions, histories and symbols in order to nourish mutual cultural awareness and respect. Far from being a threat to liberal values, the recognition and protection of cultural diversity is a necessary condition of the primary good of self respect, and so of the individual freedom and autonomy that it underpins, in a manner appropriate to a post-imperial age.

It is also worth noting that the protection of cultural diversity is compatible with the principle of liberal neutrality. As we have seen in many classic liberal theories, the feigned cultural indifference of the constitution served to reinforce the dominant, European male culture at the expense of all others. In hindsight, it is obvious that the stages view of cultural development served to prop up the self respect, and so the autonomy of the members of the dominant society and to undermine the self respect, and so the ability to participate fully of the other members. If a contemporary constitution is to be culturally neutral, it should not promote one culture at the expense of others, but mutually recognise and accommodate the cultures of all the citizens in an agreeable manner.

A closely related worry is that legal and political diversity will shield illiberal and undemocratic enclaves. The consistent application of the conventions of mutual recognition, continuity and consent renders such an outcome impossible for, as we have seen, the conventions which protect the provinces and nations of a multinational confederation also apply to the citizens within them. Nevertheless, I would like to answer the objection by taking up the case of the recognition of the sovereignty of Aboriginal peoples by the non-Aboriginal states that have been erected over them. If treaty constitutionalism does not lead to undemocratic forms of government, then the lesser degrees of self government necessary to accommodate cultural diversity in other cases are unlikely to as well.

Before proceeding, I would like to enter a disclaimer. The presumption that non-Aboriginal people may sit in judgement, from the unquestioned superiority of their constitutions and traditions of interpretation, and guard the transition of the Aboriginal peoples from colonialism to self government smacks of the imperial attitude that contemporary constitutionalism aims to dislodge. Given the historical record, it is not Aboriginal people who need guarding. To avoid this undignified stance, I will try to proceed in a way that leads non-Aboriginal readers to see their role, not as superior judges and guardians but as treaty partners in an intercultural dialogue.

Two of the primary goods of constitutionalism are civic participation and the civic dignity that accompanies it. They cannot be realised by assimilating Aboriginal peoples to non-Aboriginal forms of government. This is unjust and the cause of the alienation and resistance that come to any free people who are forcefully governed by alien laws and ways. Self government enables Aboriginal peoples, just as it enables non-Aboriginal peoples, to participate in governing their societies in accord with their own laws and cultural understandings of self rule, and so regain their dignity as equal and active citizens.

These two goods are not realised only in one canonical form of institution and charter. The practice of government should rest on the sovereignty of the people, enabling them to exercise their powers of self rule in culturally appropriate ways and to amend or overthrow the government if it thwarts their powers. Accordingly, the constitutional forms of democratic participation and citizen dignity vary with the cultures and circumstances of the peoples of the world. In many cases Aboriginal peoples, with their smaller, oral societies, tend to place greater emphasis on direct participation by all and government by consensus. As J. Anthony Long explains, in a large number of Aboriginal nations, political authority rests on the ability of the chief or council to sustain the continuous consent of the citizens. With their respect for family, tradition and place, the methods of election also vary. When consent dissipates due to distrust, the citizens often form sovereign bodies, such as healing circles, to reform defective practices and elect a new chief or council.

Although these forms of face to face government have often served as an ideal in Western political thought, modern theorists condemn them as primitive, ancient and incompatible with modern constitutions. Locke, Kant, Constant and their followers took the size and institutional formation of European societies as the norm and held that representative government, aggregate majority rule, the concentration of sovereignty and compulsory obedience are essential features of a modern constitution. This was yet another hasty and parochial generalisation. The democratic goods of participation, free expression and reform are realised better for Aboriginal peoples in their culturally distinct forms of constitution. The attempt to impose European institutions would create resistance and undermine the democratic goods the institutions are meant to secure, just as earlier attempts have done for the last four centuries.

This response, however, does not address the immediate concern. The fear is that, as the administrative dictatorships over Aboriginal peoples are dismantled, they may leave a class of Aboriginal male elites in power. They may use their sovereignty to rule despotically over their own people and shield themselves from constitutional limits. They have gained so much power under the cloak of the Indian Act and other administrative arrangements that Aboriginal people may not be able to control them. This is a genuine concern that is also shared by many Aboriginal people, especially Aboriginal women who have suffered physical abuse and discrimination on reserves.

First, the patriarchal structures that the elites occupy were set up by colonial administrators. They destroyed the wide variety of forms of rule by women and men that Aboriginal peoples previously enjoyed. The existence of such elites, then, is scarcely an argument for continuing to subject Aboriginal people to non-Aboriginal rule. Quite the contrary. The solution is to ensure that Aboriginal peoples are able to draw on and innovate with their older constitutions and traditions in order to limit or overthrow the elites in the transition to self government. The character of sovereignty in contemporary constitutionalism makes this possible.

In the theories of Hobbes and Pufendorf, sovereignty signifies a single locus of political power that is absolute or autonomous. It is not conditioned by any other political power. A sovereign ruler or body of people (such as a legislature) exercises political power over others (subjects) but is not subject or accountable to the exercise of political power by others. Absolute sovereignty arose in the age of absolute monarchy and passed to absolute nation states in the eighteenth century. This sense of sovereignty generates the problem of undemocratic enclaves. However, it is a false depiction of sovereignty today.

The concept of sovereignty has undergone a change in the transition from Hobbes to contemporary constitutionalism. First, the exercise of political power is dependent on and limited by the consent or agreement of the people. This limit, required by the convention of consent, is marked by the phrase "popular sovereignty." It is the single most important condition of legitimacy in the contemporary world. No constitutional association is considered legitimate unless government rests on the consent, and so the sovereignty, of the people. Although the expressions sovereign "nations" and sovereign "states" continue to be used, they imply the proviso that the exercise of political power in them has the consent of the people. Popular sovereignty takes two forms: either the people exercise political power themselves or they delegate political power to their representatives. The people place more constraints on the exercise of political power by charters of rights.

Second, sovereignty is limited by a degree of interdependency on, but not subordination to, international relations of various kinds. All contemporary nations are involved in complex relations of interdependence, yet they are still recognised as sovereign. The Maastricht treaty, the North American Free Trade Agreement, the General Agreement on Tariffs and Trade, international laws, treaties, environmental accords and agreements on human and Indigenous rights all limit the exercise of political power. None the less, the continued use of the term "sovereignty" signals that there are limits to external independence. These are hard to define and are always open to debate, but there seem to be two widely held conditions. As Chief Justice Marshall explained ... the relations of interdependency should be voluntarily taken on and they should fall short of colonial dependency. If either of these two conditions of consent and continuity is not met, then it is standardly said that sovereignty has been lost.

Finally, political power is divided among a number of representative bodies, thereby forming varieties of federal and confederal associations, rather than being concentrated in one supreme body, as in the classic modern theories.... The majority of contemporary societies divide power in various ways to allow regions, peoples and nations to govern themselves to different degrees, as in Australia, the United Kingdom and Germany and, concurrently, to place checks on the corrupting tendency of concentrating power in a single, central body.

It does not follow from the demise of the absolute sense of sovereignty that "the end of sovereignty" is near, as some scholars have hastily concluded.4 Rather, a concept of sovereignty remains which incorporates these three limits and is appropriate to the contemporary age. Sovereignty in this non-absolute sense means the authority of a culturally diverse people or association of peoples to govern themselves by their own laws and ways free from external subordination. It is a concept of sovereignty that accords with the overlapping and interdependent terrain of constitutionalism [...] . As the politics of cultural recognition continues to submit governments to the three conventions, it will be limited further.

Once it is realised that the recognition of sovereignty in a post-imperial age can mean no more than this, the normative problem of a despotic elite dissolves, for such an elite could not survive the application of the limits to sovereignty. This concept of sovereignty is not alien to Aboriginal constitutionalism, for it is the concept of sovereignty embodied in the treaty system. Furthermore, the argument applies analogously to any recognition of sovereignty in diverse federalism. No sovereign member is shielded from these limits, just as no independent country is, for they are prescribed by the three conventions which justify the recognition of their sovereignty.

The most common objection to the recognition and accommodation of cultural diversity is that it will lead to disunity. The connections between uniformity and unity on one hand and diversity and disunity on the other are so firmly forged in the language of modern constitutionalism that it seems unreasonable to raise doubts. In the theories of Hobbes and Pufendorf, uniformity leads to unity and so to the strength and power needed to hold out in the competition with other European powers over the wealth and labour of the non-European world. Diversity leads to disunity, weakness, dissolution and death. The "crasie house," Hobbes concluded, "hardly lasting out their own time, must assuredly fall upon the heads of their posterity."5 We have noticed the same connection drawn in the *Federalist papers* between uniformity, unity and imperial expansion, this time over the Aboriginal nations, and the disunity and weakness that would befall a diverse confederation. Lord Durham in Canada was no less concerned to insist that the unity created by cultural uniformity would empower the British empire to expand across the continent. In fact, it is difficult to find a classic text of modern constitutionalism which does not contrast uniformity, unity and power to diversity, disunity and weakness....

Although these imperial arguments were originally served to us as reasons for uniformity, I humbly submit that they may now simply be returned as reasons against it. Further, even if cultural uniformity were necessary to unity, the only just way it can be obtained is through consent of those affected. More decisively, the inference is false. The imposition of uniformity does not lead to unity but to resistance, further repression and disunity. The proof is the dismal record in practice.

Knox's comparison of Ireland and Minorca remains relevant today as it was in 1774, as we have seen in example after example. Aboriginal peoples are exemplary. Every imaginable means of destruction of their cultures and assimilation into uniform European ways has been tried. Yet, after five hundred years of repression and attempted genocide, they are still here and as multiform as ever. The other cultures I have mentioned have suffered suppression and assimilation as well. They too have resisted, like so many bent but unbreakable twigs, to use Sir Isaiah Berlin's phrase, for cultural recognition is a deep and abiding human need. The suppression of cultural difference in the name of uniformity and unity is one of the leading causes of civil strife, disunity and dissolution today.

Conversely, where cultural diversity has been recognised and accommodated in various ways, confrontation and conflict have eased and the members of a constitutional association have been able to work together on their common problems. As we have seen, resources of legal and political pluralism and culturally sensitive constitutional reasoning are available in the history of common constitutionalism to handle situations. Their use demonstrates that the unity of a constitutional association derives from the protection and concordance, rather than the discontinuity and assimilation, of the cultural identities of its members. The strength of the constitutional fabric consists in the interweaving of different threads—a crazy quilt rather than a crazy house.

The mutual recognition of the cultures of citizens engenders allegiance and unity for two reasons. Citizens have a sense of belonging to, and identification with, a constitutional association in so far as, first, they have a say in the formation and governing of the association and, second, they see their own cultural ways publicly acknowledged and affirmed in the basic institutions of their society. No matter how diverse or confederal it is, these two features nurture a strong sense of pride in the association. There is no irreconcilable conflict between allegiance to the constitution and one's culture or cultures, for the constitution and its public institutions and traditions of interpretation are the protectors, rather than the destroyers, of the cultures and rights of the members. If these two conditions are not met, the association is experienced as an alien and imposed yoke that suppresses the members' liberty and cultural identities, causing resistance and disunity. As Said pragmatically replies to Schlesinger, "it is better to explore history than to repress or deny it." The fact that the United States contains so many histories, many of them now clamouring for attention, is by no means to be suddenly feared since many of them were always there, and out of them an American society and politics were created. If the "old and habitual ideas of the main group" are not "flexible enough to admit new groups, then these ideas need changing, a far better thing to do than reject the emerging groups."[6]

This is the oldest lesson of Western and Aboriginal constitutionality. The politics of cultural recognition is the response to the flouting of the lesson in modern constitutionalism. If the twenty-first century is to be different from the devastating cultural conflicts of the late twentieth century, this lesson will have to be relearned. The courageous citizens of Palestine and Israel, including the dissidents, may prove in practice that this lesson can be learned even after long periods of bitter conflict and imperfect negotiations.

Two Public Goods of Contemporary Constitutionalism: Belonging and Critical Freedom

Why, then, in the face of injustice and inefficacy, is modern constitutional politics dominated by the will to impose uniformity in the name of unity and power? Why is the first step of mutual recognition so difficult? There are many answers to this question. The pursuit of property and the splendour of empire, the misunderstanding and fear of others different from oneself and other explanations have been raised.... Since I am dealing with language, I want to take up the reason why the *language* of modern constitutionalism disposes its users to uniformity.

... [T]he language of modern constitutionalism is informed by the mistaken assumption that the general terms of constitutionalism are applied identically in every instance. This assumption predisposes the theorists and citizens who use the language to look for and insist upon a uniformity and unity that the diverse and aspectival constitutional phenomena it is supposed to represent do not exhibit. They predicate of the phenomena what lies in the language of representation. When the association and its constituents fail to live up to the ideal they are said to be suffering an identity crisis.

In the course of his many attempts to dislodge the assumption that a concept is identical to itself in every instance, Wittgenstein paused to suggest one explanation for the powerful hold of this widespread "paradigm of identity." His interlocutor insists, surely, "a thing is identical with itself." Wittgenstein replies, there "is no finer example of a useless proposition, which yet is connected with a certain play of the imagination. It is as if in imagination we put a thing into its own shape and saw that it fitted."7

This explanation applies to the concepts of modern constitutionalism, for the image of a thing fitting into its own shape is exemplified in the idea that there are necessary and sufficient conditions for the application of a general term of constitutionalism. When the identity of a constitutional association and its constituents is imagined in this way, it is thought of as identical to itself, for example, that a nation must fit into its own shape, like it fits into its borders on a map. The thought that it is not identical to itself, but a complicated network of similarities, overlapping, criss-crossing and open to negotiation offends against the imaginary unity of the nation. This play of the imagination is held in place and reinforced by the habitual use of the language of modern constitutionalism.

The captivating role of this imaginary paradigm of identity in modern constitutionalism has been noted by many observers. Descartes mentions how the early modern constitutional reformers were driven by the classical images of the unity of Sparta and the vision of the mythical legislator who makes the constitution to fit his ideal plan. These republican images have been supplemented by the individualist and communitarian sovereign people of Locke and Rousseau, the modern constitutional monoculture of Kant and Constant, the veil of ignorance, the homogeneous community, the transcultural ideal speech-situation and the shared understandings of those who followed....

It is not too extravagant to suggest, therefore, that the failure mutually to recognise and live with cultural diversity is a failure of imagination; a failure to look on human associations in ways not ruled by these dubious images.

I have invited you to see the terms of constitutionalism as never quite identical to themselves. I have described them overlapping, interacting and negotiated in use because these are the ways they are handled in practice, thereby constituting the aspectival and diverse identity of the constitutional associations they describe. These descriptions free us to regard constitutionalism differently, providing an alternative "paradigm of identity" and evoking a play of the imagination more congenial to recognising and negotiating cultural diversity in a post-imperial age.

The best evocation of this alternative play of the imagination is *The spirit of Haida Gwaii.* If contemporary constitutionalism is imagined in the light of this wonderful sculpture, the two public goods it harbours come into sharp relief.... [T]hey are the critical freedom to question in thought and challenge in practice one's inherited cultural ways, on one hand, and the aspiration to belong to a culture and place, and so to be at home in the world, on the other. The differences between these invaluable goods have been settled in the black canoe. Their concord is indicated by Bill Reid's epigram, "the boat goes on forever anchored in the same place," and by the various aspects of the constitutional organisation of the members on board....

In modern constitutionalism, critical freedom and adherence to custom are thought of as the mutually exclusive and irreconcilable goods which underlie the conflicts of our time over cultural recognition. The ancient constitution is said to have provided a sense of belonging, by the deference to custom, but excluded the critical freedom essential to modern identity. Modern constitutionalism enthrones the freedom of critical enquiry and dissent by excluding the authority of custom. This opposition between ancient authority and modern examination was at the heart of the great early struggles for modern constitutionalism and it continues to inform debate among liberals, nationalists, communitarians, postmoderns, cultural feminists and interculturalists today....

Imagine the large father grizzly bear at the bow of the canoe addressing the other passengers. He describes his vision of the constitutional association in his terms and traditions, explaining how bears exercise their rights, govern themselves, care for each other and relate to others. Instead of then listening to the others, becoming aware of and marvelling at the diversity of cultural ways, enjoying the reflective disequilibrium the dialogue engenders, and negotiating a peaceful arrangement of their similarities and differences, he unjustly demands that everyone adopt the ways of the bear clan, as male bears see them. He claims that the ways of the bear clan are superior to all the others in their civility or efficiency. Alternatively, he may claim that they are not bear ways at all, but universal ways that the bears, being at a higher stage, are able to discern. Or he confidently asserts that his articulation of the association comprehends and sublimates the constitutional ways of the others in a higher synthesis. The other passengers would accept these ways if they too were reasonable, if they would think through the following thought experiment, or if they would only speak in the language of constitutionalism he uses.

The injustice of not applying the conventions of recognition and continuity mutually is glaringly obvious. The various strategies of the bear manifest the imperial attitude of speaking for rather than with others, the anti-democratic attitude which informs the imperial features of modern constitutionalism. This attitude of superiority is supported by the background image that the association must exhibit uniformity, that some such vision must capture its identity. And, alas, if the other passengers accept his modern language, they too will find it difficult to imagine otherwise.

From the perspectives of *The spirit of Haida Gwaii*, it is unimaginable that this attitude could be seen as just. The passengers are arranged to subvert this imperial attitude at every turn. Of course, the bear ways are indispensable to the beauty of the canoe, but they would become monstrous if they were to gain hegemony and efface the living cultures of the other members. The beauty of the bear, and of any other member of the ensemble, comes from his place among the others. The aesthetic justice involved is precisely that of rendering each member his or her due.

As one walks around the sculpture and is drawn to imagine oneself aboard, one is constantly made aware that the passengers never fit into their own shape. The play of one's imagination is never allowed to settle on this possibility. This *Xuuya* play is orchestrated by the endless juxtaposition of these diverse and interrelated creatures, the identity of each consisting in the innumerable ways it relates to and interacts with the others. As the assemblage is viewed from one point of view, certain aspects are recognised and they give a vision to the whole. For example, take in the breathtaking view from the raven's position. Then view the multiplicity from the bear's locale. Other aspects and relations come to light, and a different vision of the whole. Now, look at how the mother bear, according to Bill Reid, appears to be cautioning her husband that his vision overlooks some important aspect of the confederation. Then walk around and see how each member and the ensemble are transformed from the neighbourhood of *hlkkyaan qqusttaan*, the frog, or the borough of *Qaganjaat*, the mouse woman. The imperious attempt to colonise this celebration of diversity in one form of recognition—whether of one passenger, of the comprehension of all passengers, or of a form which transcends their differences—is resisted and defeated by the play of the irreducible diversity of the work of art on one's imagination. *Xuuya*, the raven, is at the helm as a reminder that this play is the spirit of the voyage.

If we now view ourselves as members of the black canoe, the diversity of our fellow citizens evokes a sense of belonging to a constitutional association in which one's own culture (or cultures) is recognised as a constituent and interrelated part of the justice of the whole association. This specific sense of belonging and civic pride would be lost if one's culture were excluded, identified in isolation from the others or imposed on all the members. The sense of belonging comes from being associated with the other cultures.

The good of belonging typical of ancient constitutionalism is thus transformed in a manner appropriate to a culturally diverse age.... The sense of belonging and allegiance comes not only from the public recognition of one's culture, but also because one's culture is respected among others and woven into the public fabric of the association, gaining its strength and splendour from its accommodation among, and interrelations with, the others. This is more than a civic awareness that citizens of other cultures exist in one's polity. One's own identity as a citizen is inseparable from a shared history with other citizens who are irreducibly different; whose cultures have interacted with and enriched one's own and made their mark on the basic institutions of society. The loss or assimilation of any of the other cultures is experienced as an impoverishment of one's own identity.

I imagine that many citizens of the four nations of the United Kingdom have a very similar sense of belonging to their multiple kingdom. As interculturalists argued ..., the sensibility should be extended analogously to the other cultures of contemporary societies. Such a post-imperial understanding of belonging is incompatible with assimilation and the best bulwark against it. The pride of belonging to a culture that gains its splendour and reputation from its association with others encourages citizens to care for the survival and conservation of all cultures. The surviving cultural multiplicity constitutes the secure place of anchorage.

At the same time, the black canoe evokes a sense of estrangement from one's own cultural outlook by seeing it juxtaposed to a multiplicity of others. Although the myth creatures view the whole from their own individual points of view, their overlap, interaction and negotiation ensure that they cannot help but be aware that their own viewpoint is one among many, and that the others are not exotic and separate, but near at hand and interrelated to their own in a variety of ways. Their entangled arrangement, graphically highlighted by the wolf and eagle, creates the disequilibrium with respect to one's settled cultural self understanding.

The sense of being at home in the multiplicity yet at the same time playfully estranged by it awakes an attitude of wonder. The Haida myths Bill Reid retells in *The raven steals the light* overflow with examples of how the creatures of the black canoe revel in this wonderful cultural freedom....

Now, the ability to free ourselves from what is most familiar and to wonder again at the sheer diversity of things is just as highly valued in contemporary, non-Aboriginal civilisations. However, as George Marcus and Michael Fischer submit in *Anthropology as cultural critique*, it is thought to require an exotic experience: atonal music, cubist or surreal painting, *Waiting for Godot* or, especially, an encounter with a primitive culture. The juxtaposition of the myth creatures reveals that this invaluable attitude of world reversal and wonder can be awakened just by doing what Wittgenstein does in the *Philosophical investigations* and what they do aboard the canoe: exchange and juxtapose their myths, narratives and further descriptions of their interrelated histories together. The wonderfulness of *The spirit of Haida Gwaii* thus ushers in the other public good of contemporary constitutionalism: the ability to see one's own ways as strange and unfamiliar, to stray from and take up a critical attitude towards them and so open cultures to question, reinterpretation, negotiation, transformation and non-identity.

The theorists of modern constitutionalism define critical freedom and dissent as their primary good. Yet, after a critical survey, the settled forms of critical freedom and dissent within modern constitutionalism and its three traditions of interpretation turn out to be much narrower than they first appear. They are exercised within the uncriticised horizons of seven features which look increasingly contingent and parochial as the vestiges of the imperial age recede. Moreover, the presumption of a comprehensive theory forecloses the possibility of an intercultural dialogue in which diversity awareness and broader critical freedom could be engendered and exercised.

A constitutional association which recognises and accommodates cultural diversity, in contrast, provides the social basis for critical reflection on and dissent from one's own cultural institutions and traditions of interpretation. Citizens are made aware of cultural diversity at home, as something related to and overlapping with their own culture, but nevertheless different. The possibility of crossing from one culture to another is available and unavoidable, for each citizen is a member of more than one culture. The diverse legal and political institutions of the association create an environment in which one's own institutions and traditions can scarcely be taken for granted. The mutual respect for and affirmation of cultural diversity in the civic life of a society further enhance a critical attitude to one's own culture and a tolerant and critical attitude towards others. An ethos of critical freedom is also sustained by the public acknowledgement that the constitution is open to review and that discussion of it is a valuable dimension of citizenship. Most importantly, engagement in intercultural dialogues on the constitution, like Aboriginal exchanges of stories, is itself the exercise of critical freedom, as citizens tell and mediate their stories of the association. In these and other ways, contemporary constitutionalism provides a broader and more cosmopolitan forum for a civic life of critical freedom than modern constitutionalism....

NOTES

1   Clifford Geertz, "The strange estrangement: Taylor and the natural sciences," *Philosophy in an Age of Pluralism: The Philosophy of Charles Taylor in Question,* ed. James Tully (Cambridge: Cambridge University Press, 1994) 83–95.
2   Octavio Paz, *The Labyrinth of Solitude* (London: Penguin, 1967), cited in Jamake Highwater, *The Primal Mind: Vision and Reality in Indian America* (New York: Meridian, 1981) motto and 9.
3   Bill Reid, verbal statement to the Wilderness Advisory Committee, Vancouver B.C., January 1986; Doris Shadbolt, *Bill Reid* (Vancouver: Douglas and McIntyre, 1986) 178.
4   Joseph A. Camilleri and Jim Falk, *The End of Sovereignty? The Politics of a Shrinking and Fragmenting World* (Aldershot: Edward Arnold, 1992).
5   Hobbes, *Leviathan,* ed. Richard Tuck (Cambridge: Cambridge University Press, 1991) 221.
6   Edward Said, *Culture and Imperialism* (New York: Knopf, 1993) xxvi.
7   Wittgenstein, *Philosophical Investigations,* tr. G.E.M. Anscombe (Oxford: Basil Blackwell, 1967), ss. 215, 216.

FURTHER READING

Tully's *A Discourse on Property: John Locke and his Adversaries* (Cambridge: Cambridge University Press, 1980) is a radical re-interpretation of Locke's philosophical defence of private property. Closely analysing Locke's account with an eye on the political context of late eighteenth-century Britain, Tully suggests that Locke's conclusions point to a much more conditional and circumscribed defence of private property than that normally ascribed to Locke. In Chapter Five of *Strange Multiplicity* (Cambridge: Cambridge University Press, 1995), too, Tully gives an excellent account of how Locke's theory of property was used to justify the conquest of indigenous peoples. Tully expands his work on Locke in *An Approach to Political Philosophy: Locke in Contexts* (Cambridge: Cambridge University Press, 1993); and his interest in cultural recognition and globalization is reflected in *Multinational Democracies,* edited with Alain Gagnon (Cambridge: Cambridge University Press, 2001).

CHAPTER 17

WILL KYMLICKA

INTRODUCTION

Will Kymlicka is the theorist who has best defined and examined the nature of multicultural citizenship within liberal democracies. Kymlicka argues that certain discrete cultural groups in modern liberal states can justifiably claim unique rights as a group. Because of the fundamental importance of cultural identity to the development of the autonomous liberal, he argues, contemporary liberals cannot coherently neglect the preservation of distinct ways of life that may be overwhelmed by a dominant mainstream culture. Like Charles Taylor, Kymlicka attempts to balance the resonance of individualism with the vibrancy and transcendence of social life.

THE GOOD, THE BAD, AND THE INTOLERABLE: MINORITY GROUP RIGHTS (1996)

Ethnocultural minorities around the world are demanding various forms of recognition and protection, often in the language of "group rights." Many commentators see this as a new and dangerous trend that threatens the fragile international consensus on the importance of individual rights. Traditional human rights doctrines are based on the idea of the inherent dignity and equality of all individuals. The emphasis on group rights, by contrast, seems to treat individuals as the mere carriers of group identities and objectives, rather than as autonomous personalities capable of defining their own identity and goals in life. Hence it tends to subordinate the individual's freedom to the group's claim to protect its historical traditions or cultural purity.

I believe that this view is overstated. In many cases, group rights supplement and strengthen human rights, by responding to potential injustices that traditional rights doctrine cannot address. These are the "good" group rights. There are cases, to be sure, where illiberal groups seek the right to restrict the basic liberties of their members. These are the "bad" group rights. In some cases, these illiberal practices are not only bad, but intolerable, and the larger society has a right to intervene to stop them. But in other cases, liberal states must tolerate unjust practices within a minority group. Drawing the line between the bad and the intolerable is one of the thorniest issues liberal democracies face.

I want to look at the relationship between group and individual rights in the context of the claims of indigenous peoples in North America. In both the United States and Canada, these peoples have various group rights. For example, they have rights of self-government, under which they exercise control over health, education, family law, policing, criminal justice, and resource development. They also have legally recognized land claims, which reserve certain lands for their exclusive use and provide guaranteed representation on certain regulatory bodies. And in some cases, they have rights relating to the use of their own language.

The situation of indigenous peoples is a useful example, I think, for several reasons. For one thing, they have been at the forefront of the movement toward recognizing group rights at the international level—reflected in the Draft Universal Declaration on Indigenous Rights at the United Nations. The case of indigenous peoples also shows that group rights are not a new issue. From the very beginning of European colonization, the "natives" fought for rights relating to their land, languages, and self-government. What has changed in recent years is not that indigenous peoples have altered their demands, but rather that these demands have become more visible, and that the larger society has started to listen to them.

Reflecting on this long history should warn us against the facile assumption that the demand for group rights is somehow a byproduct of current intellectual fashions, such as postmodernism, or of ethnic entrepreneurs pushing affirmative action programs beyond their original intention. On the contrary, the consistent historical demands of indigenous peoples suggest that the issue of group rights is an enduring and endemic one for liberal democracies.

Group rights, as I will use the term, refer to claims to something more than, or other than, the common rights of citizenship. The category is obviously very large and can be subdivided into any number of more refined categories, reflecting the different sorts of rights sought by different sorts of groups.

Two Kinds of Group Rights

For my purposes, however, the most important distinction is between two kinds of group rights: one involves the claim of an indigenous group against its own members; the other involves the claim of an indigenous group against the larger society. Both of these can be seen as protecting the stability of indigenous communities, but they respond to different sources of instability. The first is intended to protect a group from the destabilizing impact of internal dissent (that is, the decision of individual members not to follow traditional practices or customs), whereas the second is intended to protect the group from the impact of external decisions (that is, the economic or political policies of the larger society). I will call the first "internal restrictions" and the second "external protections."

Both are "group rights," but they raise very different issues. Internal restrictions involve intra-group relations. An indigenous group may seek the use of state power to restrict the liberty of its own members in the name of group solidarity. For example, a tribal government might discriminate against those members who do not share the traditional religion. This sort of internal restriction raises the danger of individual oppression. Group rights in this sense can be invoked by patriarchal and theocratic cultures to justify the oppression of women and the legal enforcement of religious orthodoxy.

Of course, all forms of government involve restricting the liberty of those subject to their authority. In all countries, no matter how liberal and democratic, people are required to pay taxes to support public goods. Most democracies also require people to undertake jury duty or to perform some amount of military or community service, and a few countries require people to vote. All governments expect and sometimes require a minimal level of civic responsibility and participation from their citizens.

But some groups seek to impose much greater restrictions on the liberty of their members. It is one thing to require people to do jury duty or to vote, and quite another to compel people to attend a particular church or to follow traditional gender roles. The former are intended to uphold liberal rights and democratic

institutions, the latter restrict these rights in the name of orthodoxy or cultural tradition. It is these latter cases that I have in mind
when talking about internal restrictions.

Obviously, groups are free to require respect for traditional norms
and authorities as terms of membership in private, voluntary associations. A Catholic organization can insist that its members be
Catholics in good standing, and the same applies to voluntary religious organizations within indigenous communities. The problem
arises when a group seeks to use *governmental* power, or the distribution of public benefits, to restrict the liberty of members.

On my view, such legally imposed internal restrictions are almost
always unjust. It is a basic tenet of liberal democracy that whoever
exercises political power within a community must respect the civil
and political rights of its members, and any attempt to impose internal restrictions that violate this condition is unjust.

External protections, by contrast, involve inter-group relations.
In these cases, the indigenous group seeks to protect its distinct
existence and identity by limiting its vulnerability to the decisions
of the larger society. For example, reserving land for the exclusive
use of indigenous peoples ensures that they are not outbid for this
resource by the greater wealth of outsiders. Similarly, guaranteeing representation for indigenous peoples on various public regulatory bodies reduces the chance that they will be outvoted on
decisions that affect their community. And allowing indigenous
peoples to control their own health care system ensures that critical decisions are not made by people who are ignorant of their
distinctive health needs or their traditional medicines.

On my view, these sorts of external protections are often consistent with liberal democracy, and may indeed be necessary for democratic justice. They can be seen as putting indigenous peoples and
the larger society on a more equal footing, by reducing the extent
to which the former is vulnerable to the latter.

Of course, one can imagine circumstances where the sorts of
external protections demanded by a minority group are unfair.
Under the apartheid system in South Africa, for example, whites,
who constituted less than 20 percent of the population, demanded
87 percent of the land mass of the country, monopolized all the
political power, and imposed Afrikaans and English throughout the
entire school system. They defended this in the name of reducing

their vulnerability to the decisions of other larger groups, although the real aim was to dominate and exploit these groups.

However, the sorts of external protections sought by indigenous peoples hardly put them in a position to dominate others. The land claims, representation rights, and self-government powers sought by indigenous peoples do not deprive other groups of their fair share of economic resources or political power, nor of their language rights. Rather, indigenous peoples simply seek to ensure that the majority cannot use its superior numbers or wealth to deprive them of the resources and institutions vital to the reproduction of their communities. And that, I believe, is fully justified. So, whereas internal restrictions are almost inherently in conflict with liberal democratic norms, external protections are not—so long as they promote equality between groups rather than allowing one group to oppress another.

The Group Rights of Indigenous Peoples

Which sorts of claims are indigenous peoples making? This is not always an easy question to answer. Self-government rights can be used either to secure external protections or to impose internal restrictions, and some indigenous groups use these rights in both ways.

But most indigenous peoples seek group rights primarily for the external protections they afford. Most groups are concerned with ensuring that the larger society does not deprive them of the resources and institutions necessary for their survival, not with controlling the extent to which their own members engage in untraditional or unorthodox practices. Under these circumstances, there is no conflict between external protections and individual rights. Groups that have these external protections may fully respect the civil and political rights of their own members. Indeed, many indigenous groups have adopted their own internal constitutional bills of rights, guaranteeing freedom of religion, speech, press, conscience, association, and a speedy and public trial.

In these cases, group rights supplement, even strengthen, standard human rights. Far from limiting the basic civil and political rights of individual Indians, they help to protect the context within which those rights have their meaning and efficacy. The long history of European-indigenous relations suggests that even if indigenous peoples have citizenship rights in the mainstream society, they tend to be politically impotent and culturally marginalized.

Some readers might think that I am underestimating the illiberal tendencies of indigenous groups. I have argued that many Indian communities are committed to respecting the rights of their individual members. Why then are most indigenous peoples in the United States opposed to the idea that their internal decisions should be subject to judicial review under the U.S. Bill of Rights?

This is an important question, which goes to the heart of the relationship between group and individual rights, and which is worth exploring in some depth. As part of their self-government, tribal councils in the United States have historically been exempted from the constitutional requirement to respect the Bill of Rights. Various efforts have been made by federal legislators to change this, most recently the 1968 Indian Civil Rights Act. According to this Act, which was passed by Congress despite vociferous opposition from most Indian groups, tribal governments are now required to respect most (but not all) constitutional rights. However, there are still limits on judicial review of the actions of tribal councils. If a member of an Indian tribe feels that her rights have been violated by her tribal council, she can seek redress in a tribal court, but she cannot (except under exceptional circumstances) seek redress from the Supreme Court.

Indian groups remain strongly opposed to the 1968 Act, and would almost certainly resist any attempt to extend the jurisdiction of federal courts over Indian governments. Similarly, Indian bands in Canada have argued that their self-governing councils should not be subject to judicial review under the Canadian Charter of Rights and Freedoms. They do not want their members to be able to challenge band decisions in the courts of the mainstream society.

These limits on the application of constitutional bills of rights suggest that individuals or subgroups within Indian communities could be oppressed in the name of group solidarity or cultural purity. For example, concern has been expressed that Indian women in the United States and Canada might be discriminated against under certain systems of self-government, if these communities are exempt from the constitutional requirement of sexual equality. Demanding exemption from judicial review in the name of self government, for many people, is a smokescreen behind which illiberal groups hide their oppressive practices.

Before jumping to this conclusion, however, we should consider the reasons why groups that believe in individual rights would nonetheless be distrustful of judicial review. In the case of indigenous peoples, these reasons are, I think, painfully obvious. After all, the federal courts have historically accepted and legitimated the colonization and dispossession of Indian peoples and lands. Why should Indians trust the federal courts to act impartially now?

But there are other, more specific concerns. Many Indians argue that their self-government needs to be exempt from the Bill of Rights, not in order to restrict the liberty of women or religious dissidents, but to defend the external protections of Indians vis-à-vis the larger society. Their special rights to land, or to hunting, or to group representation, which reduce their vulnerability to external economic and political decisions, could be struck down as discriminatory under the Bill of Rights. Such protections do not, in my view, violate equality. On the contrary, a powerful case could be made that they promote equality, by protecting Indians from unjust majority decisions. But Indians rightly worry that the Supreme Court could take a different and more formalistic view of equality rights.

Indian leaders also fear that white judges might interpret certain rights in culturally biased ways. For example, traditional Indian forms of consensual political decision making could be seen as denying democratic rights. These traditional procedures do not violate the underlying democratic principle of the Constitution— namely, that legitimate authority requires the consent of the governed, subject to periodic review. However, they do not use the particular method for securing consent envisioned by the Constitution—namely, periodic election of representatives. Rather, they rely on time-honored procedures for ensuring consensual decision making. Indian leaders worry that white judges will impose their own culturally specific form of democracy, without considering whether traditional Indian practices are an equally valid interpretation of democratic principles.

It is often difficult for outsiders to assess the likelihood that self-government for an indigenous minority will lead to the suppression of basic individual rights. The identification of oppression requires sensitivity to the specific context, particularly when dealing with other cultures, and so it is not surprising that Indians would want these questions settled in a forum where judges are familiar with the situation.

Hence many Indian leaders seek exemption from the Bill of Rights, but at the same time affirm their commitment to basic human rights and freedoms. They endorse the principles, but object to the particular institutions and procedures that the larger society has established to enforce these principles. They seek to create or maintain their own procedures for protecting rights, specified in tribal constitutions (some of which are based on the provisions of international protocols).

Of course, not all Indian groups accept the commitment to respect individual rights. One example of internal restrictions concerns freedom of religion on the Pueblo reservation. Because they are not subject to the Bill of Rights, tribal governments are not required to obey its strict separation of church and state. The Pueblo have, in effect, established a theocratic government that discriminates against those members who do not share the tribal religion. For example, housing benefits have been denied to members of the community who have converted to Protestantism. In this case, self-government powers are being used to limit the freedom of members to question and revise traditional practices.

The Pueblo also use sexually discriminatory membership rules. If female members marry outside the tribe, their children are denied membership. But if men marry outside the tribe, the children are members. Here again, the rights of individuals are being restricted to preserve a communal practice (although there is some debate about whether this membership rule is in fact the "traditional" one, or whether it was adopted by the Pueblo at the behest of the American government, which hoped thereby to minimize its financial obligations).

In other cases, tribal governments have become profoundly undemocratic, governed by strongmen who ignore traditional ideals of consensus and govern by a combination of intimidation and corruption.

In these cases, not surprisingly, members of the Indian community often seek some form of outside judicial review. These cases put liberals on the horns of a serious dilemma. This is no longer a case of whites imposing "our" norms on Indians, who would prefer to live by "their" norms. The problem, rather, is that Indians themselves are deeply divided, not only about their traditional norms, but also about the ability of their traditional decision-making procedures to deal with these divisions. In some cases, reformers seeking federal judicial review may form a sizable minority, if not a majority, within their community. For example, the Native Women's Association of Canada, worried about the danger of sexual discrimination on their reserves, has demanded that the decisions of Aboriginal governments be subject to the Canadian Charter.

The Limits of Toleration

How should liberal states respond in such cases? It is right and proper, I think, for liberals to criticize oppressive practices within indigenous communities, just as we should criticize foreign countries that oppress their citizens. These oppressive practices may be traditional (although many aren't), but tradition is not self-validating. Indeed, that an oppressive practice is traditional may just show how deep the injustice goes.

But should we intervene and impose a liberal regime on the Pueblo, forcing them to respect the religious liberty of Protestants and the sexual equality of women? Should we insist that indigenous governments be subject to the Bill of Rights, and that their decisions be reviewable by federal courts?

It's important here to distinguish two questions: (1) Are internal restrictions consistent with liberal principles? and (2) Should liberals impose their views on minorities that do not accept some or all of these principles? The first is the question of *identifying* a defensible liberal theory of group rights; the second is the question of *imposing* that theory.

The first question is easy: internal restrictions are illiberal and unjust. But the answer to the second question is less clear. That liberals cannot automatically impose their principles on groups that do not share them is obvious enough, I think, if the illiberal group is another country. The Saudi Arabian government unjustly denies political rights to women or non-Muslims. But it doesn't follow that liberals outside Saudi Arabia should forcibly intervene to compel the Saudis to give everyone the vote. Similarly, the German government unjustly denies political rights to the children and grandchildren of Turkish "guest-workers," born and raised on German soil. But it doesn't follow that liberals outside Germany should use force to compel Germany to change its citizenship laws.

What isn't clear is the proper remedy for rights violations. What third party (if any) has the authority to intervene in order to force the government to respect those rights? The same question arises when the illiberal group is a self-governing indigenous community within a single country. The Pueblo tribal council violates the rights of its members by limiting freedom of conscience and by employing sexually discriminatory membership rules. But what third party (if any) has the authority to compel the Pueblo council to respect those rights?

Liberal principles tell us that individuals have certain claims that their government must respect, such as individual freedom of conscience. But having identified those claims, we now face the very different question of imposing liberalism. If a particular government fails to respect those claims, who can legitimately step in and force compliance? (By "imposing" liberalism, I am referring to forcible intervention by a third party. Noncoercive intervention is a different matter, which I discuss below.)

The attitude of liberals toward imposing liberalism has changed over the years. In the international context, they have become increasingly skeptical about using force to compel foreign states to obey liberal principles. Many nineteenth-century liberals thought that liberal states were justified in colonizing and instructing foreign countries. Woodrow Wilson defended the American colonization of the Philippines in 1902 on the grounds that "they are children and we are men in these matters of government and justice." Contemporary liberals, however, have abandoned this doctrine as both imprudent and illegitimate, and sought instead to promote liberal values through persuasion and financial incentives.

In the case of self-governing indigenous minorities, however, liberals have been much more willing to endorse coercive intervention. Many American liberals assume that the Supreme Court has the legitimate authority to overturn any decisions of the Pueblo tribal council that violate individual rights. They commonly assume that to have a "right" means not only that legislators should respect one's claim, but also that there should be a system of judicial review to ensure that respect. Moreover, this judicial review should occur at a country-wide level. That is, in addition to the various state and tribal courts that review the laws of state and tribal governments, there should also be a Supreme Court to which all governments within the country are answerable. Indeed, many American liberals often talk as if it is part of the very meaning of "rights" that there should be a single court in each country with the authority to review the decisions of all governments within that country.

This is a very particularist understanding of rights. In some liberal countries (for example, Britain), there is a strong tradition of respecting individual rights, but there is no constitutional bill of rights and no basis for courts to overturn parliamentary decisions that violate individual rights. (The same was true in Canada until 1982.) In other countries, there is judicial review, but it is decentralized—that is, political subunits have their own systems of review, but there is no single bill of rights and no single court to which all levels of government are answerable. Indeed, this was true in the United States for a considerable period of time. Until the passage of the Fourteenth Amendment, state legislatures were answerable to state courts for the way they respected state constitutions, but were not answerable to the Supreme Court for respecting the Bill of Rights.

It's easy to see why American liberals are committed to giving the Supreme Court such wide authority. Historically, this sort of judicial review, backed up by federal troops, was required to overturn the racist legislation of Southern states, which state courts had upheld. Given the central role federal courts have played in the struggle against racism, American liberals have developed a deep commitment to centralized judicial review. So when a question is raised about self-governing indigenous peoples, many liberals automatically support centralized review, even though these peoples were historically exempt from any such external intervention.

In short, contemporary liberals have become more reluctant to impose liberalism on foreign countries, but more willing to impose liberalism on indigenous minorities. This, I think, is inconsistent. Both foreign states and indigenous minorities form distinct political communities, with their own claims to self-government. Attempts to impose liberal principles by force are often perceived, in both cases, as a form of aggression or paternalistic colonialism. And, as a result, these attempts often backfire. The plight of many former colonies in Africa shows that liberal institutions are likely to be unstable when they are the products of external imposition rather than internal reform. In the end, liberal institutions can work only if liberal beliefs have been internalized by the members of the self-governing society, be it an independent country or an indigenous minority.

There are, of course, important differences between foreign states and indigenous minorities. Yet, in both cases, there is relatively little scope for legitimate coercive interference. Relations between the majority society and indigenous peoples should be determined by peaceful negotiation, not force. This means searching for some basis of agreement. The most secure basis would be agreement on fundamental principles. But if the two groups do not share basic principles, and cannot be persuaded to adopt the other's principles, they will have to rely on some more minimalist modus vivendi.

The resulting agreement may well exempt the indigenous minority from the Bill of Rights and judicial review. Indeed, such exemptions are often implicit in the historical treaties by which the minority entered the larger state. This means that the majority will sometimes be unable [to] prevent the violation of individual rights within the minority community. Liberals have to learn to live with this, just as they must live with illiberal laws in other countries.

It doesn't follow that liberals should stand by and do nothing. An indigenous government that rules in an illiberal way acts unjustly. Liberals have a right, and a responsibility, to speak out against such injustice. Hence, liberal reformers inside the culture should seek to promote their principles through reason and example, and liberals outside should lend their support. Since the most enduring forms of liberalization are those that result from internal reform, the primary focus for liberals outside the group should be to support liberals inside.

Moreover, there is an important difference between coercively imposing liberalism and offering incentives for liberal reforms. Again, this is clear in the international arena. For example, the desire of former communist countries to enter the European Community (EC) has provided leverage for Western democracies to push for liberal reforms in Eastern Europe. Membership in the EC is a powerful, but noncoercive, incentive for liberal reform. Similarly, many people thought that negotiations over the North American Free Trade Agreement provided an opportunity for Canada and the United States to pressure the Mexican government into improving its human rights record.

There are many analogous opportunities for a majority to encourage indigenous peoples, in a noncoercive way, to liberalize their internal constitutions. Of course there are limits to the appropriate forms of pressure. Refusing to extend trade privileges is one thing, imposing a total embargo or blockade is quite another. The line between incentive and coercion is not a sharp one, and where to draw it is a much-debated point in the international context.

Finally, and perhaps most important, liberals can push for the development and strengthening of international mechanisms for protecting human rights. Some Indian tribes have expressed a willingness to abide by international declarations of rights, and to answer to international tribunals about complaints of rights violations within their communities. They accept the idea that their governments, like all sovereign governments, should be accountable to international norms. Indeed, they have shown greater willingness to accept this kind of review than many nation-states, which jealously guard their sovereignty in domestic affairs. Most Indian tribes do not oppose all forms of external review. What they object to is being subject to the constitution of their conquerors, which they had no role in drafting, and being answerable to federal courts composed entirely of non-Indian justices.

This shows, I think, that the assumption of American liberals that there must be one court within each country that is the ultimate defender of individual rights is doubly mistaken, at least in the case of indigenous peoples. History has proven the value of holding all governments accountable for respecting human rights. But the appropriate forum for reviewing the actions of self-governing indigenous peoples may skip the federal level, as it were. Many indigenous groups would endorse a system in which their decisions are reviewed in the first instance by their own courts and then by an international court. Federal courts, dominated by the majority, would have little or no authority over them.

These international mechanisms could arise at the regional as well as global level. European countries have agreed to establish their own multilateral human rights tribunals. Perhaps North American governments and Indian tribes could agree to establish a similar tribunal, on which both sides are fairly represented.

This isn't to say that federal intervention to protect liberal rights is never justified. In cases of gross and systematic violation of human rights, such as slavery, genocide, torture, or mass expulsions, there are grounds for intervening in the internal affairs of an indigenous group. A number of factors are relevant here, including the severity of rights violations within the community, the degree of consensus on restricting individual rights, and the ability of dissenting members to leave the community if they so desire. For example, whether intervention is justified in the case of an Indian tribe that restricts freedom of conscience surely depends on whether it is governed by a tyrant who lacks popular support and prevents people leaving the community or whether the tribal government has a broad base of support and religious dissidents are free to leave.

I should note that my arguments here do not just apply to indigenous peoples. They also apply to other national minorities—that is, other nonimmigrant groups whose homeland has been incorporated into a larger state through conquest, colonization, or the ceding of territory from one imperial power to another. Nonindigenous national minorities include the Québécois in Canada and Puerto Ricans in the United States. These groups differ from indigenous peoples in many ways, but in all these cases, the role of the federal courts in reviewing the decisions of self-governing minorities should be settled by negotiation, not imposition.

Cases involving immigrant groups are quite different. It is more legitimate to compel respect for liberal principles. I do not think it is wrong for liberal states to insist that immigration entails accepting the state's enforcement of liberalism, so long as immigrants know this in advance, and nonetheless choose to come.

Thinking Creatively about Rights

I've argued that the group rights sought by indigenous peoples need not conflict with human rights, and that the relationship between the two must be assessed carefully on a case-by-case basis. Even when the two do conflict, we cannot assume automatically that the courts and constitutions of the larger society should prevail over the self-governing decisions of the indigenous group. Indigenous peoples have good reasons, and sound legal arguments, to reject federal review of their self-government.

We should, however, think creatively about new mechanisms for enforcing human rights that will avoid the legitimate objections indigenous peoples have to federal courts. My aim is not to undermine human rights but rather to find fairer and more effective ways to promote them.

As Joseph Carens puts it, "People are supposed to experience the realization of principles of justice through various concrete institutions, but they may actually experience a lot of the institution and very little of the principle." This is exactly how many indigenous peoples perceive the supreme courts of Canada and the United States. What they experience is not the principle of human dignity and equality, but rather a social institution that has historically justified their conquest and dispossession.

Moreover, to focus exclusively on the danger of internal restrictions is often to miss the real source of injustice. The fact is that many indigenous groups feel compelled to impose internal restrictions because the larger society has denied them legitimate external protection. As Denise Réaume has noted, part of the "demonization" of other cultures is the assumption that they are naturally inclined to use coercion against their members. But insofar as some groups seem regrettably willing to use coercion to preserve traditional practices, this may be due, not to any innate illiberalism but to the fact that the larger society has failed to protect them. Unable to get protection for its lands and institutions, the minority turns to the only people it does have some control over, namely, its own members. This tendency does not justify internal restrictions, but it suggests that before we criticize a minority for imposing restrictions on its members, we should first make sure we are respecting its legitimate group rights.

Our goal, therefore, should be to find new mechanisms that will protect *both* the individual and group rights of indigenous peoples. We need to think about effective mechanisms, acceptable to indigenous peoples, for holding their governments accountable for the way individual members are treated. But we need simultaneously to think about effective mechanisms for holding the larger society accountable for respecting the group rights of indigenous peoples. Focusing on the former while neglecting the latter is counterproductive and hypocritical.

Many indigenous peoples have looked to the United Nations, and its draft declaration on indigenous rights, as a possible forum for pursuing these twin forms of accountability. Unfortunately, both the Canadian and U.S. governments have been reluctant to give any international body jurisdiction over the treaty rights, land claims, or self-government rights of indigenous peoples. Viewed in this light, the real obstacle to a more satisfactory balance of individual and group rights is not the refusal of indigenous peoples to accept external review, but rather the refusal of the larger society to accept restrictions on its sovereignty.

FURTHER READING

Because Kymlicka's writing is extraordinarily clear and accessible, it is best to read his work on its own terms, saving commentaries for critical rather than exegetical purposes. Kymlicka's ideas are best set out in *Liberalism, Community, and Culture* (Oxford: Clarendon Press, 1989), *The Rights of Minority Cultures* (Oxford and Toronto: Oxford University Press, 1995), *Multicultural Citizenship: A Liberal Theory of Minority Rights* (Oxford: Clarendon Press, 1995), and *Politics in the Vernacular: Nationalism, Multiculturalism, and Citizenship* (Oxford: Oxford University Press, 2001). He has also published a number of edited volumes, including *Ethnicity and Group Rights*, with Ian Shapiro (New York: New York University Press, 1997); *Citizenship in Diverse Societies*, with Wayne Norman (Oxford: Oxford University Press, 2000); *Can Liberal Pluralism be Exported? Western Political Theory and Ethnic Relations in Eastern Europe*, with Magda Opalski (Oxford: Oxford University Press, 2001); and *Language Rights and Political Theory*, with Alan Patten (Oxford: Oxford University Press, 2003). The best critique of the theory of minority rights based upon culture is Brian Barry's *Culture and Equality: An Egalitarian Critique of Multiculturalism* (Cambridge, MA: Harvard University Press, 2001).

18 MICHAEL IGNATIEFF

INTRODUCTION

Isaiah Berlin famously wrote that "the fox knows many things, but the hedgehog knows one big thing." Michael Ignatieff (b. 1947) is an excellent example of Berlin's fox (and evidence for this is, not coincidentally, Ignatieff's major biography of Berlin). Ignatieff has published widely not only in political theory, but also in the genres of fiction, memoir, and screenplay. While the works published by Ignatieff are diverse, he is consistent in examining the hard, substantive questions confronting the modern liberal democratic state. Two of his pre-eminent interests are human rights and modern warfare, and many of his works focus upon the complicated ethical issues underlying international relations and human security. The following excerpt was originally part of the 2000 Massey Lectures.

THE RIGHTS REVOLUTION (2000)

In the course of these lectures, I've retold the history of our country since the 1960s as a story of the struggle by different groups of citizens for rights and recognition. In this final lecture, it's time to draw together the argument and ask a basic question: Has the rights revolution brought us closer together as a nation or driven us further apart?

The answer to the question depends on whose point of view you take. In these lectures, I've taken the point of view of the rights-claimants in these struggles: women seeking sexual and economic equality, aboriginal peoples seeking recognition of their title to land, ethnic minorities seeking protection of their culture, and same-sex couples seeking rights equivalent to those afforded heterosexuals. From their perspective, the history of the past forty years is a story of freedom painfully fought for and far from achieved. Unity, by and large, has not been their concern.

From the viewpoint of the bystander majority, however, the rights revolution has often seemed less about emancipation than about fragmentation, with the Canada they once knew taken apart and reassembled into a fractious collection of rival rights communities: gays versus straights, aboriginal peoples versus non-aboriginals, French-speakers versus English-speakers, immigrants versus native-born, abled versus disabled, rich versus poor. The rights revolution empowered these groups at the price of disempowering the majority. When a majority feels it is weakened, it is natural for it to believe that the country has been weakened as well.

Minorities have won recognition, and now it is the turn of the majority to look around and ask, in astonishment, whether it recognizes itself. Where is the majority any more? Who are we? Once we thought we knew: white, heterosexual, family-oriented, native-born people who were Canadians first and anything else second. Now the population is cross-cut with identities—sexual, racial, religious, and ethnic—making it difficult to speak of a Canadian majority at all. This may be one reason for the belief, widely held among our elites, that our country has become ever more difficult to govern. The essential work of national politics is creating majorities (i.e., national coalitions of interest). As the rights revolution fragments the majority, it fragments the coalitions that keep the country together.

The rights revolution also turns politics into an exchange of recrimination between victims and their supposed oppressors. It's not that there aren't real victims out there; the problem is that the majority has genuine difficulty accepting the idea that present generations remain responsible for the harms committed by past ones. How long must the Canadian majority continue to pay for the abuses done to aboriginal peoples in times past? How long must it do penance for racism, sexism, and other forms of injustice? It is clear that for many Canadians, the debate over past injustice produces not mutual recognition but resentment. Victim and oppressor become co-dependent, locked into their roles and unable to shed them. The victim minorities resent depending on the majority for redress. The majority resents depending on the minority for forgiveness. Since forgiveness would foreclose future claims, victims tend to withhold it; since redress implies culpability, it too is withheld. So the politics of argument is replaced by a politics of blackmail and stonewalling. Many in the majority Canadian community who have felt themselves put in the dock by the incessant accusations of various victim communities do not see the rights revolution as a story of a successful fight for inclusion by the excluded. Instead they see it as a story of how a once strong country was fragmented.

Before we determine whether the rights revolution has been destructive of national unity, we should notice that focusing on the rights revolution and its consequences offers a different perspective on the unity issue than the one we became used to before the rights revolution began. The unity debate of the early 1960s was almost entirely about whether Quebec's demands could be met within the framework of the Canadian federation. No one else's claims belonged in the frame, certainly not those of aboriginal peoples, women, people of colour, and same-sex groups. None of these groups was perceived as offering any kind of political challenge to the unity of the country. The only such challenge came from Quebec, and the holy place where this challenge was addressed was the preserve of the high priests of federalism: constitutional lawyers and federal and provincial bureaucrats who knew by heart every arcane clause of the British North America Act, and could tell you, as the old joke used to have it, whether having sex in Canada was a provincial responsibility or a federal one.

The high priests went about their work for a century and a quarter, interpreting the sacred texts and waving the incense of rhetoric in the direction of the congregation, but they did not succeed in keeping the country together. Indeed in 1995, we came within 60,000 votes, in the Quebec referendum, of beginning the dissolution of our country. By then, the high priests had lost control of the rituals of unity. Quebec's battle with Canada had become fused with all the other battles for recognition. At the constitutional talks on Quebec's future, aboriginal and women's groups won a place at the negotiating table. Quebec discovered that it could not secure its demands unless aboriginal peoples and women also won theirs. As these rights claims converged in one negotiating forum, the result was deadlock. A bilateral discussion between Quebec and Canada has been transformed into a multi-dimensional chess game. This "rights frenzy"—that is, the proliferation and entanglement of rights claims—has made many commentators question our very capacity to keep the country together.[1]

But this negative point could also be put positively. Instead of fragmenting the country, rights talk has actually made the national-unity process more democratic. By forcing their way into the negotiations on national unity between 1987 and 1991, women and aboriginal peoples secured a right of participation not just for themselves but for all Canadians. Future constitutional change will have to be ratified by a national referendum. The citizens have forced their way into the inner sanctum and whatever arcane rituals of accommodation are enacted there in the future will require the citizens' consent.

This particular point about rights demands and democracy could be generalized. Not all of the battles fought by minorities have been only on behalf of their own groups. Sometimes, the rights that have been won have been won for everyone. For example, women were never fighting just for themselves; they were fighting for their children, and even for the men in their lives. Likewise, the Charter of Rights and Freedoms is not just a collection of entrenched rights for various linguistic, sexual, and aboriginal minorities. It standardized rights for all citizens. To the degree that rights struggles for particular groups enhance or clarify the rights of all citizens, they strengthen, rather than weaken, the country.

Even when the rights that are gained are exclusively for the use of a particular group, all may benefit indirectly from the fact that the political process becomes more inclusive, and therefore better able to respond to public needs and aspirations. Thus only the disabled specifically benefit when their rights of access and mobility are granted, but the rest of us benefit in a general way too. We benefit because the disabled are freed from dependency relationships that embarrass them and us. Once their mobility rights are guaranteed, they can look after themselves and establish relationships with the rest of us on a basis of genuine equality. The second benefit to us of specific mobility rights for the disabled is that they help our democracy to work better. We are not required to represent the interests of the disabled, since they can do it themselves. And those who represent themselves invariably do a better job than anybody else.[2]

In other cases, however, the majority is less convinced that it has benefited from the rights revolution. Other battles—such as those for language rights, aboriginal title, and sexual enfranchisement—have seemed not to benefit the majority, but rather to force it to cede power and cultural authority. The cultural authority in question is the right of the majority to define what the country "stands for," and how it is seen by itself and the rest of the world. So on questions of sexual morality, the impact of the rights revolution has been to diminish the power of the heterosexual majority to define what is normal and normative in personal life. On questions of our national history and self-image, the impact of the aboriginal revolution has been to force the Canadian majority to face up to the spectre of racism in our national past. When groups get rights, in other words, they also get the right to change the national story, and when they do so, the results can be painful. Once rights are granted, the majority has to live with the truth, and the truth can hurt.

In more direct and immediate ways (i.e., through tax dollars), the Canadian majority has had to pay for the rights revolution. For many in this bystander majority, it seems that the Canadian state is being treated like a kind of general store, situated at a dusty cross-roads where federal and provincial power meet, which every passing traveller feels free to loot in the name of some rights claim or other. Certainly the cost of meeting rights claims—and these claims include rights to welfare, employment insurance, pay equity, and aboriginal title—helped to increase the federal deficit. By 1995, the problem demanded a solution. But the solution—cutbacks to federal services—further weakened the welfare and regional adjustment programs that hold the country together. In this way, meeting rights claims has not always strengthened the sinews of national unity.

The revival of English-Canadian nationalism in the 1980s and 1990s is a reaction to these trends, not just to Quebec nationalism. The mood of English Canada has settled into a single angry demand: enough is enough. This anger is focused not just on Quebec, but also on aboriginal peoples and other rights-claimants. Enough concessions, enough negotiations, enough rights already. There is a new sympathy for symmetrical federalism: equal rights for all provinces and all individuals; no special status for anybody. What I've called the pool-table version of national political space seems to promise an end to the politics of victimhood and black-mail. Strict equality of individual rights would bring us together. We would cease to recognize each other as competing rights communities and instead see ourselves as fellow citizens.

In an earlier lecture, I argued that this symmetrical version of rights doesn't work. It's not true to our history. We simply are a patchwork quilt of distinctive societies. Quebec is entitled to recognition as a distinctive society and its language laws, immigration statutes, and education provisions should be different in order to protect what is different about the province. There also need to be special language laws, as well as French-language education, for New Brunswick because of the size and importance of its Acadian minority. Provinces with large aboriginal populations, like British Columbia, may have to devolve power over land and resources in ways that are different from other provinces. Each situation is different and each needs to be addressed with special provisions.

Yet recognition of distinctiveness does not have to fragment the country. What ought to balance these distinctive provisions is a politics of reciprocity. If Quebec is granted certain rights in respect of its language and culture, the rest of the country has a right to expect the province to protect the cultures, languages, and religions of its minorities. Reciprocity rather than strict symmetry for all is the way to move beyond a politics of concession and threat into a process of mutual recognition, in which each side acknowledges the distinctiveness of the other.

Aboriginal groups, to use another example, have a unique claim on the land and its resources as the original inhabitants of the country. But just as their treaties cannot be "extinguished" by later legislation, except with their consent, so the rights of other Canadians cannot be extinguished by recognition of aboriginal rights. The task is to find a way to reconcile aboriginal claims with the rights of other Canadians to use common resources and with the duty of the federal government to husband and conserve the environment. On both the Atlantic and Pacific fishing grounds, these issues have exploded. Burnt Church has joined Oka in the annals of Canadian conflict. But we would do well to remember, before we shake our heads at the loss of our civility, that rights don't create the conflict—they merely validate claims. And in the case of disputes over resource management, it is good that claims are understood as rights.[3] We don't want a return to the days when aboriginal peoples had no rights and when the federal government's management of resources went unquestioned. Equally, we don't want people defying the law or taking it into their own hands. If these are the limits of what is tolerable, then courts and legislatures will simply have to find peaceful adjudication somewhere in the middle.4 Aboriginal peoples and non-aboriginal Canadians cannot live together unless both accept the ultimate sovereignty of Canadian law. Within this common frame, distinctive aboriginal rights can be reconciled with both use rights by other groups and federal environmental controls. The overall objective for all concerned is to find a way to recognize group rights while maintaining the unity of Canadian citizenship, so that we do not have either second-class citizens or privileged ones, and we can maintain equal moral consideration for all Canadians.

This goes beyond balancing rights. It also means balancing acts of recognition. At the moment, the Canadian majority feels that it is faced with multiplying demands for recognition from various minority groups, without these groups accepting any obligation to recognize the majority. This is the heart of the bitterness in English Canada over Quebec. It is the feeling that the Canadian majority is being asked to concede recognition of Quebec's distinct status without earning any commensurate recognition of Canada in return. This perceived inequality of recognition has led many English Canadians to refuse to be party to further concessions. What has proved insupportable is not the nature of Quebec's demands, but the threat of separation that accompanies the demands. Give us what we want or we will go is not a form of recognition but an expression of contempt....

In other words, recognition is a two-way street. National unity, therefore, depends on equality of rights and equality of recognition: minorities recognize majorities; majorities recognize minorities. Both seek shelter under the arch of a law they can trust, since both have had a hand in building it. This could be called a civic nationalist vision of what should hold the country together.5 Why call it nationalist? Isn't that a dangerous word? I could call it patriotism instead, but that would reproduce an invidious distinction between positive patriotism and negative nationalism. In fact, "patriotism" is simply the name we give to our love of country, while "nationalism" is the epithet we apply to other people's.6 In fact, there is nothing intrinsically fanatical or extreme about nationalism, if we define it as a principled love of country. Canadians have good reasons to love their country, and I would argue that our rights culture is one of them. As I maintained in my first lecture, the essential distinctiveness of Canada itself lies in the fact that we are a tri-national community, trying to balance individual and collective rights without sacrificing the unity and equality of our citizenship. If you ask me what I love about my country, this is it.

It may seem strange to confess a love for something so seemingly legalistic and desiccated as rights. Yet we need to think of rights as something more than a dry enumeration of entitlements in constitutional codes, as more than a set of instruments that individuals use to defend themselves. Rights create and sustain culture and by culture we mean habits of the heart. Rights create community. They do so because once we believe in equal rights, we are committed to the idea that rights are indivisible. Defending your own rights means being committed to defending the rights of others....

The commitment to indivisibility goes with a commitment to mutual sacrifice. All rights cost us something. Even when we don't avail ourselves of our entitlements, others do, and we pay for their use.7 Belonging to a rights community implies that we surrender some portion of our freedom to sustain the collective entitlements that make our life possible. This idea of sacrifice is the very core of what it means to belong to a national community: paying taxes, obeying the law, submitting disputes to adjudication and abiding peacefully by these decisions. Sacrifice does not stop there. The reason that war memorials occupy a central symbolic place in the national life of all nations, even though the wars remembered are now far away in time, is that they represent the sacrifice that all citizens make to keep a community free.

But nationalism is more than this. It is a way of seeing, a way of recognizing fellow citizens as belonging to a shared rights community, and as being entitled to the protection and the care that the national community can provide.

The central issue for Canada, in the wake of the rights revolution, is whether a rights culture is enough to hold the country together, whether it creates a sufficiently robust sense of belonging, and a sufficiently warm-hearted kind of mutual recognition, to enable us to solve our differences peacefully. The criticism most often advanced against a civic nationalist vision of national community is that it is too thin. It bases national solidarity on rights equality, but neither rights nor equality make sufficiently deep claims on the loyalties and affections of people to bond them together over time.8

This is a very old worry about societies based on rights. When Edmund Burke, the great Anglo-Irish conservative thinker of the late eighteenth century, fulminated against the type of society he saw coming into being with the French Revolution, he warned that the revolutionaries were laying themselves open to continual rebellion.9 For these new societies were based on contract, on consent, on agreements between parties that could be dissolved. By contrast, the *ancien regime* societies, whose disappearance he lamented, had been based on tradition, history, common origins, and all the deepest sources of human affection and commitment. The enduring relevance of Burke's critique suggests that he identified a crucial weakness in rights-based societies. Clearly, rights are not enough. The elements that hold a country like Canada together run deeper than rights: the land, shared memory, shared opportunity, and shared hope. Yet Burke and his fellow conservatives underestimated the power of rights as a source of legitimacy and cohesion in modern societies, just as they sentimentalized the legitimacy of the *ancien regime*. The ancient and immemorial tissue of connections was insufficient to keep the France of the *ancien regime* together, and the democratic republic that succeeded it, which was based on consent and contract, has endured for two hundred years....

Canada faces similar challenges. It is held together not just by its constitution, but by formidably strong links of common ancestry. The problem, however, is that our ancestry is a double, even triple, inheritance. In Quebec, the majority francophone community traces its ancestry to the original French settlers, and English Canadians trace theirs to the Scottish, English, and Irish immigrants who opened the frontier from the eighteenth century onward. One million aboriginal Canadians, meanwhile, trace their ancestry back to the heritage of the tribal nations of North America. This triple inheritance doesn't necessarily weaken the country—it may even strengthen it—but it does mean that the principles of national unity cannot be found by joint appeal to common origins.

This is essentially why Canada has no choice but to gamble on rights, to found its unity on civic nationalist principles. Its unity must be derived from common principles rather than common origins. The importance of these principles of unity is only redoubled by the impact of immigration. If there are more than seventy languages spoken in the homes of only one of our major cities,

Toronto, then it is clear that we need a single common language to communicate together, and it is also clear that rights, not roots, are what will hold us together in the future.[10]

The Canadian majority in the next century will be unrecognizably different from the majority I grew up in as a child. Already Canadians of Chinese, Sikh, and Ukrainian origin have occupied the highest offices of state, and more will do so as time goes by. The new Canadian elite has no common origin, only a commitment to common values. But as "new Canadians" make their way to the top, their demands for inclusion are forcing a change in our most basic mythologies. Canadians from these new communities refuse to accept the very concept of Canada as a pact between founding races—that is, the English, the French, and the aboriginal peoples. This concept seems to accord no place to them. Most of them can accept that original inhabitants may have claims to territory and language that are withheld from newcomers. But as these communities grow in number and size, it will be rights delivery, not myths of common origin, that will hold us together. Indeed, without a common fabric of citizenship, without common rights, it is difficult to see what will enable a multicultural society to cohere....[11]

NOTES

[1] Richard Gwyn, *Nationalism without Walls: The Unbearable Lightness of Being Canadian* (Toronto: McClelland and Stewart, 1996), ch. 10.

[2] Al Etmanski, *A Good Life* (Burnaby, B.C.: Planned Lifetime Advocacy Network, 2000). I am indebted to Vancouver city councillor Sam Sullivan for discussing issues relating to the rights of the disabled with me.

[3] "Legal Lobster War Heats Up," *Globe and Mail*, 18 Aug. 2000.

[4] "Uneasy Peace Reigns over Burnt Church," *Globe and Mail*, 16 Aug. 2000.

[5] For a discussion of these terms, see my book *Blood and Belonging: Journeys into the New Nationalism* (Toronto: Penguin, 1993), introduction.

[6] Maurizio Viroli, *For Love of Country: An Essay on Patriotism and Nationalism* (Oxford: Clarendon Press, 1995).

[7] Stephen Holmes and Cass R. Sunstein, *The Cost of Rights: Why Liberty Depends on Taxes* (New York: W.W. Norton, 1999).

[8] Bernard Yack, "The Myth of the Civic Nation," in *Theorizing Nationalism*, ed. Robert Beiner (Albany: State University of New York Press, 1999), 103–19. Philip Resnick, "Civic and Ethnic Nationalism: Lessons from the Canadian Case," in *Canadian Political Philosophy: Contemporary Reflections*, ed. R. Beiner and W. Norman (Toronto: University of Toronto Press, 2000).

[9] Edmund Burke [1790], *Reflections on the Revolution in France* (New York: Oxford University Press, 1993).

[10] "Schools Fear for Immigrant Students," *Globe and Mail*, 3 Mar. 1998.

[11] Neil Bissoondath, *Selling Illusions: The Cult of Multiculturalism* (Toronto: Penguin Books, 1994).

FURTHER READING

One of Ignatieff's best early books is *Wealth and Virtue: The Shaping of Political Economy in the Scottish Enlightenment*, edited with Istvan Hont, especially the first chapter (Cambridge and New York: Cambridge University Press, 1983). Those interested in human rights should read both the full text of *The Rights Revolution* (Toronto: House of Anansi Press, 2000) and *Human Rights as Politics and Idolatry*, edited and introduced by Amy Gutman (Princeton, NJ: Princeton University Press, 2001). Those specifically interested in the moral challenges of modern political conflict ought to read *Blood and Belonging: Journeys into the New Nationalism* (Toronto: Viking, 1993), *The Warrior's Honor: Ethnic War and the Modern Conscience* (Toronto: Viking, 1998), *Empire Lite: Nation-Building in Bosnia, Kosovo, and Afghanistan* (Toronto: Penguin, 2003), and *The Lesser Evil: Political Ethics in an Age of Terror* (Toronto: Penguin, 2004).

SOURCES

"The Spectre of Annexation and the Real Danger of National Disintegration," copyright © 1912 by Henri Bourassa, Montreal: "Le Devoir," v. 42, p. 23. Reprinted with permission of Le Devoir.

"Hardy Perennials," copyright © 1915 by Nellie McClung, reprinted from *In Times Like These*, Toronto: McLeod & Allen. Reprinted with permission of Marcia McClung.

"Transportation as a Factor in Canadian Economic History," copyright © 1956 by Harold Innis, reprinted from *Essays in Canadian Economic History*, ed. Mary Q. Innis, Toronto: University of Toronto Press Inc. Reprinted with permission of the publisher.

Democracy in Alberta: Social Credit and the Party System, copyright © 1953 by C.B. Macpherson, Toronto: University of Toronto Press Inc. Reprinted with permission of the publisher.

"Medicare: The Time to Take a Stand," copyright © 1979 by Tommy Douglas, reprinted from *Tommy Douglas Speaks: Till Power is Brought to Pooling*, ed. L.D. Lovick, Lantzville: Oolichan Books. Reprinted by permission of the publisher.

"Chapter Five," copyright © 1970 by Kari Levitt, reprinted from *Silent Surrender: The Multinational Corporation in Canada*, Kari Levitt, Toronto: Macmillan. Reprinted by permission of McGill-Queen's University Press.

"Reflections on Decentralism," by George Woodcock, reprinted from *The Anarchist Reader*, ed. George Woodcock. Copyright © George Woodcock with permission from The Writers' Trust of Canada c/o the Woodcock Estate.

"Federalism, Nationalism and Reason," copyright © 1968 by Pierre Trudeau, reprinted from *Federalism and the French Canadians*, ed. Pierre Elliot Trudeau, Toronto: Macmillan. Reprinted by permission of the literary executor of the Trudeau Estate.

Excerpts from *English-Speaking Justice*, copyright © 1974, 1985 by George Parkin Grant. Reprinted by permission of House of Anansi Press, Toronto.